poetry

poetry
a thematic approach

Sam H. Henderson

James Ward Lee

North Texas State University

45323

Wadsworth Publishing Company, Inc.   Belmont, California

L. C. Cat. Card No.: 68–11209

Printed in the United States of America

Acknowledgments

BALLANTINE BOOKS, INC.—for "Hippopotamothalamion" by John Hall Wheelock. From *New Poems by American Poets*, © 1957 by Ballantine Books, Inc.

BRANDT & BRANDT—for "Nightmare Number Three" by Stephen Vincent Benét. From *The Selected Works of Stephen Vincent Benét*, published by Holt, Rinehart and Winston, Inc. Copyright 1935 by Stephen Vincent Benét. Copyright renewed © 1963 by Thomas C. Benét, Stephanie B. Mahin and Rachel Benét Lewis. Reprinted by permission of Brandt & Brandt.

CHATTO & WINDUS LTD.—for "Two Realities" by Aldous Huxley. From *Verses and Comedy*. Reprinted by permission of Mrs. Laura Huxley and the publishers.

THE CLARENDON PRESS, OXFORD—for "The Hill Pines Were Sighing" by Robert Bridges. By permission of The Clarendon Press, Oxford.

COLLINS-KNOWLTON-WING, INC.—for "A Pinch of Salt" by Robert Graves. Reprinted by permission of Collins-Knowlton-Wing, Inc. Copyright © 1917 by International Authors, N.V.

DODD, MEAD & COMPANY—for "Heaven" by Rupert Brooke. Reprinted by permission of Dodd, Mead & Company from *The Collected Poems of Rupert Brooke*. Copyright 1915 by Dodd, Mead & Company. Copyright 1943 by Edward Marsh.

DOUBLEDAY & COMPANY, INC.—for "The Waking" by Theodore Roethke, copyright 1953 by Theodore Roethke; "Child on Top of a Greenhouse" by Theodore Roethke, copyright 1946 by Editorial Publications, Inc.; "My Papa's Waltz" by Theodore Roethke, copyright 1942 by Hearst Magazine, Inc. From the book *Words for the Wind* by Theodore Roethke. Reprinted by permission of Doubleday & Company, Inc. For "Danny Deever" and "The White Man's Burden" by Rudyard Kipling from *Rudyard Kipling's Verse*: Definitive Edition. By permission of Doubleday & Company, Inc.

NORMA MILLAY ELLIS—for "Euclid Alone Has Looked on Beauty Bare," "Justice Denied in Massachusetts," and "What Lips My Lips Have Kissed" by Edna St. Vincent Millay. By permission of Norma Millay Ellis.

ACKNOWLEDGMENTS

THE EXPLICATOR—for "Dickinson's 'I Heard a Fly Buzz When I Died'" by Gerhard Friedrich, "Hopkins' 'The Windhover'" by Elisabeth Schneider, and "Marvell's 'The Picture of Little T.C. in a Prospect of Flowers'" by J. L. Simmons. Reprinted with special permission of the authors and *The Explicator*.

HARCOURT, BRACE & WORLD, INC.—for "my sweet old etcetera" by E. E. Cummings. Copyright, 1926, by Horace Liveright, copyright, 1954, by E. E. Cummings. For "Buffalo Bill's . . ." by E. E. Cummings. Copyright 1923, 1951 by E. E. Cummings. For "Gee, i like to think of dead" by E. E. Cummings. Copyright, 1925, by E. E. Cummings. For "anyone lived in a pretty how town" by E. E. Cummings. Copyright, 1940, by E. E. Cummings. For "the cambridge ladies" by E. E. Cummings. Copyright, 1923, 1951, by E. E. Cummings. All reprinted from his volume *Poems 1923–1954* by permission of Harcourt, Brace & World, Inc. For "Eighth Air Force" by Randall Jarrell. From *Losses* by Randall Jarrell, copyright, 1948, by Harcourt, Brace & World, Inc., and reprinted with their permission. For "Naming of Parts" by Henry Reed from *A Map of Verona and Other Poems,* copyright, 1947, by Henry Reed. Reprinted by permission of Harcourt, Brace & World, Inc. For "Ten Definitions of Poetry" by Carl Sandburg from *Good Morning, America* by Carl Sandburg, copyright, 1920, by Harcourt, Brace & World, Inc.; renewed, 1948, by Carl Sandburg. Reprinted by permission of the publishers. For "The Love Song of J. Alfred Prufrock" by T. S. Eliot from *Collected Poems 1909–1962* by T. S. Eliot, copyright, 1936, by Harcourt, Brace & World, Inc.; copyright © 1963, 1964, by T. S. Eliot. Reprinted by permission of the publishers.

EMORY HOLLOWAY—for permission to reprint the MS version of "A Noiseless Patient Spider" by Walt Whitman.

HOLT, RINEHART AND WINSTON, INC.—for "The Egg and the Machine," "Fire and Ice," "Choose Something Like a Star," "The Road Not Taken," "Stopping by Woods on a Snowy Evening," and "Provide, Provide" by Robert Frost. From *The Complete Poems of Robert Frost.* Copyright 1916, 1923, 1928, 1949 by Holt, Rinehart and Winston, Inc.; copyright 1936, 1944, 1951, © 1956, by Robert Frost. For "When I Was One-and-Twenty," "Loveliest of Trees," "I Hoed and Trenched and Weeded," "To an Athlete Dying Young," and "Terence, This Is Stupid Stuff" by A. E. Housman. From "A Shropshire Lad"—Authorised Edition—from *The Complete Poems of A. E. Housman.* Copyright 1939, 1940, © 1959 by Holt, Rinehart and Winston, Inc. For "When First My Way to Fair I Took," "Lancer," "The Laws of God, The Laws of Man," "The Chestnut Casts His Flambeaux," "From the Wash the Laundress Sends," and "Easter Hymn" by A. E. Housman. From *The Collected Poems of A. E. Housman.* Copyright 1922 by Holt, Rinehart and Winston, Inc. Copyright 1936, 1950 by Barclays Bank Ltd. Copyright © 1964 by Robert E. Symons. All reprinted by permission of Holt, Rinehart and Winston, Inc.

HOUGHTON MIFFLIN COMPANY—for "Ars Poetica," "The End of the World," and "You, Andrew Marvell" by Archibald MacLeish. From *Collected Poems of Archibald MacLeish.* Copyright by Archibald MacLeish. Reprinted by permission of the publisher, Houghton Mifflin Company.

INDIANA UNIVERSITY PRESS—for "Dirge" and "Readings, Forecasts, Personal Guidance" by Kenneth Fearing. From *New and Selected Poems* by Kenneth Fearing. Reprinted by permission of Indiana University Press: Bloomington, Indiana.

MRS. RANDALL JARRELL—for "Death of a Ball Turret Gunner" by Randall Jarrell.

ALFRED A. KNOPF, INC.—for "Moo" by Robert Hillyer. © Copyright 1961 by Robert Hillyer. Reprinted from *Collected Poems,* by Robert Hillyer, by permission of Alfred A. Knopf, Inc. For "Anecdote of the Jar" and "Peter Quince at the Clavier" by Wallace Stevens. Copyright 1923 and renewed 1951 by Wallace Stevens. Reprinted from *The Collected Poems of Wallace Stevens,* by permission of Alfred A. Knopf, Inc. For "Sanctuary" by Elinor Wylie. Copyright 1921 by Alfred A. Knopf, Inc., and renewed 1949 by William Rose Benét. Reprinted from *Collected*

Poems, by Elinor Wylie, by permission of Alfred A. Knopf, Inc. For "The Equilibrists" and "Blue Girls" by John Crowe Ransom. Copyright 1927 by Alfred A. Knopf, Inc., and renewed 1955 by John Crowe Ransom. Reprinted from *Selected Poems*, by John Crowe Ransom, by permission of Alfred A. Knopf, Inc. For "Bells for John Whiteside's Daughter" by John Crowe Ransom. Copyright 1924 by Alfred A. Knopf, Inc., and renewed 1952 by John Crowe Ransom. Reprinted from *Selected Poems*, by John Crowe Ransom, by permission of Alfred A. Knopf, Inc.

LITTLE, BROWN AND COMPANY—for "Kind of an Ode to Duty" by Ogden Nash. Copyright 1935 by The Curtis Publishing Company. Reprinted from *The Face Is Familiar* by Ogden Nash by permission of Little, Brown and Company.

LIVERIGHT PUBLISHING CORPORATION—for "To Brooklyn Bridge," "The Air Plant," and "Lachrymae Christi" by Hart Crane. From *The Collected Poems of Hart Crane*. By permission of Liveright, Publishers, N. Y. Copyright © Renewed, 1961 by Liveright Publishing Corporation.

THE MACMILLAN COMPANY—for "Mr. Flood's Party" by E. A. Robinson from *Collected Poems* by E. A. Robinson. Copyright 1921, Edwin Arlington Robinson, copyright renewed 1949 by Ruth Nivison. For "The Sheaves" by E. A. Robinson from *Collected Poems* by E. A. Robinson. Copyright 1925, Edwin Arlington Robinson, copyright renewed 1952 by Ruth Nivison and Barbara R. Holt. For "The Waste Places" by James Stephens from *Collected Poems*. Copyright 1915, The Macmillan Company, copyright renewed 1943 by James Stephens. For "To a Steamroller" and "Poetry" by Marianne Moore from *Collected Poems* by Marianne Moore. Copyright 1935, Marianne Moore, copyright renewed 1963 by Marianne Moore and T. S. Eliot. For "Nevertheless" by Marianne Moore. Copyright 1944 by Marianne Moore. Reprinted with permission of The Macmillan Company from *Collected Poems* by Marianne Moore. For "Eve" and "Time, You Old Gypsy Man" by Ralph Hodgson. Reprinted with permission of The Macmillan Company from *Poems* by Ralph Hodgson. Copyright 1917, The Macmillan Company, copyright renewed 1945 by Ralph Hodgson. For "The Lake Isle of Innisfree," "An Old Song Resung," and "When You Are Old" by W. B. Yeats. Reprinted with permission of The Macmillan Company from *Collected Poems* by W. B. Yeats. Copyright 1906, The Macmillan Company, copyright renewed 1934 by William Butler Yeats. For "To a Friend Whose Work Has Come to Nothing" by W. B. Yeats. Reprinted with permission of The Macmillan Company from *Collected Poems* by W. B. Yeats. Copyright 1916, The Macmillan Company, copyright renewed 1944 by Bertha Georgie Yeats. For "Easter, 1916" and "The Second Coming" by W. B. Yeats. Reprinted with permission of The Macmillan Company from *Collected Poems* by W. B. Yeats. Copyright 1924, The Macmillan Company, copyright renewed 1952 by Bertha Georgie Yeats. For "Leda and the Swan" and "Sailing to Byzantium" by W. B. Yeats. Reprinted with permission of The Macmillan Company from *Collected Poems* by W. B. Yeats. Copyright 1928, The Macmillan Company, copyright renewed 1956 by Georgie Yeats. For "Byzantium" by W. B. Yeats. Reprinted with permission of The Macmillan Company from *Collected Poems* by W. B. Yeats. Copyright 1933, The Macmillan Company, copyright renewed 1961 by Bertha Georgie Yeats. For "Why Should Not Old Men Be Mad" and "Politics" by W. B. Yeats. Reprinted with permission of The Macmillan Company from *Collected Poems* by W. B. Yeats. Copyright 1940, by Georgie Yeats. For "The Ruined Maid," "The Man He Killed," "Hap," "Drummer Hodge," "The Darkling Thrush," "The Convergence of the Twain," and "Channel Firing" by Thomas Hardy. Reprinted with permission of The Macmillan Company from *Collected Poems* by Thomas Hardy. Copyright 1925, The Macmillan Company.

THE NATIONAL COUNCIL OF TEACHERS OF ENGLISH—for "The Irony of E. E. Cummings" by David Ray (*College English*, January 1962), "No. 14 of Donne's Holy Sonnets" by John E. Parish (*College English*, January 1963), and "Intimations of Mortality: An Analysis of Hopkins' 'Spring and Fall' " by John A. Myers, Jr. (*College English*, November 1962). Reprinted with the permission of the National Council of Teachers of English and the authors.

NEW DIRECTIONS PUBLISHING CORPORATION—for "Arms and the Boy" and "Dulce et Decorum Est" by Wilfred Owen from *The Collected Poems of Wilfred Owen*. Copyright © by Chatto and Windus, Ltd., 1963. Reprinted by permission of the publisher, New Directions Publishing Corporation. For "The River Merchant's Wife: A Letter," "Portrait d'une Femme," and "A Pact" by Ezra Pound. From *Personae* by Ezra Pound. Copyright, 1926, 1954, by Ezra Pound. Reprinted by permission of the publisher, New Directions Publishing Corporation. For "Ballad for Gloom" by Ezra Pound from *Personae 1909* by Ezra Pound. All rights reserved. Reprinted by permission of New Directions Publishing Corporation, for The Committee for Ezra Pound. For "Fern Hill," "And Death Shall Have No Dominion," and "Do Not Go Gentle into That Good Night" by Dylan Thomas from *Collected Poems* by Dylan Thomas. Copyright, 1953, by Dylan Thomas. © 1957 by New Directions. Reprinted by permission of the publisher, New Directions Publishing Corporation. For "The Poor" and "Daisy" by William Carlos Williams from *The Collected Earlier Poems of William Carlos Williams*. Copyright, 1938, 1951, by William Carlos Williams. Reprinted by permission of the publisher, New Directions Publishing Corporation. For "Before Disaster" from *The Giant Weapon* by Yvor Winters. Copyright 1943 by New Directions. Reprinted by permission of the publisher, New Directions Publishing Corporation.

NEW STATESMAN—for "The Pleasures of a Technological University" by Edwin Morgan. Reprinted from the *New Statesman*, London, by permission.

OCTOBER HOUSE—for "Leg in a Subway" by Oscar Williams. Reprinted with permission.

OXFORD UNIVERSITY PRESS—for "The Fury of Aerial Bombardment" by Richard Eberhart. From *Collected Poems 1930–1960* by Richard Eberhart. © 1960 by Richard Eberhart. For "Felix Randal" and "Pied Beauty" by Gerard Manley Hopkins. From *Poems by Gerard Manley Hopkins*, Third Edition, edited by W. H. Gardner. Copyright 1948 by Oxford University Press, Inc. For "Birmingham," "Museums," and "The British Museum Reading Room" by Louis MacNeice. Reprinted from *Collected Poems, 1925–1948*, by Louis MacNeice, Oxford University Press, Inc., 1963. All reprinted by permission of Oxford University Press.

RANDOM HOUSE—for "An Elementary School Class-Room" and "Two Armies" by Stephen Spender. Copyright 1942 by Stephen Spender. Reprinted from *Collected Poems 1928–1953*, by Stephen Spender, by permission of Random House, Inc. For "The Landscape Near an Aerodrome," "The Express," and "My Parents Kept Me from Children Who Were Rough" by Stephen Spender. Copyright 1934 and renewed 1961 by Stephen Spender. Reprinted from *Collected Poems 1928–1953*, by Stephen Spender, by permission of Random House, Inc. For "Musée des Beaux Arts" and "September 1, 1939" by W. H. Auden. Copyright 1940 by W. H. Auden. Reprinted from *The Collected Poetry of W. H. Auden*, by permission of Random House, Inc. For "Age in Prospect" by Robinson Jeffers. Copyright 1925 and renewed 1953 by Robinson Jeffers. Reprinted from *Roan Stallion, Tamar and Other Poems*, by Robinson Jeffers, by permission of Random House, Inc. For "Auto Wreck," "Buick," and "Hollywood" by Karl Shapiro. Copyright 1941 by Karl Shapiro. Reprinted from *Poems 1940–1953*, by Karl Shapiro, by permission of Random House, Inc. For "Poet" by Karl Shapiro. Copyright 1942 by Karl Shapiro. Reprinted from *Poems 1940–1953*, by Karl Shapiro, by permission of Random House, Inc. For "The Progress of Faust" by Karl Shapiro. Copyright 1946 by Karl Shapiro. Reprinted from *Poems 1940–1953*, by Karl Shapiro, by permission of Random House, Inc. Originally appeared in *The New Yorker*.

SCHOCKEN BOOKS INC.—for "Break of Day in the Trenches" by Isaac Rosenberg. Reprinted by permission of Schocken Books Inc. from *Collected Poems* by Isaac Rosenberg, copyright © 1949 by Schocken Books Inc.

CHARLES SCRIBNER'S SONS—for "Miniver Cheevy" (Copyright 1907 Charles Scribner's Sons; renewal copyright 1935) and "How Annandale Went Out" by E. A. Robinson, reprinted with permission of Charles Scribner's Sons from *The Town Down the River* by Edwin Arlington Robinson. Copyright 1910 Charles Scribner's Sons; renewal copyright 1938 Ruth Nivison. "Cliff

Klingenhagen," "Luke Havergal," "Credo," and "Richard Cory" by E. A. Robinson are reprinted with the permission of Charles Scribner's Sons from *The Children of the Night* by Edwin Arlington Robinson (1897).

THE SOCIETY OF AUTHORS—for "The Listeners," "The Miracle," and "Silver" by Walter de la Mare. Permission granted by The Literary Trustees of Walter de la Mare and The Society of Authors.

THE UNIVERSITY OF KANSAS CITY REVIEW—for "Crossroads" and "Hart Crane's 'Lachrymae Christi' " by Martin Staples Shockley.

PETER VIERECK—for "Poet" and "Kilroy." From *Terror and Decorum*, New York, 1948, Pulitzer Prize, 1949, now out of print and reprinted, 1967, in Peter Viereck's *Selected and New Poems*, Bobbs-Merrill, New York. All rights retained by Peter Viereck.

THE VIKING PRESS—for "City-Life" by D. H. Lawrence. From *The Complete Poems of D. H. Lawrence*, edited by Vivian de Sola Pinto and F. Warren Roberts. Copyright 1933 by Frieda Lawrence. All rights reserved. Reprinted by permission of The Viking Press, Inc.

THE VIRGINIA QUARTERLY REVIEW—for "The Epilogue Spoken by a Tape Recorder" by Arthur M. Sampley. Reprinted from *The Virginia Quarterly Review*, Summer 1965.

WESLEYAN UNIVERSITY PRESS—for "At the Executed Murderer's Grave" by James Wright. Copyright © 1958 by James Wright. Reprinted from *Saint Judas* by James Wright, by permission of Wesleyan University Press.

for Florence and Marcia

Preface

Of all the poetry texts available today, none seems ideally suited to the increasing number of college courses, especially on the freshman and sophomore levels, which act as general introductions to literature. Two main types of books are presently available to college teachers: the traditional historical anthology and the anthology that concentrates on poetic principles and techniques. The first of these is suitable chiefly for survey courses; the second is useful mainly when the class studies the formal aspects of poetry for an extended period. With the increasing availability of multiple texts and the tendency of instructors and departments to tailor individual courses to their needs rather than choosing a ready-made system, an alternative approach to the study of poetry is called for. *Poetry: A Thematic Approach* offers that alternative.

This text, as the title indicates, is an arrangement of poems according to dominant literary themes. Several years of teaching such courses have convinced us of the validity of the thematic approach. It is especially useful in multiple-text courses of broad range. To begin with, it facilitates the design and arrangement of introduction to literature courses. It allows the instructor to integrate the teaching of poetry with the teaching of novels, stories, and plays. Perhaps a less tangible but no less valuable factor, we found, is that the thematic approach helps the instructor overcome the indifference, the suspicion, and sometimes the outright hostility of the student as he studies poetry seriously for the first time. It does this by enabling him to see the broad associations and parallels between poetry and the other genres. Finally, we feel that a thematic approach will help correct the imbalance that is sometimes found when too much emphasis is placed on "background" or the formal aspects of poetry. In their place, of course, these things are important, and it is not our intention to "cut the heart out of the mystery." Poetry is and should remain a very special genre. It is our contention, however, that each instructor can best determine how and when the more formal and technical aspects of poetry should be taught. We maintain that a thematic arrangement, along with the apparatus we provide, can be a highly satisfactory approach to the teaching of poetry to students who have had little formal literary training and who come from disparate backgrounds.

Although the major thematic groups and overall arrangements may seem at times arbitrary, they are no more so than a chronological arrangement or a grouping according to imagery, tone, or some such technical facet of poetry. The major headings we employ, in our opinion, incorporate the major themes of literature.

We have purposely made this text as flexible as possible, accepting the fact of some arrangement, of course. It is our intent to suggest rather than dictate. We have observed that most instructors prefer, in all but highly technical poetry courses, a minimum of apparatus; and to that end we have eliminated all but the most essential notes and glossary. We have also provided, for each thematic grouping, a selected list of novels, plays, and short stories on the same theme. In addition, there are representative explications in most of the thematic groupings. Some are from critical journals; some are published here for the first time; some are written by students. The text contains also a chronological table of contents, so that an instructor may make chronological distinctions if he chooses.

We wish to thank our colleagues on the English staff of North Texas State University—especially William F. Belcher, Gerald A. Kirk, Walter Lazenby, Carroll Y. Rich, Arthur M. Sampley, Martin Shockley, and James T. F. Tanner—for their helpful advice and criticism. For help in preparing the manuscript we are indebted to Fran Allen, Mary Conklin, Ramona Perez, Gena Poore, and Carol Vaughan, and to Carol Agee of Wadsworth Publishing Company. To our wives, Marcia Henderson and Florence Lee, we owe special thanks for encouragement and practical assistance.

S. H. H.
J. W. L.

Contents

4.   THE GROWTH OF SCIENCE AND TECHNOLOGY   99

Chronological
Table of Contents

I
Innocence and Expanding Awareness

The poems in this section present a number of attitudes toward childhood and youth—nostalgia, irony, and objective reflection. In lyric poems such as those reprinted here, the theme often revolves around a child's reaction to some incident in his life that helped to shape him. Some poets celebrate the fleeting joys of childhood and youth: "Then come kiss me, sweet and twenty,/ Youth's a stuff will not endure." Others contrast the pleasures of youth with the sadness of adulthood: "The pence are here and here's the fair,/ But where's the lost young man?" Still others do much the same as fiction writers and, as Roethke does in "My Papa's Waltz," recall some crucial, life-changing experience that turned innocence into awareness. In "Spring and Fall: To a Young Child," Hopkins traces the adult's sense of anxiety back to the child's perception of his own mortality.

The Romantic poets celebrated childhood as a time when man is closest to God because he has recently come to this world, "trailing clouds of glory"; Wordsworth called the child "father of the man." In childhood and youth, according to the Romantic poet, one is naturally inclined to goodness because of his innocence and nearness to God. The older one grows, the more tinged he becomes with the evils of adulthood and civilization: He "cons his little part" to act out the drama of adulthood.

The theme of innocence and expanding awareness is a favorite subject not only of poets but of novelists and short-story writers as well. In novels and stories the theme usually takes the form of the initiation story, in which an innocent (such as Holden Caulfield or Huck Finn) learns some harsh truths about the adult world.

Below is a list of plays, novels, and short stories on the theme of innocence and expanding awareness. A similar list is included in each section of this book.

READINGS IN OTHER GENRES

PLAYS

Maxwell Anderson, *The Bad Seed*
Robert Anderson, *Tea and Sympathy*
James M. Barrie, *Peter Pan*
Lillian Hellman, *The Children's Hour*
Howard Lindsay and Russel Crouse, *Life with Father*
Eugene O'Neill, *Ah, Wilderness!*
Samuel Taylor, *The Happy Time*
John Van Druten, *I Remember Mama*

NOVELS

James Agee, *A Death in the Family*
Samuel Butler, *The Way of All Flesh*
Willa Cather, *My Ántonia*
Charles Dickens, *Great Expectations*
Henry Fielding, *Tom Jones*
William Golding, *Lord of the Flies*
Richard Hughes, *A High Wind in Jamaica*
James Joyce, *A Portrait of the Artist as a Young Man*
Oliver La Farge, *Laughing Boy*
Carson McCullers, *A Member of the Wedding*
Herman Melville, *Billy Budd, Foretopman*
Marcel Proust, *Swann's Way*
J. D. Salinger, *The Catcher in the Rye*
Mark Twain, *Huckleberry Finn*
Thomas Wolfe, *Look Homeward, Angel*

SHORT STORIES

Truman Capote, "Children on Their Birthdays"
Joseph Conrad, "Youth"
William Faulkner, "The Bear"
Ernest Hemingway, "Ten Indians," "The Capital of the World"
Herman Hesse, "Youth, Ah Youth"
James Joyce, "Araby"
Katherine Mansfield, "The Garden Party"
Katherine Anne Porter, "The Circus"
J. D. Salinger, "Down at the Dingy," "The Laughing Man"
Alan Sillitoe, "The Loneliness of the Long-Distance Runner"

John Steinbeck, "The Leader of the People"
Ruth Suckow, "A Start in Life"
Peter Taylor, "A Spinster's Tale"
Dylan Thomas, "Peaches"
Robert Penn Warren, "Blackberry Winter"

O Mistress Mine

O Mistress mine, where are you roaming?
O stay and hear! Your true-love's coming,
   That can sing both high and low;
Trip no further, pretty sweeting,
Journeys end in lovers meeting,   5
   Every wise man's son doth know.

What is love? 'tis not hereafter;
Present mirth hath present laughter;
   What's to come is still unsure;
In delay there lies no plenty;   10
Then come kiss me, sweet and twenty,
   Youth's a stuff will not endure.

WILLIAM SHAKESPEARE
(From *Twelfth Night*)

The Picture of Little T. C. in a Prospect of Flowers

See with what simplicity
This nymph begins her golden days!
In the green grass she loves to lie,
And there with her fair aspect tames
The wilder flowers, and gives them names,   5
But only with the roses plays,
        And them does tell
What colour best becomes them, and what smell.

Who can foretell for what high cause
This darling of the gods was born?   10
Yet this is she whose chaster laws
The wanton Love shall one day fear,
And, under her command severe,
See his bow broke and ensigns torn.
        Happy, who can   15
Appease this virtuous enemy of man!

O then let me in time compound
And parley with those conquering eyes,
Ere they have tried their force to wound;
Ere with their glancing wheels they drive   20
In triumph over hearts that strive,
And them that yield but more despise;
            Let me be laid
Where I may see thy glories from some shade.

Meantime, whilst every verdant thing   25
Itself does at thy beauty charm,
Reform the errors of the Spring:
Make that the tulips may have share
Of sweetness, seeing they are fair;
And roses of their thorns disarm;   30
            But most procure
That violets may a longer age endure.

But O, young beauty of the woods,
Whom nature courts with fruits and flowers,
Gather the flowers, but spare the buds,   35
Lest Flora, angry at thy crime
To kill her infants in their prime,
Do quickly make th' example yours;
            And, ere we see,
Nip in the blossom all our hopes and thee.   40

ANDREW MARVELL

Marvell's "Picture of Little T. C. in a Prospect of Flowers"

J. L. Simmons

"The Picture of Little T. C. in a Prospect of Flowers" has not received the
explication which the poem so richly rewards. It is as though editors and com-
mentators are satisfied that H. M. Margoliouth's discovery as to the identity of
T. C., explaining the "Darling of the Gods" and the strangely somber warning
of the conclusion, has exhausted a minor, if perfect, poem. (Theophila Corne-
wall's little sister, who bore the same name, had died in infancy; present in
Marvell's mind is the fear that a similar catastrophe might overtake his friend's
new daughter. See *Modern Language Review,* October, 1922.)

In the first stanza the more obvious meaning of the word *prospect* is made
evident: the poet, in the present tense, observes the child in a scene of flowers.
She is made the perfect, prelapsarian man by the words *simplicity,* describing
the state of man before the initial sin unbalanced his four equally mixed elements, and *golden,* the adjectival pureness of the days when Astraea, the goddess

of justice, lived among men—the equivalent in classical mythology of the Garden of Eden. More subtle biblical references, coyly taken over in terms of a child, back up her relationship with Adam. Lines 4 and 5 allude to Adam's duties in Eden, which the child echoes by taming and naming "The wilder flowers": ". . . and God said unto them, Be fruitful, and multiply, and replenish the earth, and subdue it . . ." (*Genesis,* I, 28); "And out of the ground the Lord God formed every beast of the field, and every fowl of the air; and brought them unto Adam to see what he would call them. . . ." (*Genesis,* II, 19). Marvell makes a further reference in lines 7 and 8 to *Genesis,* II, 15: "And the Lord God took the man, and put him into the Garden of Eden to dress it and to keep it." This passage is ingenuously reflected in having T. C. advise the roses in their toilette. That T. C. "only with the roses plays" recalls to mind that the rosary derived its name from "a place where roses grow"; and "playes" and "prayes" are as closely related in spelling and sound as their activities would be for a pure creature.

The tense in the second stanza shifts to the future, and the symbolic meaning of the word *prospect* shows itself: the contemplation of hopes for T. C.'s future. She becomes, in the poet's imagination, even more than prelapsarian man: Diana, the militant goddess of virginity, fighting Cupid, the representation of "wanton Love."

The images of battle, the fight between purity and wantonness, are carried over into the third stanza, dramatized in a projected present tense, where the poet, a mere natural man, anticipates a parley in order to avoid her "glancing wheels." The poet of "The Garden" prefers the shade—as Marvell often does as a means of escaping the sun-drenched conflict—where he can watch the glory of her fight, a successful, godlike victory over evil. This is the prospect in store for the child, the manner in which she will "flower."

The fourth stanza brings us abruptly back to the present, and with it the associations of the child as perfect man and of the garden as Eden. Since the child is perfect, she can restore nature to its perfection; and the tulips which lost their odor and the roses which gained their thorns, all as a reverberation of Adam's sin, can be reformed. The season was then, traditionally, a perpetual spring: therefore violets might indeed "a longer age endure."

The warning comes in the final stanza, and it seems impossible not to believe that Marvell had another famous source in mind which he would, to great effect, echo. Of course Adam was given a warning regarding the handling of nature's store, and the parallel with Genesis is extended; but I have in mind another famous admonition. "Gather the flowers, but spare the buds" seems almost beyond doubt to be a conscious reversal of Herrick's warning in his famous *carpe diem* poem, "Gather ye rosebuds while ye may." If taken so, then Marvell's line certainly gains a seriousness of intent scarcely felt otherwise, and with that line the whole poem. The fear behind the warning, then, is not so much owing to memories of a dead sister also named T. C. as to the fact that the child might lose the innocence and purity she now manifests through fol-

lowing Herrick's worldly advice. Her life might not be lost, but the glorious pros-
pects envisioned by the poet would never be realized. Marvell knew what he
was doing in not allowing personal biographical material to be the key to his
poem.

Childhood

I cannot reach it; and my striving eye
Dazzles at it, as at eternity.
   Were now that chronicle alive,
Those white designs which children drive,
And the thoughts of each harmless hour,   5
With their content, too, in my power,
Quickly would I make my path even,
And by mere playing go to heaven.

   Why should men love
A wolf more than a lamb or dove?   10
Or choose hell-fire and brimstone streams
Before bright stars and God's own beams?
Who kisseth thorns will hurt his face,
But flowers do both refresh and grace,
And sweetly living—fie on men!—   15
Are, when dead, medicinal then;
If seeing much should make staid eyes,
And long experience should make wise,
Since all that age doth teach is ill,
Why should I not love childhood still?   20
Why, if I see a rock or shelf,
Shall I from thence cast down myself?
Or by complying with the world,
From the same precipice be hurled?
Those observations are but foul   25
Which make me wise to lose my soul.

And yet the practice worldlings call
Business, and weighty action all,
Checking the poor child for his play,
But gravely cast themselves away.   30

   Dear, harmless age! the short, swift span
Where weeping Virtue parts with man;
Where love without lust dwells, and bends
What way we please without self-ends.

An age of mysteries! which he   35
Must live twice that would God's face see;
Which angels guard, and with it play,
Angels! which foul men drive away.

How do I study now, and scan
Thee more than e'er I studied man,   40
And only see through a long night
Thy edges and thy bordering light!
Oh for thy center and midday!
For sure that is the narrow way!

HENRY VAUGHAN

The Retreat

Happy those early days when I
Shined in my angel-infancy!
Before I understood this place
Appointed for my second race,
Or taught my soul to fancy ought   5
But a white, celestial thought;
When yet I had not walked above
A mile, or two, from my first love,
And looking back (at that short space),
Could see a glimpse of his bright face;   10
When on some gilded cloud or flower
My gazing soul would dwell an hour,
And in those weaker glories spy
Some shadows of eternity;
Before I taught my tongue to wound   15
My conscience with a sinful sound,
Or had the black art to dispense
A several sin to every sense;
But felt through all this fleshly dress
Bright shoots of everlastingness.   20
    O how I long to travel back
And tread again that ancient track!
That I might once more reach that plain,
Where first I left my glorious train,
From whence th' enlightened spirit sees   25
That shady city of palm trees;
But (ah!) my soul with too much stay
Is drunk, and staggers in the way.
Some men a forward motion love,

But I by backward steps would move,   30
And when this dust falls to the urn,
In that state I came, return.

HENRY VAUGHAN

Introduction

Piping down the valleys wild,
Piping songs of pleasant glee,
On a cloud I saw a child,
And he laughing said to me:

"Pipe a song about a Lamb!"   5
So I piped with merry cheer.
"Piper, pipe that song again";
So I piped: he wept to hear.

"Drop thy pipe, thy happy pipe;
Sing thy songs of happy cheer":   10
So I sang the same again,
While he wept with joy to hear.

"Piper, sit thee down and write
In a book, that all may read."
So he vanished from my sight   15
And I plucked a hollow reed,

And I made a rural pen,
And I stained the water clear,
And I wrote my happy songs
Every child may joy to hear.   20

WILLIAM BLAKE
(From Songs of Innocence)

A Cradle Song

Sweet dreams, form a shade
O'er my lovely infant's head;
Sweet dreams of pleasant streams
By happy, silent, moony beams.

Sweet sleep, with soft down   5
Weave thy brows an infant crown.
Sweet sleep, Angel mild,
Hover o'er my happy child.

Sweet smiles, in the night
Hover over my delight;   10
Sweet smiles, mother's smiles,
All the livelong night beguiles.

Sweet moans, dovelike sighs,
Chase not slumber from thy eyes.
Sweet moans, sweeter smiles,   15
All the dovelike moans beguiles.

Sleep, sleep, happy child,
All creation slept and smiled;
Sleep, sleep, happy sleep,
While o'er thee thy mother weep.   20

Sweet babe, in thy face
Holy image I can trace.
Sweet babe, once like thee,
Thy Maker lay and wept for me,

Wept for me, for thee, for all,   25
When He was an infant small.
Thou His image ever see,
Heavenly face that smiles on thee,

Smiles on thee, on me, on all;
Who became an infant small.   30
Infant smiles are His own smiles;
Heaven and earth to peace beguiles.

WILLIAM BLAKE
(From *Songs of Innocence*)

The Lamb

Little Lamb, who made thee?
Dost thou know who made thee?
Gave thee life, and bid thee feed,
By the stream and o'er the mead;
Gave thee clothing of delight,   5
Softest clothing, woolly, bright;

Gave thee such a tender voice,
Making all the vales rejoice?
   Little Lamb, who made thee?
   Dost thou know who made thee?   10

   Little Lamb, I'll tell thee,
   Little Lamb, I'll tell thee:
He is callèd by thy name,
For He calls Himself a Lamb.
He is meek, and He is mild;   15
He became a little child.
I a child, and thou a lamb,
We are callèd by His name.
   Little Lamb, God bless thee!
   Little Lamb, God bless thee!   20

WILLIAM BLAKE
(From *Songs of Innocence*)

The Little Black Boy

My mother bore me in the southern wild,
   And I am black, but O, my soul is white!
White as an angel is the English child,
   But I am black, as if bereaved of light.

My mother taught me underneath a tree,   5
   And sitting down before the heat of day,
She took me on her lap and kissèd me,
   And, pointing to the East, began to say:

"Look on the rising sun: there God does live,
   And gives his light, and gives his heat away;   10
And flowers and trees and beasts and men receive
   Comfort in morning, joy in the noonday.

"And we are put on earth a little space,
   That we may learn to bear the beams of love;
And these black bodies and this sun-burnt face   15
   Is but a cloud, and like a shady grove.

"For when our souls have learned the heat to bear,
   The cloud will vanish; we shall hear his voice,
Saying: 'Come out from the grove, my love and care,
   And round my golden tent like lambs rejoice.' "   20

Thus did my mother say, and kissèd me;
   And thus I say to little English boy:

When I from black, and he from white cloud free,
   And round the tent of God like lambs we joy,

I'll shade him from the heat, till he can bear   25
   To lean in joy upon our Father's knee;
And then I'll stand and stroke his silver hair,
   And be like him, and he will then love me.

WILLIAM BLAKE
(From *Songs of Innocence*)

The Echoing Green

The sun does arise,
And make happy the skies;
The merry bells ring
To welcome the spring;
The skylark and thrush,   5
The birds of the bush,
Sing louder around
To the bells' cheerful sound,
While our sports shall be seen
On the echoing green.   10

Old John, with white hair,
Does laugh away care,
Sitting under the oak,
Among the old folk.
They laugh at our play,   15
And soon they all say:
"Such, such were the joys
When we all, girls and boys,
In our youth time were seen
On the echoing green."   20

Till the little ones, weary,
No more can be merry;
The sun does descend,
And our sports have an end.
Round the laps of their mothers   25
Many sisters and brothers,
Like birds in their nest,
Are ready for rest,
And sport no more seen
On the darkening green.   30

WILLIAM BLAKE
(From *Songs of Innocence*)

Holy Thursday

'Twas on a Holy Thursday, their innocent faces clean,
The children walking two and two, in red and blue and green,
Grey-headed beadles walked before, with wands as white as snow,
Till into the high dome of Paul's they like Thames' waters flow.

O what a multitude they seemed, these flowers of London town!   5
Seated in companies they sit with radiance all their own.
The hum of multitudes was there, but multitudes of lambs,
Thousands of little boys and girls raising their innocent hands.

Now like a mighty wind they raise to Heaven the voice of song,
Or like harmonious thunderings the seat of Heaven among.   10
Beneath them sit the agèd men, wise guardians of the poor;
Then cherish pity, lest you drive an angel from your door.

WILLIAM BLAKE
(From *Songs of Innocence*)

My Heart Leaps Up When I Behold

My heart leaps up when I behold
    A rainbow in the sky:
So was it when my life began;
So is it now I am a man;
So be it when I shall grow old,   5
    Or let me die!
The Child is father of the Man;
And I could wish my days to be
Bound each to each by natural piety.

WILLIAM WORDSWORTH

I Remember, I Remember

I remember, I remember,
The house where I was born,
The little window where the sun
Came peeping in at morn;
He never came a wink too soon,   5
Nor brought too long a day,

But now, I often wish the night
Had borne my breath away!

I remember, I remember,
The roses, red and white,   10
The violets, and the lily-cups,
Those flowers made of light!
The lilacs where the robin built,
And where my brother set
The laburnum on his birthday,—   15
The tree is living yet!

I remember, I remember,
Where I was used to swing,
And thought the air must rush as fresh
To swallows on the wing   20
My spirit flew in feathers then,
That is so heavy now,
And summer pools could hardly cool
The fever of my brow!

I remember, I remember,   25
The fir trees dark and high;
I used to think their slender tops
Were close against the sky;
It was a childish ignorance,
But now 'tis little joy   30
To know I'm farther off from heaven
Than when I was a boy.

THOMAS HOOD

Lines

Here often, when a child I lay reclined,
   I took delight in this locality.
Here stood the infant Ilion of the mind,
   And here the Grecian ships did seem to be.
And here again I come, and only find   5
   The drain-cut levels of the marshy lea—
Gray sea banks and pale sunsets—dreary wind,
   Dim shores, dense rains, and heavy-clouded sea!

ALFRED, LORD TENNYSON

There Was a Child Went Forth

There was a child went forth every day,
And the first object he looked upon, that object he became,
And that object became part of him for the day or a certain part
    of the day,
Or for many years or stretching cycles of years.

The early lilacs became part of this child,   5
And grass and white and red morning-glories, and white and red
    clover, and the song of the phoebe-bird,
And the Third-month lambs and the sow's pink-faint litter, and
    the mare's foal and cow's calf,
And the noisy brood of the barnyard or by the mire of the pond-
    side,
And the fish suspending themselves so curiously below there, and
    the beautiful curious liquid,
And the water-plants with their graceful flat heads, all became
    part of him.   10

The field-sprouts of the Fourth-month and Fifth-month became
    part of him,
Winter-grain sprouts and those of the light-yellow corn and the
    esculent roots of the garden,
And the apple-tree covered with blossoms and the fruit afterward
    and wood-berries, and the commonest weeds by the road,
And the old drunkard staggering home from the outhouse of the
    tavern whence he had lately risen,
And the schoolmistress that passed on her way to the school,   15
And the friendly boys that passed, and the quarrelsome boys,
And the tidy and fresh-cheeked girls, and the barefoot negro boy
    and girl,
And all the changes of city and country wherever he went.

His own parents, he that had fathered him and she that had con-
    ceived him in her womb and birthed him,
They gave this child more of themselves than that,   20
They gave him afterward every day, they became part of him.

The mother at home quietly placing the dishes on the supper-table,
The mother with mild words, clean her cap and gown, a whole-
    some odor falling off her person and clothes as she walks by,
The father, strong, self-sufficient, manly, mean, angered, unjust,
The blow, the quick loud word, the tight bargain, the crafty lure   25
The family usages, the language, the company, the furniture, the
    yearning and swelling heart,

Affection that will not be gainsaid, the sense of what is real, the thought if after all it should prove unreal,

The doubts of day-time and the doubts of night-time, the curious whether and how,

Whether that which appears so is so, or is it all flashes and specks?

Men and women crowding fast in the streets, if they are not flashes and specks what are they?   30

The streets themselves and the façades of houses, and goods in the windows,

Vehicles, teams, the heavy-planked wharves, the huge crossing at the ferries,

The village on the highland seen from afar at sunset, the river between,

Shadows, aureola and mist, the light falling on roofs and gables of white or brown two miles off,

The schooner near by sleepily dropping down the tide, the little boat slack-towed astern,   35

The hurrying tumbling waves, quick-broken crests, slapping,

The strata of colored clouds, the long bar of maroon-tint away solitary by itself, the spread of purity it lies motionless in,

The horizon's edge, the flying sea-crow, the fragrance of salt marsh and shore mud,

These became part of that child who went forth every day, and who now goes, and will always go forth every day.

WALT WHITMAN

Spring and Fall: To a Young Child

Márgarét, are you griéving
Over Goldengrove unleaving?
Leáves, líke the things of man, you
With your fresh thoughts care for, can you?
Áh! ás the heart grows older   5
It will come to such sights colder
By and by, nor spare a sigh
Though worlds of wanwood leafmeal lie;
And yet you wíll weep and know why.
Now no matter, child, the name: 10
Sórrow's spríngs áre the same.
Nor mouth had, no nor mind, expressed
What heart heard of, ghost guessed:
It ís the blight man was born for,
It is Margaret you mourn for.   15

GERARD MANLEY HOPKINS

Intimations of Mortality:
An Analysis of Hopkins' "Spring and Fall"

John A. Myers, Jr.

Students are almost always intrigued and often excited by this poem. Even when they do not fully grasp the theme, they respond to the poem's mood and tone; and they are charmed by its simple but powerful music: its sprung rhythms, its sounds (with its skillful use of alliteration and internal rhyme), its fresh and original language. Of course, even without such Hopkins coinages as *unleaving, wanwood,* and *leafmeal,* the poem's language is deceptive: its diction is simple, but individual words are combined in startling ways, are forced to take on new meanings or to compress several possible meanings into themselves. It is this combination of simplicity and compression that teases the student and makes him feel that surely this is a poem he can master, however elusive its central meaning remains. Often he will come to class eager to confirm his own ideas but receptive to the insights toward which the teacher can direct him.

Under these conditions there are many ways of "springing" this poem for a class of eleventh or twelfth graders. I shall suggest one method of presentation which has proved successful. This might be called the thematic approach, but it is heavily dependent on a consideration of the poem's dramatic structure (which emphasizes the relationship of the speaker of the poem to the person spoken to —or about) and a close examination of the poem's language. In fact, this approach will demonstrate, as well as any other, the inseparability of form, language, and meaning in poetry and will enable the teacher to reveal the fallacy of paraphrase.

I like to start with the title, which tells us something about the setting (autumn) and the characters (a child and an older person who is addressing himself to the child) of our drama. It even tells us something of the poem's theme since it suggests that fall and spring are somehow connected or involved in one another and that there is a further connection between these two seasons and the child—or the child's feelings. All of these matters are tentative at the beginning and must be confirmed by a careful examination of the dramatic situation and the language. We will return to the title later.

Most students can grasp the dramatic situation and can understand the "plot" once they have mastered the second line. The speaker of the poem, a fond and philosophical adult, wonders that Margaret can grieve "over Goldengrove unleaving"—or a grove of trees whose yellow leaves are falling. Some students may have been thrown off by reading *unleaving* as "not leaving" rather than "deleaf-ing"! Once this matter is cleared up, the teacher can proceed rapidly with his examination of the poem. He will, of course, be able to consider many details of language, syntax, sound, and meter that cannot be dealt with in this paper. One such detail might be the capitalization of Goldengrove. Apparently Hopkins wants us to think of this as a *particular* and perhaps favorite grove known to both speaker and child by this name. But the teacher might ask what further tonal effect the poet has achieved by running the two words together.

At this point in the analysis of the role of the speaker, the teacher might ask the vital question, is the speaker actually talking *to* Margaret? A consideration of the kind of speculation the speaker is indulging in makes it clear that he is *not* but is merely musing out loud. The scene has a different meaning for him than it has for Margaret, and Margaret would hardly understand the play of his mind and his emotions. Some support for this interpretation can be gained from an analysis of the rhythm and rhyme of lines three and four. Line three seems to be an example of Hopkins' sprung rhythm. Somehow Hopkins has set up what might be called a dactylic or trochaic expectation for line four, but he surprises us by retaining the accented *you* in line three (compressing the spring, so to speak) and releases us into line four, which begins with an anapest, hovers the accent over *thoughts,* and then reverts to the trochaic pattern with "care for, can you?" "Can you" rhymes with "man, you," but it has a different beat, and the tension created by this conflict between rhyme and meter serves to emphasize the *rhetorical* nature of the question. The forced accent on *you* makes this a pivotal word, and the total effect of these two lines is to make a sharp differentiation between the speaker with *his* thoughts and the child with *hers.*

We can say, then, that it is *as if* the speaker were addressing Margaret as he observes her weeping; and this dramatic fact accounts, in part, for the tone of tenderness and wistfulness that run throughout the poem. He muses sadly ("Ah!") that although Margaret (with her *fresh* thoughts, so like the leaves when they were green) can care for leaves as if they were human ("like the things of man"), the time will come (when the heart, now in its springtime, grows colder) when she will be unmoved by such a phenomenon even though it will be witnessed on a much vaster scale and when the process has gone much further ("Worlds of wanwood leafmeal lie"). At this point teachers should invite comments from their students on the possible meanings of *wanwood* and *leafmeal.* These words hold a legitimate fascination for students; teachers can capitalize on the students' love of word games and make of their guesses an exercise in intellectual responsibility. For whatever they find in these words must fit the context of the poem. *Wanwood* I take to be a compounding of "wan," with its suggestion of the pallor of dead leaves and the sadness of the forest with its completely bare trees (possibly combined with the older meaning "dark," "livid"), and "wormwood" with its suggestion of the human counterpart in bitterness and disappointment. *Leafmeal* seems compounded of "piecemeal," the slow attrition of nature, and "leaf-mould," suggestive of utter decay.

What does line 9 signify? Does it say that Margaret *insists* on weeping and in demanding an answer? Or does it mean that Margaret will weep even when she is an adult, only then she will *know* why she weeps? Or both? I leave this ambiguity to the reader though I think my preference will emerge shortly.

Now, in line 10, contains a similar and related ambiguity. Is it simply an indication of present time, or is it the sound one makes to comfort a child ("Now, now, child")? In either case, Margaret the child should not concern herself with the *name* or the secret cause of the sorrow that she has "guessed" intuitively. After all, the sources or "springs" (ask your students how many valid meanings they can find in this word; check especially for *sorrow's springtimes*) of sorrow are the same—the same for adult or child—whether they have been articulated, consciously understood ("mouth had") or only intuited ("heart heard of, ghost guessed"—the student may need some explanation here of *ghost* as *spirit* and can be reminded of Holy Ghost). Margaret will know the name of her sorrow all too soon.

The last two lines announce what the entire poem has been building toward, the tragic fact that Margaret has guessed at and that is symbolized for her by the falling leaves. The *blight* to be suffered by the golden grove is the blight common to all mankind and implicit in his being born—*just as autumn is implicit in spring.* But what exactly *is* this blight? At this point everything depends on our interpretation of the enigmatic and climactic last line. Without knowing it, Margaret is mourning for herself. What does this mean? And why is her plight identified with that of mankind?

It is too easy to say that this blight is death—mere physical destruction—and that Margaret has somehow recognized in the death of nature an emblem of the mortality which includes her. This is only part of the meaning, for what Margaret senses must die is not so much Margaret the person as *Margaret the child.* And what the adult speaker is most keenly aware of is the inevitable loss of childhood innocence with its sense of perfection and immortality. Consciousness of death is also consciousness of human limitation and imperfection and the acceptance of these: it is consciousness of sin.

The adult will weep and *know* that he is weeping for his "childhood's faith," that "sweet golden clime" where everything was perfect and everything was possible. We return to the title. This is not a poem about fall alone; it is a poem about spring *and* fall. Is it too much to suggest that it is about innocence and the fall from innocence?

Loveliest of Trees

Loveliest of trees, the cherry now
Is hung with bloom along the bough,
And stands about the woodland ride
Wearing white for Eastertide.

Now, of my threescore years and ten,   5
Twenty will not come again,
And take from seventy springs a score,
It only leaves me fifty more.

And since to look at things in bloom
Fifty springs are little room,   10
About the woodlands I will go
To see the cherry hung with snow.

A. E. HOUSMAN

When I Was One-and-Twenty

When I was one-and-twenty
  I heard a wise man say,
"Give crowns and pounds and guineas
  But not your heart away;
Give pearls away and rubies   5
  But keep your fancy free."
But I was one-and-twenty,
  No use to talk to me.

When I was one-and-twenty
  I heard him say again,   10
"The heart out of the bosom
  Was never given in vain;
'Tis paid with sighs a-plenty
  And sold for endless rue."
And I am two-and-twenty,   15
  And oh, 'tis true, 'tis true.

A. E. HOUSMAN

From the Wash the Laundress Sends

From the wash the laundress sends
My collars home with ravelled ends;
I must fit, now these are frayed,
My neck with new ones, London-made.

Homespun collars, homespun hearts,   5
Wear to rags in foreign parts.
Mine at least's as good as done,
And I must get a London one.

A. E. HOUSMAN

When First My Way to Fair I Took

When first my way to fair I took
    Few pence in purse had I,
And long I used to stand and look
    At things I could not buy.

Now times are altered: if I care   5
    To buy a thing, I can;
The pence are here and here's the fair,
    But where's the lost young man?

—To think that two and two are four
    And neither five nor three   10
The heart of man has long been sore
    And long 'tis like to be.

              A. E. HOUSMAN

Age in Prospect

Praise youth's hot blood if you will, I think that happiness
Rather consists in having lived clear through
Youth and hot blood, on to the wintrier hemisphere
Where one has time to wait and to remember.

Youth and hot blood are beautiful, so is peacefulness.   5
Youth had some islands in it, but age is indeed
An island and a peak; age has infirmities,
Not few, but youth is all one fever.

To look around and to love in his appearances,
Though a little calmly, the universal God's   10
Beauty is better I think than to lip eagerly
The mother's breast or another woman's.

And there is no possession more sure than memory's;
But if I reach that gray island, that peak,
My hope is still to possess with eyes the homeliness   15
Of ancient loves, ocean and mountains,

And meditate the sea-mouth of mortality
And the fountain six feet down with a quieter thirst
Than now I feel for old age; a creature progressively
Thirsty for life will be for death too.   20

           ROBINSON JEFFERS

The Ball Poem

What is the boy now, who has lost his ball,
What what is he to do? I saw it go
Merrily bouncing, down the street, and then
Merrily over—there it is in the water!
No use to say "O there are other balls":   5
An ultimate shaking grief fixes the boy
As he stands rigid, trembling, staring down
All his young days into the harbour where
His ball went. I would not intrude on him,
A dime, another ball, is worthless. Now   10
He senses first his responsibility
In a world of possessions. People will take balls,
Balls will be lost always, little boy,
And no one buys a ball back. Money is external.
He is learning, far behind his desperate eyes,   15
The epistemology of loss, how to stand up.
Knowing what every man must one day know
And most know many days, how to stand up.
And gradually light returns to the street,
A whistle blows, the ball is out of sight,   20
Soon part of me will explore the deep and dark
Floor of the harbour. I am everywhere,
I suffer and move, my mind and my heart move
With all that move me, under the water
Or whistling, I am not a little boy.   25

JOHN BERRYMAN

Child on Top of a Greenhouse

The wind billowing out the seat of my britches,
My feet crackling splinters of glass and dried putty,
The half-grown chrysanthemums staring up like accusers,
Up through the streaked glass, flashing with sunlight,
A few white clouds all rushing eastward,   5
A line of elms plunging and tossing like horses,
And everyone, everyone pointing up and shouting!

THEODORE ROETHKE

My Papa's Waltz

The whiskey on your breath
Could make a small boy dizzy;

But I hung on like death:
Such waltzing was not easy.

We romped until the pans   5
Slid from the kitchen shelf;
My mother's countenance
Could not unfrown itself.

The hand that held my wrist
Was battered on one knuckle;   10
At every step you missed
My right ear scraped a buckle.

You beat time on my head
With a palm caked hard by dirt,
Then waltzed me off to bed   15
Still clinging to your shirt.

THEODORE ROETHKE

My Parents Kept Me from Children
Who Were Rough

My parents kept me from children who were rough
Who threw words like stones and who wore torn clothes.
Their thighs showed through rags. They ran in the street
And climbed cliffs and stripped by the country streams.

I feared more than tigers their muscles like iron   5
Their jerking hands and their knees tight on my arms.
I feared the salt coarse pointing of those boys
Who copied my lisp behind me on the road.

They were lithe, they sprang out behind hedges
Like dogs to bark at my world. They threw mud   10
While I looked the other way, pretending to smile.
I longed to forgive them, but they never smiled.

STEPHEN SPENDER

Fern Hill

Now as I was young and easy under the apple boughs
About the lilting house and happy as the grass was green,

The night above the dingle starry,
    Time let me hail and climb
  Golden in the heydays of his eyes,   5
And honoured among wagons I was prince of the apple towns
And once below a time I lordly had the trees and leaves
    Trail with daisies and barley
  Down the rivers of the windfall light.

And as I was green and carefree, famous among the barns   10
About the happy yard and singing as the farm was home,
    In the sun that is young once only,
    Time let me play and be
  Golden in the mercy of his means,
And green and golden I was huntsman and herdsman, the calves   15
Sang to my horn, the foxes on the hills barked clear and cold,
    And the sabbath rang slowly
  In the pebbles of the holy streams.

All the sun long it was running, it was lovely, the hay-
Fields high as the house, the tunes from the chimneys, it was air   20
    And playing, lovely and watery
     And fire green as grass.
    And nightly under the simple stars
As I rode to sleep the owls were bearing the farm away,
All the moon long I heard, blessed among stables, the nightjars   25
    Flying with the ricks, and the horses
     Flashing into the dark.

And then to awake, and the farm, like a wanderer white
With the dew, come back, the cock on his shoulder: it was all
    Shining, it was Adam and maiden,   30
     The sky gathered again
    And the sun grew round that very day.
So it must have been after the birth of the simple light
In the first, spinning place, the spellbound horses walking warm
    Out of the whinnying green stable   35
     On to the fields of praise.

And honoured among foxes and pheasants by the gay house
Under the new-made clouds and happy as the heart was long,
    In the sun born over and over,
     I ran my heedless ways,   40
    My wishes raced through the house-high hay
And nothing I cared, at my sky blue trades, that time allows
In all his tuneful turning so few and such morning songs

Before the children green and golden
   Follow him out of grace.   45

Nothing I cared, in the lamb white days, that time would take me
Up to the swallow-thronged loft by the shadow of my hand,
   In the moon that is always rising,
      Nor that riding to sleep
   I should hear him fly with the high fields   50
And wake to the farm forever fled from the childless land.
Oh as I was young and easy in the mercy of his means,
      Time held me green and dying
   Though I sang in my chains like the sea.

DYLAN THOMAS

2
Love

Variants on the theme of love have been popular with poets since the beginning of a written tradition in Western culture. And almost every age that has had a poetic tradition has produced fine love poetry. The poems in this section show something of the infinite range and the universality of the theme of love. Unlike some other poetic themes, which are of limited interest to the average reader, the concept of love is something that the poet can share with almost anyone.

One of the things that the poets have most often stressed about love is its paradoxical nature. It can be at the same time satisfying and frustrating, laughable and pathetic. But few people who are caught in the toils of love find it laughable, and few poets have had the audacity or the cynicism to laugh at or mock love. Shakespeare can get by with it in a fantasy like *A Midsummer Night's Dream*. Most poets, like Drayton, are more cautious. When he says, "come, let us kiss and part;/ Nay, I have done; you get no more of me," it is only to reverse himself later in the poem. The poets know that most lovers, no matter how much they may protest, secretly enjoy the game of love. Like John Donne in "The Bait," they enjoy being hooked. And if they are honest, they will admit with Thomas Moore that "poor Wisdom's chance/ Against a glance/ Is now as weak as ever."

As the poems in this section reveal, poets' attitudes toward love do not change much through the ages, though the external context of the love situation may change. The anonymous sixteenth-century poet who says, "Christ, if my love were in my arms,/ And I in my bed again!" is solaced by much the same thoughts as Tennyson, writing three centuries later: ". . . and slip/ Into my bosom and be lost in me."

The theme of love is treated extensively in other kinds of literature. The list below is intended mainly to stimulate thinking and to offer some indication of the theme's appeal.

READINGS IN OTHER GENRES

PLAYS

Edward Albee, *Who's Afraid of Virginia Woolf?*
William Congreve, *The Way of the World*
Euripides, *Hippolytus*
Henrik Ibsen, *A Doll's House*
Federico García Lorca, *Blood Wedding*
Somerset Maugham, *The Circle*
Eugene O'Neill, *Desire under the Elms*
Jean Racine, *Phaedra*
Edmond Rostand, *Cyrano de Bergerac*
William Shakespeare, *Antony and Cleopatra, Romeo and Juliet*
August Strindberg, *Miss Julie*
Ivan Turgenev, *A Month in the Country*
Tennessee Williams, *The Rose Tattoo*

NOVELS

Emily Brontë, *Wuthering Heights*
Lawrence Durrell, *The Alexandria Quartet*
Gustave Flaubert, *Madame Bovary*
Ernest Hemingway, *A Farewell to Arms*
Henry James, *Washington Square*
D. H. Lawrence, *Sons and Lovers, Women in Love*
Somerset Maugham, *Of Human Bondage*
Abbé Prévost, *Manon Lescaut*
Leo Tolstoy, *Anna Karenina*

SHORT STORIES

Kay Boyle, "Astronomer's Wife"
James B. Hall, "Us He Devours"
James Joyce, "The Dead"
Ring Lardner, "Ex Parte," "The Love Nest"
D. H. Lawrence, "The Blind Man," "The Horse Dealer's Daughter"
Thomas Mann, "Death in Venice"
Katherine Mansfield, "Bliss," "Marriage à la Mode"
Guy de Maupassant, "Love: Three Pages from a Sportsman's Book"
Carson McCullers, "A Domestic Dilemma"
Katherine Anne Porter, "María Concepción," "Rope"

Western Wind, When Wilt Thou Blow

Western wind, when wilt thou blow?
The small rain down can rain.
Christ, if my love were in my arms,
And I in my bed again!

ANONYMOUS
(Sixteenth Century)

A Renouncing of Love

Farewell, love, and all thy laws for ever,
Thy baited hooks shall tangle me no more;
Senec and Plato call me from thy lore,
To perfect wealth, my wit for to endeavor;
In blind error when I did perséver,   5
Thy sharp repulse, that pricketh aye so sore
Taught me in trifles that I set no store,
But scape forth thence, since liberty is lever.
Therefore, farewell! Go trouble younger hearts,
And in me claim no more authority;   10
With idle youth go use thy property,
And thereon spend thy many brittle darts.
For hitherto though I have lost my time,
Me list no longer rotten boughs to climb.

SIR THOMAS WYATT

Cupid and My Campaspe Played

Cupid and my Campaspe played
At cards for kisses; Cupid paid.
He stakes his quiver, bow, and arrows,
His mother's doves and team of sparrows,

Loses them too; then down he throws   5
The coral of his lip, the rose
Growing on's cheek (but none knows how),
With these the crystal of his brow,
And then the dimple of his chin:
All these did my Campaspe win.   10
At last he set her both his eyes;
She won, and Cupid blind did rise.
   O Love! has she done this to thee?
   What shall, alas, become of me?

JOHN LYLY
(From *Campaspe*)

When in Disgrace with Fortune and Men's Eyes

When in disgrace with fortune and men's eyes,
I all alone beweep my outcast state,
And trouble deaf heaven with my bootless cries,
And look upon myself, and curse my fate,
Wishing me like to one more rich in hope,   5
Featured like him, like him with friends possessed,
Desiring this man's art, and that man's scope,
With what I most enjoy contented least;
Yet in these thoughts myself almost despising,
Haply I think on thee, and then my state,   10
Like to the lark at break of day arising
From sullen earth, sings hymns at heaven's gate;
   For thy sweet love remembered such wealth brings
   That then I scorn to change my state with kings.

WILLIAM SHAKESPEARE

Let Me Not to the Marriage of True Minds

Let me not to the marriage of true minds
Admit impediments. Love is not love
Which alters when it alteration finds,
Or bends with the remover to remove.
O, no! it is an ever-fixèd mark,   5
That looks on tempests and is never shaken;
It is the star to every wand'ring bark,
Whose worth's unknown, although his height be taken.

Love's not Time's fool, though rosy lips and cheeks
Within his bending sickle's compass come;   10
Love alters not with his brief hours and weeks,
But bears it out even to the edge of doom.
   If this be error and upon me proved,
    I never writ, nor no man ever loved.

WILLIAM SHAKESPEARE

When to the Sessions of Sweet Silent Thought

When to the sessions of sweet silent thought
I summon up remembrance of things past,
I sigh the lack of many a thing I sought,
And with old woes new wail my dear time's waste;
Then can I drown an eye, unused to flow,   5
For precious friends hid in death's dateless night,
And weep afresh love's long-since-cancelled woe,
And moan th' expense of many a vanished sight;
Then can I grieve at grievances foregone,
And heavily from woe to woe tell o'er   10
The sad account of fore-bemoanèd moan,
Which I new pay as if not paid before.
   But if the while I think on thee, dear friend,
    All losses are restored and sorrows end.

WILLIAM SHAKESPEARE

My Love Is as a Fever

My love is as a fever, longing still
For that which longer nurseth the disease,
Feeding on that which doth preserve the ill,
The uncertain sickly appetite to please.
My reason, the physician to my love,   5
Angry that his prescriptions are not kept,
Hath left me, and I desperate now approve
Desire is death, which physic did except.
Past cure I am, now reason is past care,
And frantic-mad with evermore unrest.   10
My thoughts and my discourse as madmen's are,
At random from the truth vainly expressed,
   For I have sworn thee fair, and thought thee bright
    Who art as black as Hell, as dark as night.

WILLIAM SHAKESPEARE

Shakespeare's Sonnet 147: An Explication*

Karen Alexander

Shakespeare addressed Sonnet 147 to his mysterious "dark lady." It seems to have been written during a period of self-disgust and disenchantment with his lover. It must be assumed that the attitude expressed in this sonnet was only temporary, since the sonnet immediately following this one resumes the poet's praises of the lady and his amazement at his own blindness.

My love, says the poet in Sonnet 147, is a disease that has permeated my whole being. Reason is unable to control it and has abdicated to my desire. My desire has made me mad and blind to your appearance and to your character. At last, he says, I realize that I have been deceiving myself about you. My desire has been stronger than my reason, and I am suffering because of it. The triumph of desire over reason, with the attending pain and self-disgust, is in essence the central idea of this poem. It manifests itself in the two-pronged metaphor which equates love with disease and reason with the physician whose instructions are ignored.

The first quatrain introduces the main metaphor of the poem. The poet's love is like a fever, a disease, that yearns for the very poison which will only continue and increase the fever. The play on the word "long" suggests yearning for, but also implies continuation of a condition of long standing. His love gains nourishment only from that which makes him sicker, and he continues to love because it feeds his desire which must, therefore, be unhealthy, too.

The metaphor is expanded in the second quatrain when his reason steps in as his physician. His reason, however, leaves him because its remedies and medicines have not been used; its advice has not been heeded. Now he is proving by experience that his desire, which reason has forbidden, is death to him.

The third quatrain is a description of his present condition. His love-disease is past cure, and his reason has deserted him. He is frantic with all the turmoil and unrest that he is going through. His thoughts and his speech are like a madman's because they have aimed in all directions but at the truth that many have uselessly pointed out to him.

In the couplet he admits the truth about himself and about her. He has deceived himself by thinking her beautiful and full of charm when she is, in reality, as unattractive and as despicable as everyone has said she is.

The lover's sickness is obviously not to be taken lightly. He is not melancholy in the tradition of Courtly Love as was Romeo over Rosaline. His love is a disease too serious to be euphemistically or romantically referred to as a *malade*. His love is unhealthy; it is an illness which consumes him, a cancer "feeding" on itself to please his appetite. His "sickly appetite" has been the

* Student theme.

sadistic father of his unrest. Indeed, all of the words used to carry out the metaphor—"fever," "nurseth," "disease," "feeding," "ill," "sickly," "physician," "prescription," "death," "physic," "cure"—point to a physical reason for his madness. He seems to be more in heat than in love. The phrasing of the sonnet generally is such as one uses when he is upbraiding himself, when he is disgusted with himself, when he is rebuking himself for his foolishness. They are not words that ask for sympathy; they evoke no romantic sentiments. Even the word "frantic," as the *Oxford English Dictionary* reveals, lends support to this tone of the sonnet, for it was once used as "a term of reproach imputing extreme folly."

The lover's sickness seems at least to allow him to gain a certain insight; as the phrase "At random from the truth" indicates, it is but a short step from "vainly" to "vanity." It is not illogical in the context to think of the word "vainly" in two senses: as the "objective" truth expressed in vain by others and as the lover's "truth" dictated by his vanity. The closing couplet supports these two points of view, but in the end the lover's "truth" yields to "objective" truth.

His attitude toward his lover as revealed at the end of the sonnet is still somewhat ambivalent. He has thought her "bright" and sworn her "fair," but seems in the light of objective truth to have found out otherwise. Yet the descending order of climax in both lines of the final couplet makes for deliberate ambiguity. The second part of the last line especially is not as damning as it might at first seem. Even though one takes into consideration that "night" had connotations of mischief and evil, it would appear that he is relenting a bit in his harsh judgment, for it would be logical to suppose that his judgments of her would be written in ascending order of harshness.

While it is not one of the great sonnets, Sonnet 147 is, I think, successful. The love/fever metaphor is not particularly impressive in itself until it is extended; then one discovers that the words used to complete the metaphor are words that qualify the metaphor and shape the tone of the poem. The central idea of the triumph of desire over reason is, as I have mentioned, enormously restrained and qualified by his disgust at the triumph. Perhaps the most powerful aspect of the metaphor, however, is that it so sharply defines the duality of man in love.

Young and Simple Though I Am

Young and simple though I am,
I have heard of Cupid's name:
Guess I can what thing it is
Men desire when they do kiss.
Smoke can never burn, they say,   5
But the flames that follow may.

I am not so foul or fair
To be proud nor to despair;
Yet my lips have oft observed
Men that kiss them press them hard,   10
As glad lovers use to do
When their new-met loves they woo.

Faith, 'tis but a foolish mind,
Yet methinks, a heat I find,
Like thirst longing, that doth bide   15
Ever on my weaker side,
Where they say my heart doth move.
Venus, grant it be not love.

If it be, alas, what then?
Were not women made for men?   20
As good 'twere a thing were past
That must needs be done at last.
Roses that are over-blown,
Grow less sweet, then fall alone.

Yet not churl, nor silken gull,   25
Shall my maiden blossom pull;
Who shall not I soon can tell;
Who shall, would I could as well!
This I know, whoe'er he be,
Love he must or flatter me.   30

THOMAS CAMPION

Come, You Pretty False-Eyed Wanton

Come, you pretty false-eyed wanton,
    Leave your crafty smiling!
Think you to escape me now
    With slipp'ry words beguiling?
No; you mocked me th' other day;   5
    When you got loose, you fled away;
But, since I have caught you now,
I'll clip your wings for flying:
Smoth'ring kisses fast I'll heap
    And keep you so from crying.   10

Sooner may you count the stars
    And number hail down-pouring,

Tell the osiers of the Thames,
   Or Goodwin sands devouring,
Than the thick-showered kisses here   15
   Which now thy tired lips must bear.
Such a harvest never was
   So rich and full of pleasure,
But 'tis spent as soon as reaped,
   So trustless is love's treasure.   20

THOMAS CAMPION

Since There's No Help

Since there's no help, come let us kiss and part;
Nay, I have done; you get no more of me,
And I am glad, yea glad with all my heart
That thus so cleanly I myself can free;
Shake hands forever, cancel all our vows,   5
And when we meet at any time again,
Be it not seen in either of our brows
That we one jot of former love retain.
Now at the last gasp of love's latest breath,
When, his pulse failing, passion speechless lies,   10
When faith is kneeling by his bed of death,
And innocence is closing up his eyes,
   Now if thou wouldst, when all have given him over,
   From death to life thou mightst him yet recover.

MICHAEL DRAYTON

The Bait

Come live with me, and be my love,
And we will some new pleasures prove,
Of golden sands, and crystal brooks,
With silken lines, and silver hooks.

There will the river whispering run,   5
Warmed by the eyes more than the sun,
And there the enamored fish will stay,
Begging themselves they may betray.

When thou wilt swim in that live bath,
Each fish, which every channel hath,   10

Will amorously to thee swim,
Gladder to catch thee, than thou him.

If thou, to be so seen, beest loth,
By sun or moon, thou darkenest both;
And if myself have leave to see,   15
I need not their light, having thee.

Let others freeze with angling reeds,
And cut their legs with shells and weeds,
Or treacherously poor fish beset
With strangling snare, or windowy net.   20

Let coarse bold hands from slimy nest
The bedded fish in banks out-wrest,
Or curious traitors, sleave-silk flies,
Bewitch poor fishes' wandering eyes.

For thee, thou need'st no such deceit,   25
For thou thyself art thine own bait;
The fish that is not catched thereby,
Alas, is wiser far than I.

                                    JOHN DONNE

Go and Catch a Falling Star

Go and catch a falling star,
    Get with child a mandrake root,
Tell me where all past years are,
    Or who cleft the devil's foot;
Teach me to hear the mermaids singing,   5
Or to keep off envy's stinging,
                And find
                What wind
Serves to advance an honest mind.

If thou be'st born to strange sights,   10
    Things invisible to see,
Ride ten thousand days and nights
    Till age snow white hairs on thee;
Thou, when thou return'st, wilt tell me
All strange wonders that befell thee,   15
                And swear
                No where
Lives a woman true and fair.

If thou find'st one, let me know,
    Such a pilgrimage were sweet;   20
Yet do not, I would not go,
    Though at next door we might meet;
Though she were true when you met her,
And last till you write your letter,
        Yet she   25
        Will be
False, ere I come, to two or three.

JOHN DONNE

The Good-Morrow

I wonder, by my troth, what thou and I
Did, till we loved? Were we not weaned till then?
But sucked on country pleasures, childishly?
Or snorted we in the Seven Sleepers' den?
'Twas so; but this, all pleasures fancies be;   5
If ever any beauty I did see,
Which I desired, and got, 'twas but a dream of thee.

And now good-morrow to our waking souls,
Which watch not one another out of fear;
For love all love of other sights controls,   10
And makes one little room an everywhere.
Let sea-discoverers to new worlds have gone;
Let maps to others, worlds on worlds have shown;
Let us possess one world; each hath one, and is one.

My face in thine eye, thine in mine appears,   15
And true plain hearts do in the faces rest;
Where can we find two better hemispheres
Without sharp North, without declining West?
Whatever dies was not mixed equally;
If our two loves be one, or thou and I   20
Love so alike that none do slacken, none can die.

JOHN DONNE

The Canonization

For God's sake hold your tongue and let me love,
    Or chide my palsy or my gout,

My five gray hairs or ruined fortune flout,
  With wealth your state, your mind with arts improve,
    Take you a course, get you a place,   5
    Observe his Honor, or his Grace,
Or the king's real, or his stamped face
  Contemplate; what you will, approve,
  So you will let me love.

Alas, alas, who's injured by my love?   10
  What merchant's ships have my sighs drowned?
Who says my tears have overflowed his ground?
  When did my colds a forward spring remove?
    When did the heats which my veins fill
    Add one more to the plaguy bill?   15
Soldiers find wars, and lawyers find out still
  Litigious men, which quarrels move,
  Though she and I do love.

Call us what you will, we are made such by love;
  Call her one, me another fly,   20
We are tapers too, and at our own cost die,
  And we in us find the eagle and the dove.
    The phoenix riddle hath more wit
    By us: we two being one, are it.
So to one neutral thing both sexes fit,   25
  We die and rise the same, and prove
  Mysterious by this love.

We can die by it, if not live by love,
  And if unfit for tombs and hearse
Our legend be, it will be fit for verse;   30
  And if no piece of chronicle we prove,
    We'll build in sonnets pretty rooms;
    As well a well-wrought urn becomes
The greatest ashes, as half-acre tombs,
  And by these hymns, all shall approve   35
  Us *canonized* for love:

And thus invoke us: You whom reverend love
  Made one another's hermitage;
You, to whom love was peace, that now is rage;
  Who did the whole world's soul contract, and drove   40
    Into the glasses of your eyes
    (So made such mirrors and such spies
That they did all to you epitomize)

Countries, towns, courts: Beg from above
A pattern of your love!   45

JOHN DONNE

Sweetest Love, I Do Not Go

Sweetest love, I do not go,
   For weariness of thee,
Nor in hope the world can show
   A fitter love for me;
     But since that I   5
Must die at last, 'tis best,
To use myself in jest
   Thus by feigned deaths to die.

Yesternight the sun went hence,
   And yet is here today;   10
He hath no desire nor sense,
   Nor half so short a way.
     Then fear not me;
But believe that I shall make
Speedier journeys, since I take   15
   More wings and spurs than he.

O how feeble is man's power,
   That if good fortune fall,
Cannot add another hour,
   Nor a lost hour recall!   20
     But come bad chance,
And we join to it our strength,
And we teach it art and length,
   Itself o'er us to advance.

When thou sigh'st, thou sigh'st not wind,   25
   But sigh'st my soul away,
When thou weepest, unkindly kind,
   My life's blood doth decay.
     It cannot be
That thou lovest me, as thou say'st,   30
If in thine my life thou waste,
   Thou art the best of me.

Let not thy divining heart
   Forethink me any ill;

Destiny may take thy part,   35
    And may thy fears fulfill;
        But think that we
    Are but turned aside to sleep;
    They who one another keep
        Alive, ne'er parted be.   40

JOHN DONNE

A Valediction: Forbidding Mourning

As virtuous men pass mildly away,
    And whisper to their souls to go,
Whilst some of their sad friends do say,
    "The breath goes now," and some say, "no";

So let us melt, and make no noise,   5
    No tear-floods, nor sigh-tempests move;
'Twere profanation of our joys
    To tell the laity our love.

Moving of the earth brings harms and fears;
    Men reckon what it did, and meant;   10
But trepidation of the spheres,
    Though greater far, is innocent.

Dull sublunary lovers' love
    (Whose soul is sense) cannot admit
Absence, because it doth remove   15
    Those things which elemented it.

But we by a love so much refined
    That ourselves know not what it is,
Inter-assurèd of the mind,
    Care less, eyes, lips, and hands to miss. 20

Our two souls therefore, which are one,
    Though I must go, endure not yet
A breach, but an expansion,
    Like gold to airy thinness beat.

If they be two, they are two so   25
    As stiff twin compasses are two;
Thy soul, the fixed foot, makes no show
    To move, but doth, if the other do.

And though it in the center sit,
   Yet, when the other far doth roam,   30
It leans, and hearkens after it,
   And grows erect, as that comes home.

Such wilt thou be to me, who must,
   Like the other foot, obliquely run;
Thy firmness makes my circle just,   35
   And makes me end where I begun.

                JOHN DONNE

Out Upon It! I Have Loved

Out upon it! I have loved
   Three whole days together;
And am like to love three more,
   If it prove fair weather.

Time shall moult away his wings,   5
   Ere he shall discover
In the whole wide world again
   Such a constant lover.

But the spite on't is, no praise
   Is due at all to me: 10
Love with me had made no stays
   Had it any been but she.

Had it any been but she,
   And that very face,
There had been at least ere this   15
   A dozen dozen in her place.

          SIR JOHN SUCKLING

After the Pangs of a Desperate Lover

After the pangs of a desperate lover,
   When day and night I have sighed all in vain,
Ah what a pleasure it is to discover
   In her eyes pity, who causes my pain!

When with unkindness our love at a stand is,   5
    And both have punished ourselves with the pain,
Ah what a pleasure the touch of her hand is,
    Ah what a pleasure to press it again!

When the denial comes fainter and fainter,
    And her eyes give what her tongue does deny,   10
Ah what a trembling I feel when I venture,
    Ah what a trembling does usher my joy!

When, with a sigh, she accords me the blessing,
    And her eyes twinkle 'twixt pleasure and pain;
Ah what a joy 'tis, beyond all expressing,   15
    Ah what a joy to hear, shall we again!

                                        JOHN DRYDEN

Green Grow the Rashes

Green grow the rashes, O;
    Green grow the rashes, O;
The sweetest hours that e'er I spend,
    Are spent amang the lasses, O!

There's nough but care on ev'ry han',   5
    In ev'ry hour that passes, O:
What signifies the life o' man,
    An' 'twere na for the lasses, O.

The war'ly race may riches chase,
    An' riches still may fly them, O;   10
An' though at last they catch them fast,
    Their hearts can ne'er enjoy them, O.

But gie me a canny[1] hour at e'en,
    My arms about my dearie, O;
An' war'ly cares, an' war'ly men,   15
    May a' gae tapsalteerie,[2] O!

For you sae douce,[3] ye sneer at this,
    Ye're nought but senseless asses, O:
The wisest man the warl' e'er saw,
    He dearly loved the lasses, O.   20

---

[1] Quiet.   [2] Topsy-turvy.   [3] Serious.

Auld nature swears, the lovely dears
  Her noblest work she classes, O:
Her prentice han' she tried on man,
  An' then she made the lasses, O.

ROBERT BURNS

O, Wert Thou in the Cauld Blast

O, wert thou in the cauld blast,
  On yonder lea, on yonder lea,
My plaidie to the angry airt,
  I'd shelter thee, I'd shelter thee.
Or did misfortune's bitter storms   5
  Around thee blaw, around thee blaw,
Thy bield[1] should be my bosom,
  To share it a', to share it a'.

Or were I in the wildest waste,
  Sae black and bare, sae black and bare,   10
The desert were a paradise,
  If thou wert there, if thou wert there.
Or were I monarch o' the globe,
  Wi' thee to reign, wi' thee to reign,
The brightest jewel in my crown   15
  Wad be my queen, wad be my queen.

ROBERT BURNS

[1] Shelter.

The Banks o' Doon

Ye flowery banks o' bonnie Doon,
  How can ye blume sae fair!
How can ye chant, ye little birds,
  And I sae fu' o' care!

Thou'll break my heart, thou bonnie bird,   5
  That sings upon the bough;
Thou minds me o' the happy days
  When my fause luve was true.

Thou'll break my heart, thou bonnie bird,
  That sings beside thy mate;   10

For sae I sat, and sae I sang,
   And wistna o' my fate.

Aft hae I roved by bonnie Doon,
   To see the woodbine twine;
And ilka bird sang o' its luve,   15
   And sae did I o' mine.

Wi' lightsome heart I pu'd a rose
   Upon a morn in June;
And sae I flourished on the morn,
   And sae was pu'd or' noon.   20

Wi' lightsome heart I pu'd a rose
   Upon its thorny tree;
But my fause luver staw my rose,
   And left the thorn wi' me.

ROBERT BURNS

A Red, Red Rose

O, my luve's like a red, red rose,
   That's newly sprung in June;
O, my luve's like the melodie
   That's sweetly played in tune.

As fair art thou, my bonnie lass,   5
   So deep in luve am I;
And I will luve thee still, my dear,
   Till a' the seas gang dry.

Till a' the seas gang dry, my dear,
   And the rocks melt wi' the sun;   10
And I will luve thee still, my dear,
   While the sands o' life shall run.

And fare thee weel, my only luve,
   And fare thee weel awhile!
And I will come again, my luve,   15
   Though it were ten thousand mile.

ROBERT BURNS

Mary Morison

O Mary, at thy window be,
    It is the wished, the trysted hour!
Those smiles and glances let me see,
    That make the miser's treasure poor:
How blythely wad I bide the stoure,   5
    A weary slave frae sun to sun,
Could I the rich reward secure,
    The lovely Mary Morison.

Yestreen, when to the trembling string
    The dance gaed thro' the lighted ha',   10
To thee my fancy took its wing,
    I sat, but neither heard nor saw:
Tho' this was fair, and that was braw,
    And yon the toast of a' the town,
I sighed, and said amang them a',   15
    "Ye are na Mary Morison."

O Mary, canst thou wreck his peace,
    Wha for thy sake wad gladly die?
Or canst thou break that heart of his,
    Whase only faut is loving thee?   20
If love for love thou wilt na gie,
    At least be pity to me shown!
A thought ungentle canna be
    The thought o' Mary Morison.

                              ROBERT BURNS

My Silks and Fine Array

My silks and fine array,
    My smiles and languished air,
By love are driven away;
    And mournful lean Despair
Brings me yew to deck my grave: 5
Such end true lovers have.

His face is fair as heaven
    When springing buds unfold;
O why to him was't given
    Whose heart is wintry cold?   10

His breast is love's all-worshipped tomb,
Where all love's pilgrims come.

Bring me an axe and spade,
    Bring me a winding sheet;
When I my grave have made   15
    Let winds and tempests beat:
Then down I'll lie as cold as clay.
True love doth pass away!

WILLIAM BLAKE

Never Seek to Tell Thy Love

Never seek to tell thy love,
Love that never told can be;
For the gentle wind does move
Silently, invisibly.

I told my love, I told my love,   5
I told her all my heart;
Trembling, cold, in ghastly fears.
Ah! she doth depart.

Soon as she was gone from me,
A traveller came by,   10
Silently, invisibly:
He took her with a sigh.

WILLIAM BLAKE

The Garden of Love

I went to the Garden of Love,
And saw what I never had seen:
A Chapel was built in the midst,
Where I used to play on the green.

And the gates of this Chapel were shut,   5
And "Thou shalt not" writ over the door;
So I turned to the Garden of Love
That so many sweet flowers bore;

And I saw it was fillèd with graves,
And tomb-stones where flowers should be;   10
And priests in black gowns were walking their rounds,
And binding with briars my joys and desires.

WILLIAM BLAKE

The Time I've Lost in Wooing

The time I've lost in wooing,
In watching and pursuing
  The light that lies
  In woman's eyes
Has been my heart's undoing.   5
Though Wisdom oft has sought me,
I scorned the lore she brought me,
  My only books
  Were woman's looks,
And folly's all they've taught me.   10

Her smile when Beauty granted,
I hung with gaze enchanted,
  Like him, the Sprite,
  Whom maids by night
Oft meet in glen that's haunted.   15
Like him, too, Beauty won me,
But while her eyes were on me;
  If once their ray
  Was turned away,
O! winds could not outrun me.   20

And are those follies going?
And is my proud heart growing
  Too cold or wise
  For brilliant eyes
Again to set it glowing?   25
No, vain, alas! the endeavor
From bonds so sweet to sever;
  Poor Wisdom's chance
  Against a glance
Is now as weak as ever.   30

THOMAS MOORE

There Be None of Beauty's Daughters

1

There be none of Beauty's daughters
   With a magic like thee;
And like music on the waters
   Is thy sweet voice to me:
When, as if its sound were causing   5
The charmed ocean's pausing,
The waves lie still and gleaming,
And the lulled winds seem dreaming;

2

And the midnight moon is weaving
   Her bright chain o'er the deep;   10
Whose breast is gently heaving,
   As an infant's asleep:
So the spirit bows before thee,
To listen and adore thee;
With a full but soft emotion,   15
Like the swell of summer's ocean.

GEORGE GORDON, LORD BYRON

Maid of Athens, Ere We Part

Maid of Athens, ere we part,
Give, oh give me back my heart!
Or, since that has left my breast,
Keep it now, and take the rest!
Hear my vow before I go,   5
Ζωή μου, σᾶς ἀγαπῶ.[1]

By those tresses unconfined,
Wooed by each Aegean wind;
By those lids whose jetty fringe
Kiss thy soft cheeks' blooming tinge;   10
By those wild eyes like the roe,
Ζωή μου, σᾶς ἀγαπῶ.

By that lip I long to taste;
By that zone-encircled waist;

[1] "My life, I love you."

By all the token-flowers that tell   15
What words can never speak so well;
By Love's alternate joy and woe,
Ζωή μου, σᾶς ἀγαπῶ.

Maid of Athens! I am gone:
Think of me, sweet! when alone.   20
Though I fly to Istambol,
Athens holds my heart and soul:
Can I cease to love thee? No!
Ζωή μου, σᾶς ἀγαπῶ.

GEORGE GORDON, LORD BYRON

To _____

I

One word is too often profaned
   For me to profane it,
One feeling too falsely disdained
   For thee to disdain it.
One hope is too like despair   5
   For prudence to smother,
And pity from thee more dear
   Than that from another.

II

I can give not what men call love,
   But wilt thou accept not   10
The worship the heart lifts above
   And the Heavens reject not,—
The desire of the moth for the star,
   Of the night for the morrow,
The devotion to something afar   15
   From the sphere of our sorrow?

PERCY BYSSHE SHELLEY

Now Sleeps the Crimson Petal

Now sleeps the crimson petal, now the white;
Nor waves the cypress in the palace walk;
Nor winks the gold fin in the porphyry font:
The fire-fly wakens: waken thou with me.

Now droops the milkwhite peacock like a ghost,   5
And like a ghost she glimmers on to me.

Now lies the Earth all Danaë to the stars,
And all thy heart lies open unto me.

Now slides the silent meteor on, and leaves
A shining furrow, as thy thoughts in me.   10

Now folds the lily all her sweetness up,
And slips into the bosom of the lake:
So fold thyself, my dearest, thou, and slip
Into my bosom and be lost in me.

ALFRED, LORD TENNYSON

How Do I Love Thee

How do I love thee? Let me count the ways.
I love thee to the depth and breadth and height
My soul can reach, when feeling out of sight
For the ends of Being and ideal Grace.
I love thee to the level of every day's   5
Most quiet need, by sun and candlelight.
I love thee freely, as men strive for Right;
I love thee purely, as they turn from Praise.
I love thee with the passion put to use
In my old griefs, and with my childhood's faith.   10
I love thee with a love I seemed to lose
With my lost saints,—I love thee with the breath,
Smiles, tears, of all my life!—and, if God choose,
I shall but love thee better after death.

ELIZABETH BARRETT BROWNING

A Reading of Elizabeth Barrett Browning's "How Do I Love Thee"

Winfred S. Emmons

"How Do I Love Thee" has had its critical ups and downs during the hundred-odd years of its existence. At first regarded as a good poem by a good poet, at a time when poems were supposed to be read, not solved, it fell into critical disfavor in certain circles which may be exemplified by a short article by Robert B.

Heilman in *The Explicator,* IV (October 1945), 3. Some part of the disfavor of the poem may be attributed to the disfavor with which Mrs. Browning herself is viewed, based on the huge amount of bad poetry she wrote. The poem is, moreover, Victorian, sentimental, and religious, and all of these are bad words in the mouths of many critics. Many a reader who had the poem spoiled for him in the first place by having it read to him by an intense lady with a throaty contralto voice must have, doubtless, seized on criticisms like Mr. Heilman's with glad hosannahs. Yet Mr. Heilman's criticism was unfair, impressionistic, and largely inaccurate.

Comparing "How Do I Love Thee" to Goneril's speech from *King Lear,* I, i, 56–62, Mr. Heilman finds Shakespeare's imagery sharper than Mrs. Browning's and says, "E. B. B.'s sonnet is as embarrassing as all platform rhetoric; she can find no images to realize, to prove her experience. Ironically, she relies on personal sincerity to give body to her words, whereas Goneril relies on comparable words to suggest a body of sincerity." One regrets that Mr. Heilman is embarrassed by platform rhetoric (which is what he means); but his embarrassment is no basis for any objective condemnation of the poem. In a narrowly technical sense the poem may be deficient in images, but only a small minority of professional critics are entitled to experience rising of the gorge at such a lack, especially when in a less technical sense it is *not* deficient in images. The exact meaning of Mr. Heilman's remarks about sincerity is not clear; perhaps he means that he does not like the words Mrs. Browning chose to build into her poem. Granted that it is less good than most of Shakespeare, and most poems are, Mrs. Browning's words are for the most part well chosen, and her poem is as closely related to experience as Shakespeare's, though experience by a different kind of person.

Speaking in her own person, Mrs. Browning seems to be not only religious but also probably an orthodox Christian, though the "ways" in which she loves her husband are not all directly related to her religion; if they were, the poem would not be as good as it is. First:

> I love thee to the depth and breadth and height
> My soul can reach, when feeling out of sight
> For the ends of Being and ideal Grace.

Mr. Heilman finds the poem full of "gusty protestations," and this is doubtless one of them; he is presumably repelled by the lack of concreteness that might be ascribed to a soul "reaching" and "feeling." But reaching and feeling are in themselves concrete images of search, and when "feeling out of sight," the search is being carried on in terms of faith. This "way" in which Mrs. Browning loved Robert Browning was involved in longing for the infinite, an experience not known to many readers, and it illustrates the fact that longing for the infinite can best be realized in terms of longing or love for something finite. Thus does

Mrs. Browning introduce her love, on a note of high abstraction but an abstraction that is immediately related to the concrete by the context in which it is presented. Whatever else one might say of Robert Browning, he was indeed concrete.

The second "way" deliberately leaves the realm of lofty philosophical speculation and yearning and goes to the commonplace and the domestic:

> I love thee to the level of every day's
> Most quiet need, by sun and candlelight.

At this point one needs a little memory and imagination; she also loves her husband as she loves her breakfast, her books, the creature comforts of her home. If the reader knows a little more about her, her love for her husband is even involved in the affection she feels for Flush, her dog, who never quite shared that affection. To those familiar with romantic love, the loved object has the quality of coloring the entire universe. All the little things in her world which are enjoyable, whether in the broad light of day or in the more intimate world of lighted candles, become more enjoyable because they exist in the same world which her husband inhabits.

The third and fourth "ways," however, are harder to pin down:

> I love thee freely, as men strive for Right;
> I love thee purely, as they turn from Praise.

Is "freely" the quality with which men "strive for Right"? (Not all men do so strive.) And is there any inevitability in the "pureness" with which they "turn from Praise"? These are doubtless the two worst lines in the poem, and it is well that they are buried almost in the exact middle; if the reader has been in any sense captivated by the preceding lines, he is apt to coast through them and not realize their vagueness, or even their lack of meaning, unless he is doing a formal analysis of the poem, like this one.

One might object to the fifth "way" on the basis that it seems to be two ways:

> I love thee with the passion put to use
> In my old griefs, and with my childhood's faith.

But perhaps it is the reader who has miscounted, not the poet; this may be only one "way." And a complexity is injected with "the passion put to use/ In my old griefs"; until now the reader has assumed only joy in the poet's love, but any mature person knows that love is inseparable from grief, which may be related to the actual or potential loss of the loved one or to the loss of love itself.

It is ladylike and indeed Victorian that Mrs. Browning associates "passion" here with grief, not with the lustier emotions, as did Algernon Swinburne in "Dolores":

> By the ravenous teeth that have smitten
> Through the kisses that blossom and bud,
> By the lips intertwisted and bitten
> Till the foam has a savour of blood . . .

And it is possible that there are critics who might feel that Mrs. Browning has somehow fallen short of the mark in not incorporating such manifestations of passion in her poem. I am not one of them.

How old are her "old griefs," and what were they? One might read Mrs. Browning's published letters and find out, but a better procedure, which the competent reader will already have followed anyway, is to use one's own experience. Most people have endured sorrows of their own which may be brought to bear on a reading of these lines. The following phrase, "and with my childhood's faith," may tend to localize the griefs themselves in the author's childhood, a period in which all things are experienced more passionately than later.

The love which she relates to her childhood's faith, Mrs. Browning restates in "I love thee with a love I seemed to lose/ With my lost saints." Her list of "ways" has now come full circle, back to the religious, but the religious element that was first stated in terms of a kind of mystical craving for the infinite is now stated in terms of personal belief and restored faith; the love she "seemed to lose" with her "lost saints," which actually continued to exist but without anything very concrete to relate to, now again has a foundation. The implication that Robert Browning is himself a saint (in the Catholic sense) is hyperbolical; but anyone who can bear the brand of hyperbole found in sonnets to one's mistress's eyebrow ought to be able to tolerate Mrs. Browning's.

". . . I love thee with the breath,/ Smiles, tears, of all my life!" recapitulates and concludes the poem as it has dealt with her love itself. The religious element, powerful throughout, has a conclusion of its own: ". . . and, if God choose,/ I shall but love thee better after death" builds an unobtrusive paradox on the notion of grief introduced earlier. No lover who is also religious can separate his love for the loved one from his love and knowledge of God.

I Cannot Live with You

> I cannot live with you.
> It would be life,
> And life is over there
> Behind the shelf
>
> The sexton keeps the key to,   5
> Putting up
> Our life, his porcelain,
> Like a cup

Discarded of the housewife,
Quaint or broken;   10
A newer Sèvres pleases,
Old ones crack.

I could not die with you,
For one must wait
To shut the other's gaze down,   15
You could not.

And I, could I stand by
And see you freeze,
Without my right of frost,
Death's privilege?   20

Nor could I rise with you,
Because your face
Would put out Jesus',
That new grace

Glow plain and foreign   25
On my homesick eye,
Except that you, than he
Shone closer by.

They'd judge us—how?
For you served Heaven, you know,   30
Or sought to;
I could not,

Because you saturated sight,
And I had no more eyes
For sordid excellence   35
As Paradise.

And were you lost, I would be,
Though my name
Rang loudest
On the heavenly fame.   40

And were you saved,
And I condemned to be
Where you were not,
That self were hell to me.

So we must keep apart,   45
You there, I here,

With just the door ajar
That oceans are,
And prayer,
And that pale sustenance,   50
Despair!

EMILY DICKINSON

Never the Time and the Place

Never the time and the place
    And the loved one all together!
This path—how soft to pace!
    This May—what magic weather!
Where is the loved one's face?   5
In a dream that loved one's face meets mine,
    But the house is narrow, the place is bleak
Where, outside, rain and wind combine
    With a furtive ear, if I strive to speak,
    With a hostile eye at my flushing cheek,   10
With a malice that marks each word, each sign!
O enemy sly and serpentine,
    Uncoil thee from the waking man!
      Do I hold the Past
        Thus firm and fast   15
    Yet doubt if the Future hold I can?
This path so soft to pace shall lead
Through the magic of May to herself indeed!
Or narrow if needs the house must be,
Outside are the storms and strangers; we—   20
Oh, close, safe, warm sleep I and she—
    I and she!

ROBERT BROWNING

Thus Piteously Love Closed What He Begat

Thus piteously Love closed what he begat:
The union of this ever-diverse pair!
These two were rapid falcons in a snare,
Condemned to do the flitting of the bat.
Lovers beneath the singing sky of May,   5
They wandered once; clear as the dew on flowers;
But they fed not on the advancing hours:

Their hearts held cravings for the buried day.
Then each applied to each that fatal knife,
Deep questioning, which probes to endless dole.   10
Ah, what a dusty answer gets the soul
When hot for certainties in this our life!—
In tragic hints here see what evermore
Moves dark as yonder midnight ocean's force,
Thundering like ramping hosts of warrior horse,   15
To throw that faint thin line upon the shore!

GEORGE MEREDITH

The Harlot's House

We caught the tread of dancing feet,
We loitered down the moonlit street,
And stopped beneath the Harlot's House.

Inside, above the din and fray,
We heard the loud musicians play   5
The "Treues Liebes Herz"[1] of Strauss.

Like strange mechanical grotesques,
Making fantastic arabesques,
The shadows raced across the blind.

We watched the ghostly dancers spin   10
To sound of horn and violin,
Like black leaves wheeling in the wind.

Like wire-pulled Automatons,
Slim silhouetted skeletons
Went sidling through the slow quadrille.   15

They took each other by the hand,
And danced a stately saraband;
Their laughter echoed thin and shrill.

Sometimes a clockwork puppet pressed
A phantom lover to her breast,   20
Sometimes they seemed to try to sing.

Sometimes a horrible Marionette
Came out, and smoked its cigarette
Upon the steps like a live thing.

1 "True Love's Heart."

Then, turning to my love, I said,   25
"The dead are dancing with the dead,
The dust is whirling with the dust."

But she—she heard the violin,
And left my side, and entered in:
Love passed into the House of Lust.   30

Then suddenly the tune went false,
The dancers wearied of the waltz,
The shadows ceased to wheel and whirl.

And down the long and silent street,
The dawn, with silver-sandalled feet,   35
Crept like a frightened girl.

OSCAR WILDE

The Dark-Eyed Gentleman

I pitched my day's leazings[1] in Crimmercrock Lane,
To tie up my garter and jog on again,
When a dear dark-eyed gentleman passed there and said,
In a way that made all o' me color rose-red,
     "What do I see—   5
     O pretty knee!"
And he came and he tied up my garter for me.

'Twixt sunset and moonrise it was, I can mind:
Ah, 'tis easy to lose what we nevermore find!—
Of the dear stranger's home, of his name, I knew nought,   10
But I soon knew his nature and all that it brought.
     Then bitterly
     Sobbed I that he
Should ever have tied up my garter for me!

Yet now I've beside me a fine lissom lad,   15
And my slip's nigh forgot, and my days are not sad;
My own dearest joy is he, comrade, and friend,
He it is who safe-guards me, on him I depend;
     No sorrow brings he,
     And thankful I be
That his daddy once tied up my garter for me!   20

THOMAS HARDY

[1] Bundles of gleaned wheat.

An Old Song Resung

Down by the salley[1] gardens my love and I did meet;
She passed the salley gardens with little snow-white feet.
She bid me take love easy, as the leaves grow on the tree;
But I, being young and foolish, with her would not agree.

In a field by the river my love and I did stand,   5
And on my leaning shoulder she laid her snow-white hand.
She bid me take life easy, as the grass grows on the weirs;
But I was young and foolish, and now am full of tears.

WILLIAM BUTLER YEATS

[1] Sallow, a kind of willow.

When You Are Old

When you are old and grey and full of sleep,
And nodding by the fire, take down this book,
And slowly read, and dream of the soft look
Your eyes had once, and of their shadows deep;

How many loved your moments of glad grace,   5
And loved your beauty with love false or true,
But one man loved the pilgrim soul in you,
And loved the sorrows of your changing face;

And bending down beside the glowing bars,
Murmur, a little sadly, how Love fled   10
And paced upon the mountains overhead
And hid his face amid a crowd of stars.

WILLIAM BUTLER YEATS

Luke Havergal

Go to the western gate, Luke Havergal,
There where the vines cling crimson on the wall,
And in the twilight wait for what will come.
The leaves will whisper there of her, and some,
Like flying words, will strike you as they fall;   5

But go, and if you listen, she will call.
Go to the western gate, Luke Havergal—
Luke Havergal.

No, there is not a dawn in eastern skies
To rift the fiery night that's in your eyes;   10
But there, where western glooms are gathering,
The dark will end the dark, if anything:
God slays himself with every leaf that flies,
And hell is more than half of paradise.
No, there is not a dawn in eastern skies—   15
In eastern skies.

Out of a grave I come to tell you this,
Out of a grave I come to quench the kiss
That flames upon your forehead with a glow
That blinds you to the way that you must go.   20
Yes, there is yet one way to where she is,
Bitter, but one that faith may never miss.
Out of a grave I come to tell you this—
To tell you this.

There is the western gate, Luke Havergal,   25
There are the crimson leaves upon the wall.
Go, for the winds are tearing them away,—
Nor think to riddle the dead words they say,
Nor any more to feel them as they fall;
But go, and if you trust her she will call.   30
There is the western gate, Luke Havergal—
Luke Havergal.

EDWIN ARLINGTON ROBINSON

What Lips My Lips Have Kissed

What lips my lips have kissed, and where, and why,
I have forgotten, and what arms have lain
Under my head till morning; but the rain
Is full of ghosts tonight, that tap and sigh
Upon the glass and listen for reply;   5
And in my heart there stirs a quiet pain
For unremembered lads that not again
Will turn to me at midnight with a cry.

Thus in the winter stands the lonely tree,
Nor knows what birds have vanished one by one,   10
Yet knows its boughs more silent than before:
I cannot say what loves have come and gone;
I only know that summer sang in me
A little while, that in me sings no more.

                                        EDNA ST. VINCENT MILLAY

The River-Merchant's Wife: A Letter
(After Rihaku)[1]

While my hair was still cut straight across my forehead
I played about the front gate, pulling flowers.
You came by on bamboo stilts, playing horse,
You walked about my seat, playing with blue plums.
And we went on living in the village of Chokan: 5
Two small people, without dislike or suspicion.

At fourteen I married My Lord you.
I never laughed, being bashful.
Lowering my head, I looked at the wall.
Called to, a thousand times, I never looked back.   10

At fifteen I stopped scowling,
I desired my dust to be mingled with yours
Forever and forever and forever.
Why should I climb the lookout?

At sixteen you departed,   15
You went into far Ku-to-yen, by the river of swirling eddies,
And you have been gone five months.
The monkeys make sorrowful noise overhead.
You dragged your feet when you went out.
By the gate now, the moss is grown, the different mosses,   20
Too deep to clear them away!
The leaves fall early this autumn, in wind.
The paired butterflies are already yellow with August
Over the grass in the West garden;
They hurt me. I grow older.   25
If you are coming down through the narrows of the river Kiang,
Please let me know beforehand,
And I will come out to meet you
        As far as Cho-fu-sa.

                                        EZRA POUND

[1] Done in the manner of Rihaku, the Japanese rendering of the name of Li-Po, an eighth-
century Chinese poet.

The Love Song of J. Alfred Prufrock

S'io credesse che mia risposta fosse
A persona che mai tornasse al mondo,
Questa fiamma staria senza piu scosse.
Ma perciocche giammai di questo fondo
Non torno vivo alcun, s'i'odo il vero,
Senza tema d'infamia ti rispondo.[1]

Let us go then, you and I,
When the evening is spread out against the sky
Like a patient etherised upon a table;
Let us go, through certain half-deserted streets,
The muttering retreats   5
Of restless nights in one-night cheap hotels
And sawdust restaurants with oyster-shells:
Streets that follow like a tedious argument
Of insidious intent
To lead you to an overwhelming question . . .   10
Oh, do not ask, "What is it?"
Let us go and make our visit.

In the room the women come and go
Talking of Michelangelo.

The yellow fog that rubs its back upon the window-panes,   15
The yellow smoke that rubs its muzzle on the window-panes
Licked its tongue into the corners of the evening,
Lingered upon the pools that stand in drains,
Let fall upon its back the soot that falls from chimneys,
Slipped by the terrace, made a sudden leap,   20
And seeing that it was a soft October night,
Curled once about the house, and fell asleep.

And indeed there will be time
For the yellow smoke that slides along the street,
Rubbing its back upon the window-panes;   25
There will be time, there will be time
To prepare a face to meet the faces that you meet;
There will be time to murder and create,
And time for all the works and days of hands

---

[1] The epigraph (from Dante's *Inferno*, XXVII, 61–66) is the first six lines of Guido da Montefeltro's answer to Dante's question about his identity: "If I thought that my answer were given to anyone who would ever return to the world, this flame would stand still; but because no one returned from this pit, if what I hear is true, I will answer you without fear of infamy."

That lift and drop a question on your plate;   30
Time for you and time for me,
And time yet for a hundred indecisions,
And for a hundred visions and revisions,
Before the taking of a toast and tea.

In the room the women come and go   35
Talking of Michelangelo.

And indeed there will be time
To wonder, "Do I dare?" and, "Do I dare?"
Time to turn back and descend the stair,
With a bald spot in the middle of my hair—   40
[They will say: "How his hair is growing thin!"]
My morning coat, my collar mounting firmly to the chin,
My necktie rich and modest, but asserted by a simple pin—
[They will say: "But how his arms and legs are thin!"]
Do I dare   45
Disturb the universe?
In a minute there is time
For decisions and revisions which a minute will reverse.

For I have known them all already, known them all:—
Have known the evenings, mornings, afternoons,   50
I have measured out my life with coffee spoons;
I know the voices dying with a dying fall
Beneath the music from a farther room.
      So how should I presume?

And I have known the eyes already, known them all—   55
The eyes that fix you in a formulated phrase,
And when I am formulated, sprawling on a pin,
When I am pinned and wriggling on the wall,
Then how should I begin
To spit out all the butt ends of my days and ways?   60
      And how should I presume?

And I have known the arms already, known them all—
Arms that are braceleted and white and bare
[But in the lamplight, downed with light brown hair!]
Is it perfume from a dress   65
That makes me so digress?
Arms that lie along a table, or wrap about a shawl.
      And should I then presume?
      And how should I begin?

Shall I say, I have gone at dusk through narrow streets   70
And watched the smoke that rises from the pipes
Of lonely men in shirt-sleeves, leaning out of windows? . . .

I should have been a pair of ragged claws
Scuttling across the floors of silent seas.

                              .   .   .

And the afternoon, the evening, sleeps so peacefully!   75
Smoothed by long fingers,
Asleep . . . tired . . . or it malingers,
Stretched on the floor, here beside you and me.
Should I, after tea and cakes and ices,
Have the strength to force the moment to its crisis?   80
But though I have wept and fasted, wept and prayed,
Though I have seen my head [grown slightly bald] brought in upon a
    platter,
I am no prophet—and here's no great matter;
I have seen the moment of my greatness flicker,
And I have seen the eternal Footman hold my coat, and snicker,   85
And in short, I was afraid.

And would it have been worth it, after all,
After the cups, the marmalade, the tea,
Among the porcelain, among some talk of you and me,
Would it have been worth while,   90
To have bitten off the matter with a smile,
To have squeezed the universe into a ball
To roll it toward some overwhelming question,
To say: "I am Lazarus, come from the dead,
Come back to tell you all, I shall tell you all"—   95
If one, settling a pillow by her head,
        Should say: "That is not what I meant at all.
        That is not it, at all."

And would it have been worth it, after all,
Would it have been worth while,   100
After the sunsets and the dooryards and the sprinkled streets,
After the novels, after the teacups, after the skirts that trail along the
    floor—
And this, and so much more?—
It is impossible to say just what I mean!
But as if a magic lantern threw the nerves in patterns on a screen: 105
Would it have been worth while
If one, settling a pillow or throwing off a shawl,
And turning toward the window, should say:

"That is not it at all,
That is not what I meant, at all."   110

                    .   .   .

No! I am not Prince Hamlet, nor was meant to be;
Am an attendant lord, one that will do
To swell a progress, start a scene or two,
Advise the prince; no doubt, an easy tool,
Deferential, glad to be of use,   115
Politic, cautious, and meticulous;
Full of high sentence, but a bit obtuse;
At times, indeed, almost ridiculous—
Almost, at times, the Fool.

I grow old . . . I grow old . . .   120
I shall wear the bottoms of my trousers rolled.

Shall I part my hair behind? Do I dare to eat a peach?
I shall wear white flannel trousers, and walk upon the beach.
I have heard the mermaids singing, each to each.

I do not think that they will sing to me.   125

I have seen them riding seaward on the waves
Combing the white hair of the waves blown back
When the wind blows the water white and black.

We have lingered in the chambers of the sea
By sea-girls wreathed with seaweed red and brown   130
Till human voices wake us, and we drown.

                                        T. S. ELIOT

Hippopotamothalamion

A hippopotamus had a bride
   Of rather singular beauty,
When he lay down at her side
   'Twas out of love, not duty—
    Hers was an exceptional beauty.   5
Take, oh take those lips away, etc.

He met her in Central Nigeria,
   While she was resident there,
Where life is distinctly superior
   And a hippo can take down her hair—   10

And, God, but she was fair!
Take, oh take those lips away, etc.

She was coming up from her morning swim
    When first they chanced to meet:
He looked at her, she looked at him,   15
    And stood with reluctant feet
    Where mud and river meet.
Take, oh take those lips away, etc.

Their eye-beams, twisted on one thread,
    Instantaneously did twine,   20
And he made up poetry out of his head,
    Such as: "Dear heart, be mine"—
    And he quoted, line for line,
"Hail to thee, blithe spirit," etc.

Now, hippopotamoid courtesy   25
    Is strangely meticulous—
A beautiful thing, you will agree,
    In a hippopotamus—
    And she answered, briefly, thus:
"Hail to thee, blithe spirit," etc.   30

Perhaps she was practicing the arts
    That grace old Hippo's daughter,
The coquetries that win all hearts,
    For even as he besought her
    She slid into the water.   35
Out, out, brief candle, etc.

Now on the borders of the wood,
    Whence love had drawn him hither,
He paces in an anguished mood,
    Darting hither and thither   40
    In a terrific dither.
Out, out, brief candle, etc.

The course of true love never yet
    Ran smooth, so we are told,
With thorns its pathway is beset   45
    And perils manifold,
    And has been from of old.
Out, out, brief candle, etc.

Yet soon a happier morning smiles,
   The marriage feast is spread—   50
The flower girls were crocodiles
    When hippopotamus led
    Hippopotamus, with firm tread
    A bride to the bridal bed.
Milton, thou should'st be living at this hour.   55

JOHN HALL WHEELOCK

The Equilibrists

Full of her long white arms and milky skin
He had a thousand times remembered sin.
Alone in the press of people travelled he,
Minding her jacinth, and myrrh, and ivory.

Mouth he remembered: the quaint orifice   5
From which came heat that flamed upon the kiss,
Till cold words came down spiral from the head,
Grey doves from the officious tower illsped.

Body: it was a white field ready for love,
On her body's field, with the gaunt tower above,   10
The lilies grew, beseeching him to take,
If he would pluck and wear them, bruise and break.

Eyes talking: Never mind the cruel words,
Embrace my flowers, but not embrace the swords.
But what they said, the doves came straightway flying   15
And unsaid: Honor, Honor, they came crying.

Importunate her doves. Too pure, too wise,
Clambering on his shoulder, saying, Arise,
Leave me now, and never let us meet,
Eternal distance now command thy feet.   20

Predicament indeed, which thus discovers
Honor among thieves, Honor between lovers.
O such a little word is Honor, they feel!
But the grey word is between them cold as steel.

At length I saw these lovers fully were come   25
Into their torture of equilibrium;
Dreadfully had forsworn each other, and yet
They were bound each to each, and they did not forget.

And rigid as two painful stars, and twirled
About the clustered night their prison world,   30
They burned with fierce love always to come near,
But Honor beat them back and kept them clear.

Ah, the strict lovers, they are ruined now!
I cried in anger. But with puddled brow
Devising for those gibbeted and brave   35
Came I descanting: Man, what would you have?

For spin your period out, and draw your breath,
A kinder saeculum begins with Death.
Would you ascend to Heaven and bodiless dwell?
Or take your bodies honorless to Hell?   40

In Heaven you have heard no marriage is,
No white flesh tinder to your lecheries,
Your male and female tissue sweetly shaped
Sublimed away, and furious blood escaped.

Great lovers lie in Hell, the stubborn ones   45
Infatuate of the flesh upon the bones;
Stuprate, they rend each other when they kiss,
The pieces kiss again, no end to this.

But still I watched them spinning, orbited nice.
Their flames were not more radiant than their ice.   50
I dug in the quiet earth and wrought the tomb
And made these lines to memorize their doom:—

Epitaph

Equilibrists lie here; stranger, tread light;
Close, but untouching in each other's sight;
Mouldered the lips and ashy the tall skull,   55
Let them lie perilous and beautiful.

                                        JOHN CROWE RANSOM

3
Nature

Generally speaking, poets are more in touch with nature than are writers in other genres. On the least sophisticated level, the poet writing about nature simply describes the beauties of flowers or sunsets or changes in seasons. Or perhaps, like Wordsworth, he relates the things of nature to his own life. Some see in nature God's goodness; others see the harshness and unpleasantness of a godless universe.

Wordsworth, probably the most nature-conscious of all English poets, says that nature is man's best nurse, guide, and moralist. By observing and imitating the natural world, man learns to act decently and morally. Wordsworth's attitude epitomizes the Romantic view of nature, whether in the nineteenth century or today. In contrast is the concept of nature as an evil arena, where a bloody struggle for survival occurs.

It has often been observed that art—in its arrangements and shadings—imitates nature. Oscar Wilde, on the other hand, said that nature imitates art, meaning that writers and painters have taught us to see the world around us more acutely. Many of the poems in this section do cause the reader to take a deeper and more penetrating view of the natural world.

Literary critics do not usually speak of a "nature play" or a "nature novel" as they sometimes do of a "nature poem"; for in few, if any, plays or novels is nature the dominant theme. Even so, as the list below indicates, nature can be important thematically in plays and novels. Sometimes, as in Synge's *Riders to the Sea* or in Rolvaag's *Giants in the Earth*, to change the natural setting would be to change the whole concept of the work.

READINGS FROM OTHER GENRES

PLAYS

James M. Barrie, *The Admirable Crichton*
Federico García Lorca, *Blood Wedding*
Sean O'Casey, *Cock-a-Doodle Dandy*
Eugene O'Neill, *Moon of the Caribbees, The Emperor Jones*

Robert Sherwood, *The Petrified Forest*
John Millington Synge, *Riders to the Sea*

NOVELS

Willa Cather, *O Pioneers!*
James Fenimore Cooper, *The Leatherstocking Tales*
Daniel Defoe, *Robinson Crusoe*
André Gide, *Symphonie Pastorale*
Ellen Glasgow, *Barren Ground*
Knut Hamsun, *Growth of the Soil*
Thomas Hardy, *The Return of the Native*
Ernest Hemingway, *The Old Man and the Sea*
W. H. Hudson, *Green Mansions*
Jack London, *The Call of the Wild*
Herman Melville, *Moby Dick*
O. E. Rolvaag, *Giants in the Earth*
Mikhail Sholokhov, *And Quiet Flows the Don*
John Steinbeck, *To a God Unknown*
Giovanni Verga, *The House by the Medlar Tree*

SHORT STORIES

Honoré Balzac, "A Passion in the Desert"
Stephen Crane, "The Open Boat"
William Faulkner, "The Bear"
E. M. Forster, "The Story of the Siren"
Ernest Hemingway, "Big Two-Hearted River," "The Snows of Kilimanjaro"
Jack London, "To Build a Fire"
Guy de Maupassant, "At Sea"
John Steinbeck, "Flight"

Sumer Is Icumen In

Sumer is icumen in,
    Lhudè sing cuccu;
Groweth sed and bloweth med
    And springth the wudè nu.
        Sing cuccu!   5
Awè bleteth after lomb,
    Lhouth after calvè cu;

Bulluc sterteth,[1] bucke verteth;[2]
  Murie sing cuccu.
        Cuccu, cuccu,   10
    Wel singès thu, cuccu,
    Ne swik[3] thu naver nu.
  Sing cuccu nu! Sing cuccu!
  Sing cuccu! Sing cuccu nu!

ANONYMOUS
(c. 1300)

[1] Leaps.   [2] Breaks wind.   [3] Stop.

Corinna's Going a-Maying

Get up, get up for shame, the blooming morn
Upon her wings presents the god unshorn.
  See how Aurora throws her fair
  Fresh-quilted colors through the air:
  Get up, sweet slug-a-bed, and see   5
  The dew bespangling herb and tree.
Each flower has wept and bowed toward the east
Above an hour since; yet you not dressed,
  Nay! not so much as out of bed?
  When all the birds have matins said,   10
  And sung their thankful hymns, 'tis sin,
  Nay, profanation to keep in,
Whenas a thousand virgins on this day,
Spring, sooner than the lark, to fetch in May.

Rise, and put on your foliage, and be seen   15
To come forth, like the spring-time, fresh and green,
  And sweet as Flora. Take no care
  For jewels for your gown or hair:
  Fear not; the leaves will strew
  Gems in abundance upon you;   20
Besides, the childhood of the day has kept,
Against you come, some orient pearls unwept;
  Come, and receive them while the light
  Hangs on the dew-locks of the night,
  And Titan on the eastern hill   25
  Retires himself, or else stands still
Till you come forth. Wash, dress, be brief in praying;
Few beads are best, when once we go a-Maying.

Come, my Corinna, come; and coming, mark
How each field turns a street; each street a park   30
    Made green, and trimmed with trees; see how
    Devotion gives each house a bough,
    Or branch: each porch, each door, ere this,
    An ark, a tabernacle is,
Made up of white-thorn neatly interwove,   35
As if here were those cooler shades of love.
    Can such delights be in the street,
    And open fields, and we not see't?
    Come, we'll abroad; and let's obey
    The proclamation made for May,   40
And sin no more, as we have done, by staying;
But my Corinna, come, let's go a-Maying.

There's not a budding boy or girl this day,
But is got up, and gone to bring in May.
    A deal of youth, ere this, is come   45
    Back, and with white-thorn laden home.
    Some have dispatched their cakes and cream
    Before that we have left to dream,
And some have wept, and wooed, and plighted troth,
And chose their priest, ere we can cast off sloth;   50
    Many a green-gown has been given;
    Many a kiss, both odd and even;
    Many a glance too has been sent
    From out the eye, love's firmament;
Many a jest told of the keys betraying   55
This night, and locks picked, yet we're not a-Maying.

Come, let us go, while we are in our prime,
And take the harmless folly of the time.
    We shall grow old apace, and die
    Before we know our liberty.   60
    Our life is short, and our days run
    As fast away as does the sun;
And as a vapor, or a drop of rain
Once lost, can ne'er be found again,
    So when or you or I are made   65
    A fable, song, or fleeting shade,
    All love, all liking, all delight
    Lies drowned with us in endless night.
Then while time serves, and we are but decaying,
Come, my Corinna, come, let's go a-Maying.   70

ROBERT HERRICK

The Country Life[1]

Sweet country life, to such unknown
Whose lives are others', not their own!
But, serving courts and cities, be
Less happy less enjoying thee.
Thou never plow'st the ocean's foam   5
To seek and bring rough pepper home;
Nor to the Eastern Ind dost rove
To bring from thence the scorchèd clove;
Nor, with the loss of thy loved rest,
Bring'st home the ingot from the West.   10
No, thy ambition's masterpiece
Flies no thought higher than a fleece;
Or how to pay thy hinds, and clear
All scores, and so to end the year;
But walk'st about thine own dear bounds,   15
Not envying others' larger grounds,
For well thou know'st 'tis not the extent
Of land makes life, but sweet content.
When now the cock, the plowman's horn,
Calls forth the lily-wristed morn,   20
Then to thy corn-fields thou dost go,
Which, though well soiled, yet thou dost know
That the best compost for the lands
Is the wise master's feet and hands.
There at the plow thou find'st thy team,   25
With a hind whistling there to them,
And cheer'st them up by singing how
The kingdom's portion is the plow.
This done, then to the enameled meads
Thou go'st, and as thy foot there treads   30
Thou seest a present godlike power
Imprinted in each herb and flower,
And smell'st the breath of great-eyed kine,
Sweet as the blossoms of the vine.
Here thou behold'st thy large, sleek neat[2]   35
Unto the dewlaps up in meat;
And as thou look'st, the wanton steer,
The heifer, cow, and ox draw near
To make a pleasing pastime there.

[1] The poem is written to "The Honored Mr. End. Porter, Groom of the Bedchamber to His Majesty."

[2] Cow or ox.

These seen, thou go'st to view thy flocks   40
Of sheep, safe from the wolf and fox,
And find'st their bellies there as full
Of short, sweet grass as backs with wool,
And leav'st them, as they feed and fill,
A shepherd piping on a hill.   45
For sports, for pageantry, and plays,
Thou hast thy eves and holydays,
On which the young men and maids meet
To exercise their dancing feet,
Tripping the comely country round,   50
With daffodils and daisies crowned.
Thy wakes, thy quintals,[3] here thou hast,
Thy Maypoles, too, with garlands graced,
Thy morris-dance, thy Whitsun-ale,
Thy shearing-feast, which never fail;   55
Thy harvest-home, thy wassail bowl,
That's tossed up after fox-i'-the-hole,
Thy mummeries, thy Twelfth-tide kings
And queens, thy Christmas revelings,
Thy nut-brown mirth, thy russet wit,   60
And no man pays too dear for it.
To these thou hast thy times to go,
And trace the hare i' the treacherous snow;
Thy witty wiles to draw, and get
The lark into the trammel net;   65
Thou hast thy cockrood and thy glade,
To take the precious pheasant made;
Thy lime-twigs, snares, and pitfalls then,
To catch the pilfering birds, not men.
O happy life! if that their good   70
The husbandmen but understood,
Who all the day themselves do please,
And younglings, with such sports as these;
And, lying down, have naught to affright
Sweet sleep, that makes more short the night.   75

                                        ROBERT HERRICK

[3] An object for tilting.

The Spring

Now that the winter's gone, the earth hath lost
Her snow-white robes; and now no more the frost
Candies the grass, or casts an icy cream

Upon the silver lake or crystal stream.
But the warm sun thaws the benumbèd earth,   5
And makes it tender; gives a sacred birth
To the dead swallow; wakes in hollow tree
The drowsy cuckoo and the humblebee.
Now do a choir of chirping minstrels bring,
In triumph to the world, the youthful spring.   10
The valleys, hills, and woods in rich array
Welcome the coming of the longed-for May.
Now all things smile; only my love doth lour;
Nor hath the scalding noonday sun the power
To melt that marble ice, which still doth hold   15
Her heart congealed, and makes her pity cold.
The ox, which lately did for shelter fly
Into the stall, doth now securely lie
In open fields; and love no more is made
By the fireside; but in the cooler shade   20
Amyntas now doth with his Chloris sleep
Under a sycamore, and all things keep
Time with the season; only she doth carry
June in her eyes, in her heart January.

THOMAS CAREW

Sweet Afton

Flow gently, sweet Afton, among thy green braes!
Flow gently, I'll sing thee a song in thy praise!
My Mary's asleep by thy murmuring stream,
Flow gently, sweet Afton, disturb not her dream!

Thou stock-dove, whose echo resounds through the glen,   5
Ye wild whistling blackbirds in yon thorny den,
Thou green-crested lapwing, thy screaming forbear,
I charge you disturb not my slumbering fair!

How lofty, sweet Afton, thy neighboring hills,
Far marked with the courses of clear winding rills;   10
There daily I wander as noon rises high,
My flocks and my Mary's sweet cot in my eye.

How pleasant thy banks and green valleys below,
Where wild in the woodlands the primroses blow!
There oft, as mild evening weeps over the lea,   15
The sweet-scented birk shades my Mary and me.

Thy crystal stream, Afton, how lovely it glides,
And winds by the cot where my Mary resides!
How wanton thy waters her snowy feet lave,
As gathering sweet flowerets she stems thy clear wave!   20

Flow gently, sweet Afton, among thy green braes!
Flow gently, sweet river, the theme of my lays!
My Mary's asleep by thy murmuring stream,
Flow gently, sweet Afton, disturb not her dream!

ROBERT BURNS

To Spring

O Thou with dewy locks, who lookest down
Through the clear windows of the morning, turn
Thine angel eyes upon our western isle,
Which in full choir hails thy approach, O Spring!

The hills tell each other, and the listening   5
Valleys hear; all our longing eyes are turned
Up to thy bright pavilions; issue forth,
And let thy holy feet visit our clime.

Come o'er the eastern hills, and let our winds
Kiss thy perfumèd garments; let us taste   10
Thy morn and evening breath; scatter thy pearls
Upon our love-sick land that mourns for thee.

O deck her forth with thy fair fingers; pour
Thy soft kisses on her bosom; and put
Thy golden crown upon her languished head,   15
Whose modest tresses were bound up for thee!

WILLIAM BLAKE

She Dwelt among the Untrodden Ways

She dwelt among the untrodden ways
    Beside the springs of Dove,
A Maid whom there were none to praise
    And very few to love:

A violet by a mossy stone   5
    Half hidden from the eye!
—Fair as a star, when only one
    Is shining in the sky.

She lived unknown, and few could know
    When Lucy ceased to be;   10
But she is in her grave, and, oh,
    The difference to me!

WILLIAM WORDSWORTH

Three Years She Grew in Sun and Shower

Three years she grew in sun and shower,
Then Nature said, "A lovelier flower
On earth was never sown;
This child I to myself will take;
She shall be mine, and I will make   5
A lady of my own.

"Myself will to my darling be
Both law and impulse: and with me
The girl, in rock and plain,
In earth and heaven, in glade and bower,   10
Shall feel an overseeing power
To kindle or restrain.

"She shall be sportive as the fawn
That wild with glee across the lawn
Or up the mountain springs;   15
And hers shall be the breathing balm,
And hers the silence and the calm
Of mute insensate things.

"The floating clouds their state shall lend
To her; for her the willow bend;   20
Nor shall she fail to see
Even in the motions of the storm
Grace that shall mould the maiden's form
By silent sympathy.

"The stars of midnight shall be dear   25
To her; and she shall lean her ear
In many a secret place
Where rivulets dance their wayward round,

And beauty born of murmuring sound
Shall pass into her face.   30

"And vital feelings of delight
Shall rear her form to stately height,
Her virgin bosom swell;
Such thoughts to Lucy I will give
While she and I together live   35
Here in this happy dell."

Thus Nature spake—the work was done—
How soon my Lucy's race was run!
She died, and left to me
This heath, this calm, and quiet scene;   40
The memory of what has been,
And never more will be.

WILLIAM WORDSWORTH

A Slumber Did My Spirit Seal

A slumber did my spirit seal;
    I had no human fears:
She seemed a thing that could not feel
    The touch of earthly years.

No motion has she now, no force;   5
    She neither hears nor sees;
Rolled round in earth's diurnal course,
    With rocks, and stones, and trees.

WILLIAM WORDSWORTH

Composed upon Westminster Bridge
September 3, 1802

Earth has not anything to show more fair:
Dull would he be of soul who could pass by
A sight so touching in its majesty:
This City now doth, like a garment, wear
The beauty of the morning; silent, bare,   5
Ships, towers, domes, theatres, and temples lie
Open unto the fields, and to the sky;

All bright and glittering in the smokeless air.
Never did sun more beautifully steep
In his first splendor, valley, rock, or hill;   10
Ne'er saw I, never felt, a calm so deep!
The river glideth at his own sweet will:
Dear God! the very houses seem asleep;
And all that mighty heart is lying still!

WILLIAM WORDSWORTH

It Is a Beauteous Evening, Calm and Free

It is a beauteous evening, calm and free,
The holy time is quiet as a Nun
Breathless with adoration; the broad sun
Is sinking down in its tranquility;
The gentleness of heaven broods o'er the Sea: 5
Listen! the mighty Being is awake,
And doth with his eternal motion make
A sound like thunder—everlastingly.
Dear child! dear girl! that walkest with me here,
If thou appear untouched by solemn thought,   10
Thy nature is not therefore less divine:
Thou liest in Abraham's bosom all the year;
And worshipp'st at the Temple's inner shrine,
God being with thee when we know it not.

WILLIAM WORDSWORTH

I Wandered Lonely as a Cloud

I wandered lonely as a cloud
That floats on high o'er vales and hills,
When all at once I saw a crowd,
A host, of golden daffodils;
Beside the lake, beneath the trees,   5
Fluttering and dancing in the breeze.

Continuous as the stars that shine
And twinkle on the milky way,
They stretched in never-ending line
Along the margin of a bay: 10
Ten thousand saw I at a glance,
Tossing their heads in sprightly dance.

The waves beside them danced; but they
Out-did the sparkling waves in glee:
A poet could not but be gay,   15
In such a jocund company:
I gazed—and gazed—but little thought
What wealth the show to me had brought:

For oft, when on my couch I lie
In vacant or in pensive mood,   20
They flash upon that inward eye
Which is the bliss of solitude;
And then my heart with pleasure fills,
And dances with the daffodils.

WILLIAM WORDSWORTH

Ode to the West Wind

I

O, wild West Wind, thou breath of Autumn's being,
Thou, from whose unseen presence the leaves dead
Are driven, like ghosts from an enchanter fleeing,

Yellow, and black, and pale, and hectic red,
Pestilence-stricken multitudes: O, thou,   5
Who chariotest to their dark wintry bed

The wingèd seeds, where they lie cold and low,
Each like a corpse within its grave, until
Thine azure sister of the spring shall blow

Her clarion o'er the dreaming earth, and fill   10
(Driving sweet buds like flocks to feed in air)
With living hues and odors plain and hill:

Wild Spirit, which art moving everywhere;
Destroyer and preserver; hear, O, hear!

II

Thou on whose stream, 'mid the steep sky's commotion,   15
Loose clouds like earth's decaying leaves are shed,
Shook from the tangled boughs of Heaven and Ocean,

Angels of rain and lightning: there are spread
On the blue surface of thine airy surge,
Like the bright hair uplifted from the head   20

Of some fierce Mænad, even from the dim verge
Of the horizon to the zenith's height
The locks of the approaching storm. Thou dirge

Of the dying year, to which this closing night
Will be the dome of a vast sepulchre,   25
Vaulted with all thy congregated might

Of vapors, from whose solid atmosphere
Black rain, and fire, and hail will burst: O, hear!

III

Thou who didst waken from his summer dreams
The blue Mediterranean, where he lay,   30
Lulled by the coil of his crystalline streams,

Beside a pumice isle of Baiae's bay,
And saw in sleep old palaces and towers
Quivering within the wave's intenser day,

All overgrown with azure moss and flowers   35
So sweet, the sense faints picturing them! Thou
For whose path the Atlantic's level powers

Cleave themselves into chasms, while far below
The sea-blooms and the oozy woods which wear
The sapless foliage of the ocean, know   40

Thy voice, and suddenly grow grey with fear,
And tremble and despoil themselves: O, hear!

IV

If I were a dead leaf thou mightest bear;
If I were a swift cloud to fly with thee;
A wave to pant beneath thy power, and share   45

The impulse of thy strength, only less free
Than thou, O, uncontrollable! If even
I were as in my boyhood, and could be

The comrade of thy wanderings over heaven,
As then, when to outstrip thy skiey speed   50
Scarce seemed a vision; I would ne'er have striven

As thus with thee in prayer in my sore need,
Oh! lift me as a wave, a leaf, a cloud!
I fall upon the thorns of life! I bleed!

A heavy weight of hours has chained and bowed   55
One too like thee: tameless, and swift, and proud.

V

Make me thy lyre, even as the forest is:
What if my leaves are falling like its own!
The tumult of thy mighty harmonies

Will take from both a deep, autumnal tone,   60
Sweet though in sadness. Be thou, spirit fierce,
My spirit! Be thou me, impetuous one!

Drive my dead thoughts over the universe
Like withered leaves to quicken a new birth!
And, by the incantation of this verse,   65

Scatter, as from an unextinguished hearth
Ashes and sparks, my words among mankind!
Be through my lips to unawakened earth

The trumpet of a prophecy! O, wind,
If Winter comes, can Spring be far behind?   70

PERCY BYSSHE SHELLEY

To One Who Has Been Long in City Pent

To one who has been long in city pent,
'Tis very sweet to look into the fair
And open face of heaven,—to breathe a prayer
Full in the smile of the blue firmament.
Who is more happy, when, with heart's content,   5
Fatigued he sinks into some pleasant lair
Of wavy grass, and reads a debonair
And gentle tale of love and languishment?
Returning home at evening, with an ear
Catching the notes of Philomel,—an eye   10
Watching the sailing cloudlet's bright career,
He mourns that day so soon has glided by:
E'en like the passage of an angel's tear
That falls through the clear ether silently.

JOHN KEATS

On the Sea

It keeps eternal whisperings around
Desolate shores, and with its mighty swell
Gluts twice ten thousand caverns, till the spell
Of Hecate leaves them their old shadowy sound.
Often 'tis in such gentle temper found,   5
That scarcely will the very smallest shell
Be moved for days from where it sometime fell,
When last the winds of Heaven were unbound.
Oh ye! who have your eye-balls vexed and tired,
Feast them upon the wideness of the sea;   10
Oh ye! whose ears are dinned with uproar rude,
Or fed too much with cloying melody—
Sit ye near some old cavern's mouth, and brood
Until ye start, as if the sea-nymphs quired!

JOHN KEATS

To Autumn

Season of mists and mellow fruitfulness,
    Close bosom-friend of the maturing sun;
Conspiring with him how to load and bless
    With fruit the vines that round the thatch-eaves run;
To bend with apples the mossed cottage trees,   5
    And fill all fruit with ripeness to the core;
        To swell the gourd, and plump the hazel shells
    With a sweet kernel; to set budding more,
And still more, later flowers for the bees,
Until they think warm days will never cease,   10
    For Summer has o'er-brimmed their clammy cells.

Who hath not seen thee oft amid thy store?
    Sometimes whoever seeks abroad may find
Thee sitting careless on a granary floor,
    Thy hair soft-lifted by the winnowing wind;   15
Or on a half-reaped furrow sound asleep,
    Drowsed with the fume of poppies, while thy hook
        Spares the next swath and all its twinèd flowers:
And sometimes like a gleaner thou dost keep
    Steady thy laden head across a brook;   20

Or by a cider-press, with patient look,
    Thou watchest the last oozings hours by hours.

Where are the songs of Spring? Aye, where are they?
    Think not of them, thou hast thy music too,—
While barrèd clouds bloom the soft-dying day,   25
    And touch the stubble plains with rosy hue;
Then in a wailful choir the small gnats mourn
    Among the river sallows, borne aloft
      Or sinking as the light wind lives or dies;
And full-grown lambs loud bleat from hilly bourn;   30
    Hedge-crickets sing; and now with treble soft
The red-breast whistles from a garden-croft;
    And gathering swallows twitter in the skies.

JOHN KEATS

The Apology

Think me not unkind and rude
    That I walk alone in grove and glen;
I go to the god of the wood
    To fetch his word to men.

Tax not my sloth that I   5
    Fold my arms beside the brook;
Each cloud that floated in the sky
    Writes a letter in my book.

Chide me not, laborious band,
    For the idle flowers I brought;   10
Every aster in my hand
    Goes home loaded with a thought.

There was never mystery
    But 't is figured in the flowers;
Was never secret history   15
    But birds tell it in the bowers.

One harvest from thy field
    Homeward brought the oxen strong;
A second crop thine acres yield,
    Which I gather in a song.   20

RALPH WALDO EMERSON

The Eagle

He clasps the crag with crooked hands;
Close to the sun in lonely lands,
Ringed with the azure world, he stands.

The wrinkled sea beneath him crawls;
He watches from his mountain walls,   5
And like a thunderbolt he falls.

ALFRED, LORD TENNYSON

I Dreaded That First Robin So

I dreaded that first robin so,
But he is mastered now,
And I'm accustomed to him grown,—
He hurts a little, though.

I thought if I could only live   5
Till that first shout got by,
Not all pianos in the woods
Had power to mangle me.

I dared not meet the daffodils,
For fear their yellow gown   10
Would pierce me with a fashion
So foreign to my own.

I wished the grass would hurry,
So when 'twas time to see,
He'd be too tall, the tallest one   15
Could stretch to look at me.

I could not bear the bees should come,
I wished they'd stay away
In those dim countries where they go:
What word had they for me?   20

They're here, though; not a creature failed,
No blossom stayed away
In gentle deference to me,
The Queen of Calvary.

Each one salutes me as he goes,   25
And I my childish plumes
Lift, in bereaved acknowledgment
Of their unthinking drums.

EMILY DICKINSON

A Light Exists in Spring

A light exists in spring
   Not present on the year
At any other period.
   When March is scarcely here

A color stands abroad   5
   On solitary hills
That science cannot overtake,
   But human nature *feels*.

It waits upon the lawn;
   It shows the furthest tree   10
Upon the furthest slope we know;
   It almost speaks to me.

Then, as horizons step,
   Or noons report away,
Without the formula of sound,   15
   It passes, and we stay:

A quality of loss
   Affecting our content,
As trade had suddenly encroached
   Upon a sacrament.   20

EMILY DICKINSON

A Narrow Fellow in the Grass

A narrow fellow in the grass
   Occasionally rides;
You may have met him—did you not?
   His notice sudden is.

The grass divides as with a comb, 5
A spotted shaft is seen;
And then it closes at your feet
And opens further on.

He likes a boggy acre,
A floor too cool for corn. 10
Yet when a child, and barefoot,
I more than once, at morn,

Have passed, I thought, a whip-lash
Unbraiding in the sun—
When, stooping to secure it, 15
It wrinkled, and was gone.

Several of nature's people
I know, and they know me;
I feel for them a transport
Of cordiality: 20

But never met this fellow,
Attended or alone,
Without a tighter breathing,
And zero at the bone.

EMILY DICKINSON

The Darkling Thrush
(December 31, 1900)

I leant upon a coppice gate
  When Frost was spectre-gray,
And Winter's dregs made desolate
  The weakening eye of day.
The tangled bine-stems scored the sky 5
  Like strings of broken lyres,
And all mankind that haunted nigh
  Had sought their household fires.

The land's sharp features seemed to be
  The Century's corpse outleant, 10
His crypt the cloudy canopy,
  The wind his death-lament.
The ancient pulse of germ and birth
  Was shrunken hard and dry,

And every spirit upon earth   15
  Seemed fervourless as I.

At once a voice arose among
  The bleak twigs overhead
In a full-hearted evensong
  Of joy illimited;   20
An aged thrush, frail, gaunt, and small,
  In blast-beruffled plume,
Had chosen thus to fling his soul
  Upon the growing gloom.

So little cause for carolings   25
  Of such ecstatic sound
Was written on terrestrial things
  Afar or nigh around,
That I could think there trembled through
  His happy good-night air   30
Some blessed Hope, whereof he knew
  And I was unaware.

THOMAS HARDY

Pied Beauty

Glory be to God for dappled things—
  For skies of couple-colour as a brinded cow;
    For rose-moles all in stipple upon trout that swim;
Fresh-firecoal chestnut-falls; finches' wings;
  Landscape plotted and pieced—fold, fallow, and plough;   5
    And all trades, their gear and tackle and trim.

All things counter, original, spare, strange;
  Whatever is fickle, freckled (who knows how?)
    With swift, slow; sweet, sour; adazzle, dim;
He fathers-forth whose beauty is past change: 10
    Praise him.

GERARD MANLEY HOPKINS

God's Grandeur

The world is charged with the grandeur of God.
  It will flame out, like shining from shook foil;
  It gathers to a greatness, like the ooze of oil
Crushed. Why do men then now not reck his rod?

Generations have trod, have trod, have trod; 5
  And all is seared with trade; bleared, smeared with toil;
  And wears man's smudge and shares man's smell: the soil
Is bare now, nor can foot feel, being shod.

And for all this, nature is never spent;
  There lives the dearest freshness deep down things; 10
And though the last lights off the black West went
  Oh, morning, at the brown brink eastward, springs—
Because the Holy Ghost over the bent
  World broods with warm breast and with ah! bright wings.

GERARD MANLEY HOPKINS

The Hill Pines Were Sighing

The hill pines were sighing,
O'ercast and chill was the day:
A mist in the valley lying
Blotted the pleasant May.

But deep in the glen's bosom 5
Summer slept in the fire
Of the odorous gorse-blossom
And the hot scent of the brier.

A ribald cuckoo clamored,
And out of the copse the stroke 10
Of the iron axe that hammered
The iron heart of the oak.

Anon a sound appalling,
As a hundred years of pride
Crashed, in the silence falling: 15
And the shadowy pine-trees sighed.

ROBERT BRIDGES

The Lake Isle of Innisfree

I will arise and go now, and go to Innisfree,
And a small cabin build there, of clay and wattles made:
Nine bean-rows will I have there, a hive for the honeybee,
And live alone in the bee-loud glade.

And I shall have some peace there, for peace comes
    dropping slow,   5
Dropping from the veils of the morning to where the
    cricket sings;
There midnight's all a glimmer, and noon a purple glow,
And evening full of the linnet's wings.

I will arise and go now, for always night and day
I hear lake water lapping with low sounds by the shore;   10
While I stand on the roadway, or on the pavements grey,
I hear it in the deep heart's core.

WILLIAM BUTLER YEATS

Pear Tree

Silver dust
lifted from the earth,
higher than my arms reach,
you have mounted.
O silver,   5
higher than my arms reach
you front us with great mass;
no flower ever opened
so staunch a white leaf,
no flower ever parted silver   10
from such rare silver;
O white pear,
your flower-tufts,
thick on the branch,
bring summer and ripe fruits   15
in their purple hearts.

H. D. (HILDA DOOLITTLE)

Silver

Slowly, silently, now the moon
Walks the night in her silver shoon;
This way, and that, she peers, and sees
Silver fruit upon silver trees;
One by one the casements catch   5
Her beams beneath the silvery thatch;

Couched in his kennel, like a log,
With paws of silver sleeps the dog;
From their shadowy cote the white breasts peep
Of doves in a silver-feathered sleep;　　　　　10
A harvest mouse goes scampering by,
With silver claws and a silver eye;
And moveless fish in the water gleam,
By silver reeds in a silver stream.

WALTER DE LA MARE

The Sheaves

Where long the shadows of the wind had rolled,
Green wheat was yielding to the change assigned;
And as by some vast magic undivined
The world was turning slowly into gold.

Like nothing that was ever bought or sold　　　　　5
It waited there, the body and the mind;
And with a mighty meaning of a kind
That tells the more the more it is not told.

So in a land where all days are not fair,
Fair days went on till on another day　　　　　10
A thousand golden sheaves were lying there,
Shining and still, but not for long to stay—
As if a thousand girls with golden hair
Might rise from where they slept and go away.

EDWIN ARLINGTON ROBINSON

The Air Plant
(Grand Cayman, W.I.)

This tuft that thrives on saline nothingness,
Inverted octopus with heavenward arms
Thrust parching from a palm-bole hard by the cove—
A bird almost—of almost bird alarms,

Is pulmonary to the wind that jars　　　　　5
Its tentacles, horrific in their lurch.
The lizard's throat, held bloated for a fly,
Balloons but warily from this throbbing perch.

The needles and hacksaws of cactus bleed
A milk of earth when stricken off the stalk;   10
But this—defenseless, thornless, sheds no blood,
Scarce shadow even—but the air's thin talk.

Angelic Dynamo! Ventriloquist of the Blue!
While beachward creeps the shark-swept Spanish Main.
By what conjunctions do the winds appoint   15
Its apotheosis, at last—the hurricane!

HART CRANE

Daisy

The dayseye hugging the earth
in August, ha! Spring is
gone down in purple,
weeds stand high in the corn,
the rainbeaten furrow   5
is clotted with sorrel
and crabgrass, the
branch is black under
the heavy mass of the leaves—
The sun is upon a   10
slender green stem
ribbed lengthwise.
He lies on his back—
it is a woman also—
he regards his former   15
majesty and
round the yellow center,
split and creviced and done into
minute flowerheads, he sends out
his twenty rays—a little   20
and the wind is among them
to grow cool there!

One turns the thing over
in his hand and looks
at it from the rear: brownedged,   25
green and pointed scales
armor his yellow.
But turn and turn,
the crisp petals remain
brief, translucent, greenfastened,   30
barely touching at the edges:
blades of limpid seashell.

WILLIAM CARLOS WILLIAMS

4
The Growth of Science and Technology

Aristophanes was uneasy about what the "new knowledge" was doing to men's attitudes toward the gods. John Donne, writing in the seventeenth century, felt that the "new philosophy calls all in doubt." With a few exceptions, however, poets did not concern themselves much with the growth of science and technology until very near our own time. The theme has become more important and the problem more acute now that man, for the first time in his existence, has the power to obliterate himself.

For the most part, poets are skeptical of the value of science. Some reveal a pronounced hostility toward it. Like Poe, many feel that science has "dragged Diana from her car." Frost, speaking through a protagonist in "The Egg and the Machine," threatens, "I am armed for war." Poets often feel that the "dark, Satanic mills" of technology have blighted the countryside, atrophied the people, and turned all the cities into Birminghams. Back of all their fears is an even graver doubt. If science forces us to admit that "All else is relative,/ This only true:/ $E = mc^2$," what happens to that special insight that is poetic truth?

Yet the picture is not entirely one-sided. Pope's couplet addressed to Newton reflects much of the early optimism engendered by science. The Brooklyn Bridge is for Hart Crane a rich and beautiful symbol. The locomotive has for Emily Dickinson a quality that is almost whimsical, and Walt Whitman sees it as a "fierce-throated beauty." The poets have also added their bit to the American love affair with the automobile, that "new high-spirited spirit" with "hips of a girl."

READINGS IN OTHER GENRES

PLAYS

Karel Čapek, *R.U.R.*
Gerhard Hauptmann, *The Weavers*
Eugene O'Neill, *Dynamo, The Hairy Ape*

Elmer Rice, *The Adding Machine, The Subway*
George Bernard Shaw, *Major Barbara*
Ernst Toller, *Man and the Masses*

NOVELS

Edward Bellamy, *Looking Backward*
Aldous Huxley, *Brave New World*
George Orwell, *1984*
C. P. Snow, *The Affair, The New Men, The Search*
Mark Twain, *A Connecticut Yankee in King Arthur's Court*
H. G. Wells, *The Time Machine*

SHORT STORIES

E. M. Forster, "The Machine Stops"
H. G. Wells, "The Lord of the Dynamos," "The Magic Shop"

Intended for Sir Isaac Newton

Nature and Nature's laws lay hid in night;
God said, Let Newton be! and all was light.

ALEXANDER POPE

Mock On, Mock On, Voltaire, Rousseau

Mock on, mock on, Voltaire, Rousseau;
Mock on, mock on; 'tis all in vain!
You throw the sand against the wind,
And the wind blows it back again.

And every sand becomes a gem   5
Reflected in the beams divine;
Blown back they blind the mocking eye,
But still in Israel's paths they shine.

The atoms of Democritus
And Newton's particles of light   10
Are sands upon the Red Sea shore,
Where Israel's tents do shine so bright.

WILLIAM BLAKE

Sonnet—To Science

Science! true daughter of Old Time thou art!
    Who alterest all things with thy peering eyes.
Why preyest thou thus upon the poet's heart,
    Vulture, whose wings are dull realities?
How should he love thee? or how deem thee wise?   5
    Who wouldst not leave him in his wandering
To seek for treasure in the jewelled skies,
    Albeit he soared with an undaunted wing?
Hast thou not dragged Diana from her car?
    And driven the Hamadryad from the wood   10
To seek a shelter in some happier star?
    Hast thou not torn the Naiad from her flood,
The Elfin from the green grass, and from me
The summer dream beneath the tamarind tree?

EDGAR ALLAN POE

To a Locomotive in Winter

Thee for my recitative,
Thee in the driving storm even as now, the snow, the winter-day declining,
Thee in thy panoply, thy measured dual throbbing and thy beat convulsive,
Thy black cylindric body, golden brass and silvery steel,
Thy ponderous side-bars, parallel and connecting rods, gyrating, shuttling
    at thy sides,   5
Thy metrical, now swelling pant and roar, now tapering in the distance,
Thy great protruding head-light fixed in front,
Thy long, pale, floating vapor-pennants, tinged with delicate purple,
The dense and murky clouds out-belching from thy smoke-stack,
Thy knitted frame, thy springs and valves, the tremulous twinkle of thy
    wheels,   10
Thy train of cars behind, obedient, merrily following,
Through gale or calm, now swift, now slack, yet steadily careering;
Type of the modern—emblem of motion and power—pulse of the con-
    tinent,
For once come serve the Muse and merge in verse, even as here I see thee,
With storm and buffeting gusts of wind and falling snow,   15
By day thy warning ringing bell to sound its notes,
By night thy silent signal lamps to swing.

Fierce-throated beauty!
Roll through my chant with all thy lawless music, thy swinging lamps at
    night,

Thy madly-whistled laughter, echoing, rumbling like an earthquake,
    rousing all,   20
Law of thyself complete, thine own track firmly holding,
(No sweetness debonair of tearful harp or glib piano thine,)
Thy trills of shrieks by rocks and hills returned,
Launched o'er the prairies wide, across the lakes,
To the free skies unpent and glad and strong.   25

WALT WHITMAN

When I Heard the Learn'd Astronomer

When I heard the learn'd astronomer,
When the proofs, the figures, were ranged in columns before me,
When I was shown the charts and diagrams, to add, divide, and measure
    them,
When I sitting heard the astronomer where he lectured with much applause
    in the lecture-room,
How soon unaccountable I became tired and sick,   5
Till rising and gliding out I wandered off by myself,
In the mystical moist night-air, and from time to time,
Looked up in perfect silence at the stars.

WALT WHITMAN

I Like to See It Lap the Miles

I like to see it lap the miles,
And lick the valleys up,
And stop to feed itself at tanks;
And then, prodigious, step

Around a pile of mountains,   5
And, supercilious, peer
In shanties by the sides of roads;
And then a quarry pare

To fit its sides, and crawl between,
Complaining all the while   10
In horrid, hooting stanza;
Then chase itself down hill

And neigh like Boanerges;
Then, punctual as a star,

Stop—docile and omnipotent—   15
At its own stable door.

EMILY DICKINSON

The Egg and the Machine

He gave the solid rail a hateful kick.
From far away there came an answering tick;
And then another tick. He knew the code:
His hate had roused an engine up the road.
He wished when he had had the track alone   5
He had attacked it with a club or stone
And bent some rail wide open like a switch.
So as to wreck the engine in the ditch.
Too late, though, now to throw it down the bank;
Its click was rising to a nearer clank.   10
Here it came breasting like a horse in skirts.
(He stood well back for fear of scalding squirts.)
Then for a moment there was only size,
Confusion, and a roar that drowned the cries
He raised against the gods in the machine.   15
Then once again the sand-bank lay serene.
The traveler's eye picked up a turtle trail,
Between the dotted feet a streak of tail,
And followed it to where he made out vague,
But certain signs of buried turtle egg;   20
And probing with one finger not too rough,
He found suspicious sand, and sure enough
The pocket of a little turtle mine.
If there was one egg in it, there were nine,
Torpedo-like, with shell of gritty leather   25
All packed in sand to wait the trump together.
"You'd better not disturb me any more,"
He told the distance. "I am armed for war.
The next machine that has the power to pass
Will get this plasm in its goggle glass."   30

ROBERT FROST

To a Steam Roller

The illustration
is nothing to you without the application.

You lack half wit. You crush all the particles down
    into close conformity, and then walk back and forth on them.

Sparkling chips of rock   5
are crushed down to the level of the parent block.
    Were not "impersonal judgment in esthetic
        matters, a metaphysical impossibility," you

might fairly achieve
it. As for butterflies, I can hardly conceive   10
    of one's attending upon you; but to question
        the congruence of the complement is vain, if it exists.

                                    MARIANNE MOORE

Nightmare Number Three

    We had expected everything but revolt
    And I kind of wonder myself when they started thinking—
    But there's no dice in that now.
                            I've heard fellows say
    They must have planned it for years and maybe they did.   5
    Looking back, you can find little incidents here and there,
    Like the concrete-mixer in Jersey eating the wop
    Or the roto press that printed "Fiddle-dee-dee!"

    In a three-color process all over Senator Sloop,
    Just as he was making a speech. The thing about that   10
    Was, how could it walk upstairs? But it *was* upstairs,
    Clicking and mumbling in the Senate Chamber.
    They had to knock out the wall to take it away
    And the wrecking-crew said it grinned.
                            It was only the best   15
    Machines, of course, the superhuman machines,
    The ones we'd built to be better than flesh and bone,
    But the cars were in it, of course . . .
                            and they hunted us
    Like rabbits through the cramped streets on that Bloody Monday, 20
    The Madison Avenue busses leading the charge.
    The busses were pretty bad—but I'll not forget
    The smash of glass when the Duesenberg left the show-room
    And pinned three brokers to the Racquet Club steps,
    Or the long howl of the horns when they saw the men run,   25
    When they saw them looking for holes in the solid ground . . .

I guess they were tired of being ridden in,
And stopped and started by pygmies for silly ends,
Of wrapping cheap cigarettes and bad chocolate bars,
Collecting nickels and waving platinum hair,   30
And letting six million people live in a town.
I guess it was that. I guess they got tired of us
And the whole smell of human hands.
                           But it was a shock
To climb sixteen flights of stairs to Art Zuckow's office   35
(Nobody took the elevators twice)
And find him strangled to death in a nest of telephones,
The octopus-tendrils waving over his head,
And a sort of quiet humming filling the air . . .
Do they eat? . . . There was red . . . But I did not stop to look.   40
And it's lonely, here on the roof.
                       For a while I thought
That window-cleaner would make it, and keep me company.
But they got him with his own hoist at the sixteenth floor
And dragged him in with a squeal.   45
You see, they cooperate. Well, we taught them that,
And it's fair enough, I suppose. You see, we built them.
We taught them to think for themselves.
It was bound to come. You can see it was bound to come.
And it won't be so bad, in the country. I hate to think   50
Of the reapers, running wild in the Kansas fields,
And the transport planes like hawks on a chickenyard,
But the horses might help. We might make a deal with the horses.
At least you've more chance, out there.
                    And they need us too.   55
They're bound to realize that when they once calm down.
They'll need oil and spare parts and adjustments and tuning up.
Slaves? Well, in a way, you know, we were slaves before.
There won't be so much real difference—honest there won't.
(I wish I hadn't looked into that beauty-parlor   60
And seen what was happening there.
But those are female machines and a bit high-strung.)
Oh, we'll settle down. We'll arrange it. We'll compromise.
It wouldn't make sense to wipe out the whole human race.
Why, I bet if I went to my old Plymouth now   65
(Of course, you'd have to do it the tactful way)
And said, "Look here! Who got you the swell French horn?"
He wouldn't turn me over to those police cars.
At least I don't *think* he would.
                    Oh, it's going to be jake.   70
There won't be so much real difference—honest, there won't—
And I'd go down in a minute and take my chance—

I'm a good American and I always liked them—
Except for one small detail that bothers me
And that's the food proposition. Because you see,   75
The concrete-mixer may have made a mistake,
And it looks like just high spirits.
But, if it's got so they like the flavor . . . well . . .

STEPHEN VINCENT BENÉT

To Brooklyn Bridge

How many dawns, chill from his rippling rest
The seagull's wings shall dip and pivot him,
Shedding white rings of tumult, building high
Over the chained bay waters Liberty—

Then, with inviolate curve, forsake our eyes   5
As apparitional as sails that cross
Some page of figures to be filed away;
—Till elevators drop us from our day . . .

I think of cinemas, panoramic sleights
With multitudes bent toward some flashing scene   10
Never disclosed, but hastened to again,
Foretold to other eyes on the same screen;

And Thee, across the harbor, silver-paced
As though the sun took step of thee, yet left
Some motion ever unspent in thy stride,—   15
Implicitly thy freedom staying thee!

Out of some subway scuttle, cell or loft
A bedlamite speeds to thy parapets,
Tilting there momently, shrill shirt ballooning,
A jest falls from the speechless caravan.   20

Down Wall, from girder into street noon leaks,
A rip-tooth of the sky's acetylene;
All afternoon the cloud-flown derricks turn . . .
Thy cables breathe the North Atlantic still.

And obscure as that heaven of the Jews,   25
Thy guerdon . . . Accolade thou dost bestow
Of anonymity time cannot raise:
Vibrant reprieve and pardon thou dost show.

O harp and altar, of the fury fused,
(How could mere toil align thy choiring strings!)   30
Terrific threshold of the prophet's pledge,
Prayer of pariah, and the lover's cry,—

Again the traffic lights that skim thy swift
Unfractioned idiom, immaculate sigh of stars,
Beading thy path—condense eternity: 35
And we have seen night lifted in thine arms.

Under thy shadow by the piers I waited;
Only in darkness is thy shadow clear.
The City's fiery parcels all undone,
Already snow submerges an iron year . . .   40

O Sleepless as the river under thee,
Vaulting the sea, the prairies' dreaming sod,
Unto us lowliest sometime sweep, descend
And of the curveship lend a myth to God.

HART CRANE
(Proem: From "The Bridge")

Before Disaster

Evening traffic homeward burns,
Swift and even on the turns,
Drifting weight in triple rows,
Fixed relation and repose.
This one edges out and by,   5
Inch by inch with steady eye.
But should error be increased,
Mass and moment are released;
Matter loosens, flooding blind,
Levels driver to its kind.   10
    Ranks of nations thus descend,
Watchful to a stormy end.
By a moment's calm beguiled,
I have got a wife and child.
Fool and scoundrel guide the State.   15
Peace is whore to Greed and Hate.
Nowhere may I turn to flee:
Action is security.
Treading change with savage heel,
We must live or die by steel.   20

YVOR WINTERS

Birmingham

Smoke from the train-gulf hid by hoardings blunders upward, the brakes
   of cars
Pipe as the policeman pivoting round raises his flat hand, bars
With his figure of a monolith Pharaoh the queue of fidgety machines
(Chromium dogs on the bonnet,[1] faces behind the triplex screens[2])
Behind him the streets run away between the proud glass of shops   5
Cubical scent-bottles artificial legs arctic foxes and electric mops
But beyond this center the slumward vista thins like a diagram:
There, unvisited, are Vulcan's forges who doesn't care a tinker's damn.

Splayed outwards through the suburbs houses, houses for rest
Seducingly rigged by the builder, half-timbered houses with lips pressed   10
So tightly and eyes staring at the traffic through bleary haws
And only a six-inch grip of the racing earth in their concrete claws;
In these houses men as in a dream pursue the Platonic Forms
With wireless and cairn terriers and gadgets approximating to the fickle
   norms
And endeavor to find God and score one over the neighbor   15
By climbing tentatively upward on jerry-built beauty and sweated labor.

The lunch hour: the shops empty, shopgirls' faces relax
Diaphanous as green glass empty as old almanacs
As incoherent with ticketed gewgaws tiered behind their heads
As the Burne-Jones windows in St. Philip's broken by crawling leads   20
Insipid color, patches of emotion, Saturday thrills—
(This theater is sprayed with "June")—the gutter take our old playbills,
Next week-end it is likely in the heart's funfair we shall pull
Strong enough on the handle to get back our money; or at any rate it is
   possible.

On shining lines the trams like vast sarcophagi move   25
Into the sky, plum after sunset, merging to duck's egg, barred with mauve
Zeppelin clouds, and pentecost-like the cars' headlights bud
Out from sideroads and the traffic signals, crème-de-menthe or bull's blood,
Tell one to stop, the engine gently breathing, or to go on
To where like black pipes of organs in the frayed and fading zone   30
Of the West the factory chimneys on sullen sentry will all night wait
To call, in the harsh morning, sleep-stupid faces through the daily gate.

LOUIS MACNEICE

---

[1] Hood.   [2] Windshield.

Crossroads

Testubicles spill blood across the page
Where symbols chart meticulously
Dimensions praecox.

Four motors thunder down the bombway
(Pulse is still)   5
A metronome tick-tocks
The measured steps of Elohim.
In the wasteland a ball of fire
A pillar of cloud.
Lead us, Dear Lord, into Thy Promised Land. 10

All else is relative,
This only true:
$E = mc^2$.

MARTIN STAPLES SHOCKLEY

The Express

After the first powerful plain manifesto
The black statement of pistons, without more fuss
But gliding like a queen, she leaves the station.
Without bowing and with restrained unconcern
She passes the houses which humbly crowd outside, 5
The gasworks and at last the heavy page
Of death, printed by gravestones in the cemetery.
Beyond the town there lies the open country
Where, gathering speed, she acquires mystery,
The luminous self-possession of ships on ocean. 10
It is now she begins to sing—at first quite low
Then loud, and at last with a jazzy madness—
The song of her whistle screaming at curves,
Of deafening tunnels, brakes, innumerable bolts.
And always light, aerial, underneath 15
Goes the elate meter of her wheels.
Steaming through metal landscape on her lines
She plunges new eras of wild happiness
Where speed throws up strange shapes, broad curves
And parallels clean like the steel of guns. 20
At last, further than Edinburgh or Rome,
Beyond the crest of the world, she reaches night
Where only a low streamline-brightness
Of phosphorus on the tossing hills is white.

Ah, like a comet through flames she moves entranced,   25
Wrapt in her music no bird song, no, nor bough
Breaking with honey buds, shall ever equal.

STEPHEN SPENDER

The Landscape near an Aerodrome

More beautiful and soft than any moth
With burring furred antennae feeling its huge path
Through dusk, the air liner with shut-off engines
Glides over suburbs and the sleeves set trailing tall
To point the wind. Gently, broadly, she falls,   5
Scarcely disturbing charted currents of air.

Lulled by descent, the travellers across sea
And across feminine land indulging its easy limbs
In miles of softness, now let their eyes trained by watching
Penetrate through dusk the outskirts of this town   10
Here where industry shows a fraying edge.
Here they may see what is being done.

Beyond the winking masthead light
And the landing ground, they observe the outposts
Of work: chimneys like lank black fingers   15
Or figures, frightening and mad: and squat buildings
With their strange air behind trees, like women's faces
Shattered by grief. Here where few houses
Moan with faint light behind their blinds,
They remark the unhomely sense of complaint, like a dog   20
Shut out, and shivering at the foreign moon.

In the last sweep of love, they pass over fields
Behind the aerodrome, where boys play all day
Hacking dead grass: whose cries, like wild birds,
Settle upon the nearest roofs   25
But soon are hid under the loud city.
Then, as they land, they hear the tolling bell
Reaching across the landscape of hysteria,
To where, larger than all those batteries
And charcoaled towers against that dying sky,   30
Religion stands, the Church blocking the sun.

STEPHEN SPENDER

Buick

As a sloop with a sweep of immaculate wing on her delicate spine
And a keel as steel as a root that holds in the sea as she leans,
Leaning and laughing, my warm-hearted beauty, you ride, you ride,
You tack on the curves with parabola speed and a kiss of goodbye,
Like a thoroughbred sloop, my new high-spirited spirit, my kiss.   5

As my foot suggests that you leap in the air with your hips of a girl,
My finger that praises your wheel and announces your voices of song,
Flouncing your skirts, you blueness of joy, you flirt of politeness,
You leap, you intelligence, essence of wheelness with silvery nose,
And your platinum clocks of excitement stir like the hairs of a fern.   10

But how alien you are from the booming belts of your birth and the
    smoke
Where you turned on the stinging lathes of Detroit and Lansing at night
And shrieked at the torch in your secret parts and the amorous tests,
But now with your eyes that enter the future of roads you forget;
You are all instinct with your phosphorous glow and your streaking hair.   15

And now when we stop it is not as the bird from the shell that I leave
Or the leathery pilot who steps from his bird with a sneer of delight,
And not as the ignorant beast do you squat and watch me depart,
But with exquisite breathing you smile, with satisfaction of love,
And I touch you again as you tick in the silence and settle in sleep.   20

KARL SHAPIRO

Auto Wreck

Its quick soft silver bell beating, beating,
And down the dark one ruby flare
Pulsing out red light like an artery,
The ambulance at top speed floating down
Past beacons and illuminated clocks   5
Wings in a heavy curve, dips down,
And brakes speed, entering the crowd.
The doors leap open, emptying light;
Stretchers are laid out, the mangled lifted
And stowed into the little hospital.   10
Then the bell, breaking the hush, tolls once,
And the ambulance with its terrible cargo
Rocking, slightly rocking, moves away,
As the doors, an afterthought, are closed.

We are deranged, walking among the cops   15
Who sweep glass and are large and composed.
One is still making notes under the light.
One with a bucket douches ponds of blood
Into the street and gutter.
One hangs lanterns on the wrecks that cling,   20
Empty husks of locusts, to iron poles.

Our throats were tight as tourniquets,
Our feet were bound with splints, but now
Like convalescents intimate and gauche,
We speak through sickly smiles and warn   25
With the stubborn saw of common sense,
The grim joke and the banal resolution.
The traffic moves around with care,
But we remain, touching a wound
That opens to our richest horror.   30

Already old, the question Who shall die?
Becomes unspoken Who is innocent?
For death in war is done by hands;
Suicide has cause and stillbirth, logic.
But this invites the occult mind,   35
Cancels our physics with a sneer,
And spatters all we knew of dénouement
Across the expedient and wicked stones.

                         KARL SHAPIRO

The Progress of Faust

He was born in Deutschland, as you would suspect,
And graduated in magic from Cracow
In Fifteen Five. His portraits show a brow
Heightened by science. The eye is indirect,
As of bent light upon a crooked soul,   5
And that he bargained with the Prince of Shame
For pleasures intellectually foul
Is known by every court that lists his name.

His frequent disappearances are put down
To visits in the regions of the damned   10
And to the periodic deaths he shammed,
But, unregenerate and in Doctor's gown,
He would turn up to lecture at the fair
And do a minor miracle for a fee.

Many a life he whispered up the stair   15
To teach the black art of anatomy.

He was as deaf to angels as an oak
When, in the fall of Fifteen Ninety-four,
He went to London and crashed through the floor
In mock damnation of the playgoing folk.   20
Weekending with the scientific crowd,
He met Sir Francis Bacon and helped draft
"Colours of Good and Evil" and read aloud
An obscene sermon at which no one laughed.

He toured the Continent for a hundred years   25
And subsidized among the peasantry
The puppet play, his tragic history;
With a white glove he boxed the Devil's ears
And with a black his own. Tired of this,
He published penny poems about his sins,   30
In which he placed the heavy emphasis
On the white glove which, for a penny, wins.

Some time before the hemorrhage of the Kings
Of France, he turned respectable and taught;
Quite suddenly everything that he had thought   35
Seemed to grow scholars' beards and angels' wings.
It was the Overthrow. On Reason's throne
He sat with the fair Phrygian on his knees
And called all universities his own,
As plausible a figure as you please.   40

Then back to Germany as the sages' sage
To preach comparative science to the young
Who came from every land in a great throng
And knew they heard the master of the age.
When for a secret formula he paid   45
The Devil another fragment of his soul,
The scholars wept, and several even prayed
That Satan would restore him to them whole.

Backwardly tolerant, Faustus was expelled
From the Third Reich in Nineteen Thirty-nine.   50
His exit caused the breaching of the Rhine,
Except for which the frontier might have held.
Five years unknown to enemy and friend
He hid, appearing on the sixth to pose
In an American desert at war's end   55
Where, at his back, a dome of atoms rose.

                                KARL SHAPIRO

Pleasures of a Technological University

magnesium and Crashaw
semiotics and ergonomics
lasers and caesuras
retro-rockets and peripeteia
sapphics and turquoise   5
sines and sememes
hubris and helium
Eliot and entropy
enjambment and switchgear
quasars and hapax legomena   10
thermodynamics and macrostylistics
anti-hero and anti-matter
bubble chambers and E. K. Chambers
H_2O and 8vo
genres and genera   15
meters and metres
litmus and anagnorisis
DNA and ABBA
DNB and TNT
bleeps and feet   20
Rhine and Poe
ficelle and cantilever
metal fatigue and dead metaphors
flyting and teratology
ergs and Bacon   25
genes and fitts
morphs and mesons
tektites and données
Möbius's ring and Freytag's pyramid
stichomythia and feedback   30
red shifts and *Tam o' Shanter*
copula and cupola
sonic booms and euphuism
osmosis and entasis
umlaut and ohm   35
Ethan Brand and ethyl fluid
wit and sodium chloride
neoaristotelianism and microminiaturisation
F3 and Fe
poem and pome.   40

EDWIN MORGAN

5
War

There was a time when war as a literary theme had a certain sweep and grandeur. Vergil's great epic begins, "Arms and the man I sing," as if arms and men were natural concomitants. At about the same time, Horace could write *dulce et decorum est pro patria mori*[1] and sound sincere. But no more. The horrors of twentieth-century war are so appalling that man can no longer think of "the glories of our blood and state" in just the same way that former ages did. When George Bernard Shaw, echoing Vergil, entitles his play *Arms and the Man,* it is to mock the phrase.

It has sometimes been possible for man to see the absurdity of war. He can sometimes laugh at the paradoxical incongruities that war produces; but when he does, it is the sardonic laughter of novels such as *Put Out More Flags, The Good Soldier Schweik,* and *Catch-22.* And not even Aristophanes' *Lysistrata* was able to laugh war off the scene. In the last analysis, perhaps war is too grim for laughter.

War as a literary theme would not have achieved the significance it has if writers had expressed only their indignation and revulsion at the senseless slaughter, the suffering, and the destruction caused by war. Much more important is their expression of the subtle and far-reaching ways in which war changes men. Wilfred Owen's boy, whose "teeth seem for laughing round an apple" and not for rending his enemies, is blood brother to Henry Reed's recruit, ritually naming the parts of his weapon. What these boys are being taught in the name of flatulent old abstractions is to blow each other to bits. They are being taught to develop the callousness that will let them, without retching, perform the task necessitated by the death of Randall Jarrell's gunner: "When I died they washed me out of the turret with a hose."

The poems in this section reveal that poetry can be especially effective when it deals with issues that are as current as today's news. The theme of war has also had its fascination for writers in other genres. The list below indicates that writers as diverse as Shakespeare and Shaw, Kipling and Faulkner, Mansfield and Salinger have been gripped by it.

[1] It is sweet and fitting to die for one's country.

READINGS IN OTHER GENRES

PLAYS

Aeschylus, *The Seven against Thebes*
Maxwell Anderson, *The Eve of St. Mark*
Maxwell Anderson and Laurence Stallings, *What Price Glory?*
Aristophanes, *Lysistrata*
Bertold Brecht, *Mother Courage*
Euripides, *The Trojan Women*
Jean Giraudoux, *Tiger at the Gates*
George Farquhar, *The Recruiting Officer*
Lillian Hellman, *Watch on the Rhine*
Arthur Laurents, *Home of the Brave*
Plautus, *Miles Gloriosus*
William Shakespeare, *Henry V*
George Bernard Shaw, *Arms and the Man*
Robert Sherwood, *There Shall Be No Night*

NOVELS

James Gould Cozzens, *Guard of Honor*
Stephen Crane, *The Red Badge of Courage*
Charles Dickens, *A Tale of Two Cities*
John Dos Passos, *Three Soldiers*
Jaroslav Hasek, *The Good Soldier Schweik*
Joseph Heller, *Catch-22*
Ernest Hemingway, *A Farewell to Arms, For Whom the Bell Tolls*
James Jones, *From Here to Eternity*
Norman Mailer, *The Naked and the Dead*
Erich Maria Remarque, *All Quiet on the Western Front*
Irwin Shaw, *The Young Lions*
Leo Tolstoy, *War and Peace*
Evelyn Waugh, *Put Out More Flags*
Herman Wouk, *The Caine Mutiny*

SHORT STORIES

Ambrose Bierce, "One Kind of Officer"
Stephen Crane, "A Mystery of Heroism"
William Faulkner, "All the Lost Young Men," "The Young Man Who Flew Past," "Two Soldiers"
Ernest Hemingway, "A Way You'll Never Be"

Rudyard Kipling, "Mary Postgate"
Katherine Mansfield, "The Fly"
Guy de Maupassant, "Boule de Souif"
Prosper Merimée, "The Taking of the Redoubt"
Luigi Pirandello, "War"
J. D. Salinger, "For Esmé, with Love and Squalor"

The Glories of Our Blood and State

The glories of our blood and state
  Are shadows, not substantial things;
There is no armor against fate;
  Death lays his icy hand on kings:
      Scepter and crown   5
      Must tumble down,
And in the dust be equal made
With the poor crooked scythe and spade.

Some men with swords may reap the field,
  And plant fresh laurels where they kill,   10
But their strong nerves at last must yield;
  They tame but one another still:
      Early or late,
      They stoop to fate,
And must give up their murmuring breath,   15
When they, pale captives, creep to death.

The garlands wither on your brow;
  Then boast no more your mighty deeds;
Upon death's purple altar now,
  See where the victor-victim bleeds: 20
      Your heads must come
      To the cold tomb;
Only the actions of the just
Smell sweet and blossom in their dust.

JAMES SHIRLEY
(from *The Contention of Ajax and Ulysses*)

On the Late Massacre in Piedmont

Avenge, O lord, thy slaughtered saints, whose bones
  Lie scattered on the Alpine mountains cold,
Even them who kept thy truth so pure of old
  When all our fathers worshipped stocks and stones.

Forget not: in thy book record their groans   5
  Who were thy sheep and in their ancient fold
  Slain by the bloody Piedmontese that rolled
  Mother with infant down the rocks. Their moans
The vales redoubled to the hills, and they
  To Heaven. Their martyred blood and ashes sow   10
  O'er all the Italian fields where still doth sway
The triple tyrant; that from these may grow
  A hundred-fold, who having learnt thy way,
  Early may fly the Babylonian woe.

                              JOHN MILTON

To Lucasta, Going to the Wars

          Tell me not, sweet, I am unkind,
              That from the nunnery
          Of thy chaste breast and quiet mind,
              To war and arms I fly.

          True, a new mistress now I chase: 5
              The first foe in the field;
          And with a stronger faith embrace
              A sword, a horse, a shield.

          Yet this inconstancy is such
              As you, too, shall adore;   10
          I could not love thee, dear, so much,
              Loved I not honor more.

                          RICHARD LOVELACE

The War-Song of Dinas Vawr

          The mountain sheep are sweeter,
          But the valley sheep are fatter;
          We therefore deemed it meeter
          To carry off the latter.
          We made an expedition;   5
          We met an host and quelled it;
          We forced a strong position,
          And killed the men who held it.

On Dyfed's richest valley,
Where herds of kine were browsing,   10
We made a mighty sally,
To furnish our carousing.
Fierce warriors rushed to meet us;
We met them, and o'erthrew them:
They struggled hard to beat us;   15
But we conquered them, and slew them.

As we drove our prize at leisure,
The king marched forth to catch us:
His rage surpassed all measure,
But his people could not match us.   20
He fled to his hall-pillars;
And, ere our force we led off,
Some sacked his house and cellars,
While others cut his head off.

We there, in strife bewildering,   25
Spilt blood enough to swim in:
We orphaned many children,
And widowed many women.
The eagles and the ravens
We glutted with our foemen: 30
The heroes and the cravens,
The spearmen and the bowmen.

We brought away from battle,
And much their land bemoaned them,
Two thousand head of cattle,   35
And the head of him who owned them:
Ednyfed, King of Dyfed,
His head was borne before us;
His wine and beasts supplied our feasts,
And his overthrow, our chorus.   40

THOMAS LOVE PEACOCK

Song of Saul before His Last Battle

Warriors and chiefs! should the shaft or the sword
Pierce me in leading the host of the Lord,
Heed not the corse, though a king's, in your path:
Bury your steel in the bosoms of Gath!

Thou who are bearing my buckler and bow,   5
Should the soldiers of Saul look away from the foe,
Stretch me that moment in blood at thy feet!
Mine be the doom which they dared not to meet.

Farewell to others, but never we part,
Heir to my royalty, son of my heart!   10
Bright is the diadem, boundless the sway,
Or kingly the death, which awaits us today!

GEORGE GORDON, LORD BYRON

The Destruction of Sennacherib

I

The Assyrian came down like the wolf on the fold,
And his cohorts were gleaming in purple and gold;
And the sheen of their spears was like stars on the sea,
When the blue wave rolls nightly on deep Galilee.

II

Like the leaves of the forest when Summer is green,   5
That host with their banners at sunset were seen:
Like the leaves of the forest when Autumn hath blown,
That host on the morrow lay withered and strown.

III

For the Angel of Death spread his wings on the blast,
And breathed in the face of the foe as he passed;   10
And the eyes of the sleepers waxed deadly and chill,
And their hearts but once heaved, and for ever grew still!

IV

And there lay the steed with his nostril all wide,
But through it there rolled not the breath of his pride;
And the foam of his gasping lay white on the turf,   15
And cold as the spray of the rock-beating surf.

V

And there lay the rider distorted and pale,
With the dew on his brow, and the rust on his mail:
And the tents were all silent, the banners alone,
The lances uplifted, the trumpet unblown.   20

VI

And the widows of Ashur are loud in their wail,
And the idols are broke in the temple of Baal;
And the might of the Gentile, unsmote by the sword,
Hath melted like snow in the glance of the Lord!

GEORGE GORDON, LORD BYRON

The Minstrel Boy

The Minstrel Boy to the war is gone,
   In the ranks of death you'll find him;
His father's sword he has girded on,
   And his wild harp slung behind him.—
"Land of song!" said the warrior-bard,   5
   "Though all the world betrays thee,
One sword, at least, thy rights shall guard,
   One faithful harp shall praise thee!"

The Minstrel fell!—but the foeman's chain
   Could not bring his proud soul under;   10
The harp he loved ne'er spoke again,
   For he tore its chords asunder;
And said, "No chains shall sully thee,
   Thou soul of love and bravery!
Thy songs were made for the pure and free,   15
   They shall never sound in slavery."

THOMAS MOORE

The Portent

Hanging from the beam,
   Slowly swaying (such the law),
Gaunt the shadow on your green,
   Shenandoah!
The cut is on the crown   5
   (Lo, John Brown),
And the stabs shall heal no more.

Hidden in the cap
   Is the anguish none can draw;
So your future veils its face,   10
   Shenandoah!

But the streaming beard is shown
  (Weird John Brown),
The meteor of the war.

HERMAN MELVILLE

Shiloh
A Requiem (April 1862)

Skimming lightly, wheeling still,
  The swallows fly low
Over the field in clouded days,
  The forest-field of Shiloh—
Over the field where April rain   5
Solaced the parched one stretched in pain
Through the pause of night
That followed the Sunday fight
  Around the church of Shiloh—
The church so lone, the log-built one,   10
That echoed to many a parting groan
    And natural prayer
  Of dying foemen mingled there—
Foemen at morn, but friends at eve—
  Fame or country least their care: 15
(What like a bullet can undeceive!)
  But now they lie low,
While over them the swallows skim,
  And all is hushed at Shiloh.

HERMAN MELVILLE

Beat! Beat! Drums!

Beat! beat! drums!—blow! bugles! blow!
Through the windows—through doors—burst like a ruthless force,
Into the solemn church, and scatter the congregation,
Into the school where the scholar is studying;
Leave not the bridegroom quiet—no happiness must he have now
  with his bride,   5
Nor the peaceful farmer any peace, ploughing his field or gathering
  his grain,

So fierce you whirr and pound you drums—so shrill you bugles
blow.

Beat! beat! drums!—blow! bugles! blow!
Over the traffic of cities—over the rumble of wheels in the streets;
Are beds prepared for sleepers at night in the houses? no sleepers
must sleep in those beds,
No bargainers' bargains by day—no brokers or speculators—would
they continue?
Would the talkers be talking? would the singer attempt to sing?
Would the lawyer rise in the court to state his case before the
judge?
Then rattle quicker, heavier drums—you bugles wilder blow.

Beat! beat! drums!—blow! bugles! blow!
Make no parley—stop for no expostulation,
Mind not the timid—mind not the weeper or prayer,
Mind not the old man beseeching the young man,
Let not the child's voice be heard, nor the mother's entreaties,
Make even the trestles to shake the dead where they lie awaiting
the hearses,
So strong you thump O terrible drums—so loud you bugles blow.

10

15

20

WALT WHITMAN

Cavalry Crossing a Ford

A line in long array where they wind betwixt green islands,
They take a serpentine course, their arms flash in the sun—hark to
the musical clank,
Behold the silvery river, in it the splashing horses loitering stop to
drink,
Behold the brown-faced men, each group, each person a picture, the
negligent rest on the saddles,
Some emerge on the opposite bank, others are just entering the ford—
while,
Scarlet and blue and snowy white,
The guidon flags flutter gayly in the wind.

5

WALT WHITMAN

A Sight in Camp in the Daybreak Gray and Dim

A sight in camp in the daybreak gray and dim,
As from my tent I emerge so early sleepless,

As slow I walk in the cool fresh air the path near by the hospital
   tent,
Three forms I see on stretchers lying, brought out there untended
   lying,
Over each the blanket spread, ample brownish woolen blanket,   5
Gray and heavy blanket, folding, covering all.

Curious I halt and silent stand,
Then with light fingers I from the face of the nearest the first just
   lift the blanket;
Who are you elderly man so gaunt and grim, with well-grayed hair,
   and flesh all sunken about the eyes?
Who are you my dear comrade?   10

Then to the second I step—and who are you my child and darling?
Who are you sweet boy with cheeks yet blooming?
Then to the third—a face nor child nor old, very calm, as of
   beautiful yellow-white ivory;
Young man I think I know you—I think this face is the face of the
   Christ himself,
Dead and divine and brother of all, and here again he lies.   15

WALT WHITMAN

Drummer Hodge

They throw in Drummer Hodge, to rest
   Uncoffined—just as found:
His landmark is a kopje-crest[1]
   That breaks the veldt around:
And foreign constellations west   5
   Each night above his mound.

Young Hodge the Drummer never knew—
   Fresh from his Wessex home—
The meaning of the broad Karoo,[2]
   The Bush, the dusty loam,   10
And why uprose to nightly view
   Strange stars amid the gloom.

Yet portion of that unknown plain
   Will Hodge forever be;

---

[1] Small hill.   [2] Large arid plateau in South Africa.

His homely Northern breast and brain   15
  Grow to some Southern tree,
And strange-eyed constellations reign
  His stars eternally.

THOMAS HARDY

Channel Firing

That night your great guns, unawares,
Shook all our coffins as we lay,
And broke the chancel window-squares,
We thought it was the Judgment-day

And sat upright. While drearisome   5
Arose the howl of wakened hounds:
The mouse let fall the altar-crumb,
The worms drew back into the mounds,

The glebe[1] cow drooled. Till God called, "No;
It's gunnery practice out at sea   10
Just as before you went below;
The world is as it used to be:

"All nations striving strong to make
Red war yet redder. Mad as hatters
They do no more for Christés sake   15
Than you who are helpless in such matters.

"That this is not the judgment-hour
For some of them's a blessed thing,
For if it were they'd have to scour
Hell's floor for so much threatening. . . .   20

"Ha, ha. It will be warmer when
I blow the trumpet (if indeed
I ever do; for you are men,
And rest eternal sorely need)."

So down we lay again. "I wonder,   25
Will the world ever saner be,"

[1] A cow that grazes on public land.

Said one, "than when He sent us under
In our indifferent century!"

And many a skeleton shook his head.
"Instead of preaching forty year,"   30
My neighbour Parson Thirdly said,
"I wish I had stuck to pipes and beer."

Again the guns disturbed the hour,
Roaring their readiness to avenge,
As far inland as Stourton Tower,   35
And Camelot, and starlit Stonehenge.

THOMAS HARDY

The Man He Killed

"Had he and I but met
    By some old ancient inn,
We should have sat us down to wet
    Right many a nipperkin![1]

"But ranged as infantry,   5
    And staring face to face,
I shot at him as he at me,
    And killed him in his place.

"I shot him dead because—
    Because he was my foe,   10
Just so: my foe of course he was;
    That's clear enough; although

"He thought he'd 'list, perhaps,
    Off-hand-like—just as I—
Was out of work—had sold his traps—   15
    No other reason why.

"Yes; quaint and curious war is!
    You shoot a fellow down
You'd treat, if met where any bar is,
    Or help to half-a-crown."   20

THOMAS HARDY

[1] Small tankard of ale.

Lancer

I 'listed at home for a lancer,
  Oh who would not sleep with the brave?
I 'listed at home for a lancer
  To ride on a horse to my grave.

And over the seas we were bidden   5
  A country to take and to keep;
And far with the brave I have ridden,
  And now with the brave I shall sleep.

For round me the men will be lying
  That learned me the way to behave,   10
And showed me my business of dying:
  Oh who would not sleep with the brave?

They ask and there is not an answer;
Says I, I will 'list for a lancer,
  Oh who would not sleep with the brave?   15

And I with the brave shall be sleeping
  At ease on my mattress of loam,
When back from their taking and keeping
  The squadron is riding at home.

The wind with the plumes will be playing,   20
  The girls will stand watching them wave,
And eyeing my comrades and saying
  Oh who would not sleep with the brave?

They ask and there is not an answer;
Says you, I will 'list for a lancer,   25
  Oh who would not sleep with the brave?

A. E. HOUSMAN

Easter, 1916

I have met them at close of day
  Coming with vivid faces
From counter or desk among grey
  Eighteenth-century houses.

I have passed with a nod of the head   5
Or polite meaningless words,
Or have lingered awhile and said
Polite meaningless words,
And thought before I had done
Of a mocking tale or a gibe   10
To please a companion
Around the fire at the club,
Being certain that they and I
But lived where motley is worn:
All changed, changed utterly: 15
A terrible beauty is born.

That woman's days were spent
In ignorant good-will,
Her nights in argument
Until her voice grew shrill.   20
What voice more sweet than hers
When, young and beautiful,
She rode to harriers?
This man had kept a school
And rode our wingèd horse;   25
This other his helper and friend
Was coming into his force;
He might have won fame in the end,
So sensitive his nature seemed,
So daring and sweet his thought.   30
This other man I had dreamed
A drunken, vainglorious lout.
He had done most bitter wrong
To some who are near my heart,
Yet I number him in the song;   35
He, too, has resigned his part
In the casual comedy;
He, too, has been changed in his turn,
Transformed utterly:
A terrible beauty is born.   40

Hearts with one purpose alone
Through summer and winter seem
Enchanted to a stone
To trouble the living stream.
The horse that comes from the road,   45
The rider, the birds that range

From cloud to tumbling cloud,
Minute by minute they change;
A shadow of cloud on the stream
Changes minute by minute;   50
A horse-hoof slides on the brim,
And a horse plashes within it;
The long-legged moor-hens dive,
And hens to moor-cocks call;
Minute by minute they live: 55
The stone's in the midst of all.

Too long a sacrifice
Can make a stone of the heart.
O when may it suffice?
That is Heaven's part, our part   60
To murmur name upon name,
As a mother names her child
When sleep at last has come
On limbs that had run wild.
What is it but nightfall?   65
No, no, not night but death;
Was it needless death after all?
For England may keep faith
For all that is done and said.
We know their dream; enough   70
To know they dreamed and are dead;
And what if excess of love
Bewildered them till they died?
I write it out in a verse—
MacDonagh and MacBride   75
And Connolly and Pearse
Now and in time to be,
Wherever green is worn,
Are changed, changed utterly:
A terrible beauty is born.   80

WILLIAM BUTLER YEATS

Break of Day in the Trenches

The darkness crumbles away—
It is the same old druid Time as ever.
Only a live thing leaps my hand—
A queer sardonic rat—

As I pull the parapet's poppy   5
To stick behind my ear.
Droll rat, they would shoot you if they knew
Your cosmopolitan sympathies.
Now you have touched this English hand
You will do the same to a German—   10
Soon, no doubt, if it be your pleasure
To cross the sleeping green between.
It seems you inwardly grin as you pass
Strong eyes, fine limbs, haughty athletes
Less chanced than you for life,   15
Bonds to the whims of murder,
Sprawled in the bowels of the earth,
The torn fields of France.
What do you see in our eyes
At the shrieking iron and flame   20
Hurled through still heavens?
What quaver—what heart aghast?
Poppies whose roots are in man's veins
Drop, and are ever dropping;
But mine in my ear is safe,   25
Just a little white with the dust.

ISAAC ROSENBERG

Arms and the Boy

Let the boy try along this bayonet-blade
How cold steel is, and keen with hunger of blood;
Blue with all malice, like a madman's flash;
And thinly drawn with famishing for flesh.

Lend him to stroke these blind, blunt bullet-heads   5
Which long to nuzzle in the hearts of lads,
Or give him cartridges of fine zinc teeth,
Sharp with the sharpness of grief and death.

For his teeth seem for laughing round an apple.
There lurk no claws behind his fingers supple;   10
And God will grow no talons at his heels,
Nor antlers through the thickness of his curls.

WILFRED OWEN

Dulce et Decorum Est

Bent double, like old beggars under sacks,
Knock-kneed, coughing like hags, we cursed through sludge,
Till on the haunting flares we turned our backs,
And towards our distant rest began to trudge.
Men marched asleep. Many had lost their boots,   5
But limped on, blood-shod. All went lame, all blind;
Drunk with fatigue; deaf even to the hoots
Of gas-shells dropping softly behind.

Gas! Gas! Quick, boys!—An ecstasy of fumbling,
Fitting the clumsy helmets just in time,   10
But someone still was yelling out and stumbling
And flound'ring like a man in fire or lime.—
Dim through the misty panes and thick green light,
As under a green sea, I saw him drowning.

In all my dreams before my helpless sight   15
He plunges at me, guttering, choking, drowning.

If in some smothering dreams, you too could pace
Behind the wagon that we flung him in,
And watch the white eyes writhing in his face,
His hanging face, like a devil's sick of sin;   20
If you could hear, at every jolt, the blood
Come gargling from the froth-corrupted lungs,
Bitter as the cud
Of vile, incurable sores on innocent tongues,—
My friend, you would not tell with such high zest   25
To children ardent for some desperate glory,
The old Lie: *Dulce et decorum est
Pro patria mori.*[1]

                                        WILFRED OWEN

[1] It is sweet and fitting to die for one's country.

Naming of Parts

To-day we have naming of parts. Yesterday,
We had daily cleaning. And to-morrow morning,
We shall have what to do after firing. But to-day,

To-day, we have naming of parts. Japonica
Glistens like coral in all of the neighbouring gardens,   5
   And to-day we have naming of parts.

This is the lower sling swivel. And this
Is the upper sling swivel, whose use you will see,
When you are given your slings. And this is the piling swivel,
Which in your case you have not got. The branches   10
Hold in the gardens their silent, eloquent gestures,
   Which in our case we have not got.

This is the safety-catch, which is always released
With an easy flick of the thumb. And please do not let me
See anyone using his finger. You can do it quite easy   15
If you have any strength in your thumb. The blossoms
Are fragile and motionless, never letting anyone see
   Any of them using their finger.

And this you can see is the bolt. The purpose of this
Is to open the breech, as you see. We can slide it   20
Rapidly backwards and forwards: we call this
Easing the spring. And rapidly backwards and forwards
The early bees are assaulting and fumbling the flowers:
   They call it easing the Spring.

They call it easing the Spring: it is perfectly easy   25
If you have any strength in your thumb: like the bolt,
And the breech, and the cocking-piece, and the point of balance,
Which in our case we have not got; and the almond-blossom
Silent in all of the gardens and the bees going backwards and forwards,
   For to-day we have naming of parts.   30

HENRY REED

my sweet old etcetera

my sweet old etcetera
aunt lucy during the recent

war could and what
is more did tell you just
what everybody was fighting   5

for,
my sister

isabel created hundreds
(and
hundreds) of socks not to   10
mention shirts fleaproof earwarmers

etcetera wristers etcetera, my
mother hoped that

i would die etcetera
bravely of course my father used   15
to become hoarse talking about how it was
a privilege and if only he
could meanwhile my

self etcetera lay quietly
in the deep mud et   20

cetera
(dreaming,
et
    cetera, of
Your smile
eyes knees and of your Etcetera)   25

E. E. CUMMINGS

The Fury of Aerial Bombardment

You would think the fury of aerial bombardment
Would rouse God to relent; the infinite spaces
Are still silent. He looks on shock-pried faces.
History, even, does not know what is meant.

You would feel that after so many centuries   5
God would give man to repent; yet he can kill
As Cain could, but with multitudinous will,
No farther advanced than in his ancient furies.

Was man made stupid to see his own stupidity?
Is God by definition indifferent, beyond us all?   10
Is the eternal truth man's fighting soul
Wherein the Beast ravens in its own avidity?

Of Van Wettering I speak, and Averill,
Names on a list, whose faces I do not recall
But they are gone to early death, who late in school   15
Distinguished the belt feed lever from the belt holding pawl.

RICHARD EBERHART

September 1, 1939

I sit in one of the dives
On Fifty-second Street
Uncertain and afraid
As the clever hopes expire
Of a low dishonest decade: 5
Waves of anger and fear
Circulate over the bright
And darkened lands of the earth,
Obsessing our private lives;
The unmentionable odour of death   10
Offends the September night.

Accurate scholarship can
Unearth the whole offence
From Luther until now
That has driven a culture mad,   15
Find what occurred at Linz,
What huge imago made
A psychopathic god:
I and the public know
What all schoolchildren learn,   20
Those to whom evil is done
Do evil in return.

Exiled Thucydides knew
All that a speech can say
About Democracy,   25
And what dictators do,
The elderly rubbish they talk
To an apathetic grave;
Analysed all in his book,
The enlightenment driven away,   30
The habit-forming pain,
Mismanagement and grief:
We must suffer them all again.

Into this neutral air
Where blind skyscrapers use   35
Their full height to proclaim
The strength of Collective Man,
Each language pours its vain
Competitive excuse:
But who can live for long   40
In an euphoric dream;
Out of the mirror they stare,
Imperialism's face
And the international wrong.

Faces along the bar   45
Cling to their average day:
The lights must never go out,
The music must always play,
All the conventions conspire
To make this fort assume   50
The furniture of home;
Lest we should see where we are,
Lost in a haunted wood,
Children afraid of the night
Who have never been happy or good.   55

The windiest militant trash
Important Persons shout
Is not so crude as our wish:
What mad Nijinsky wrote
About Diaghilev   60
Is true of the normal heart;
For the error bred in the bone
Of each woman and each man
Craves what it cannot have,
Not universal love   65
But to be loved alone.

From the conservative dark
Into the ethical life
The dense commuters come,
Repeating their morning vow;   70
"I *will* be true to the wife,
I'll concentrate more on my work,"
And helpless governors wake
To resume their compulsory game:
Who can release them now,   75

Who can reach the deaf,
Who can speak for the dumb?

Defenceless under the night
Our world in stupor lies;
Yet, dotted everywhere,   80
Ironic points of light
Flash out wherever the Just
Exchange their messages:
May I, composed like them
Of Eros and of dust,   85
Beleaguered by the same
Negation and despair,
Show an affirming flame.

                    W. H. AUDEN

Two Armies

Deep in the winter plain, two armies
Dig their machinery, to destroy each other.
Men freeze and hunger. No one is given leave
On either side, except the dead, and wounded.
These have their leave; while new battalions wait   5
On time at last to bring them violent peace.

All have become so nervous and so cold
That each man hates the cause and distant words
Which brought him here, more terribly than bullets.
Once a boy hummed a popular marching song,   10
Once a novice hand flapped the salute;
The voice was choked, the lifted hand fell,
Shot through the wrist by those of his own side.

From their numb harvest all would flee, except
For discipline drilled once in an iron school   15
Which holds them at the point of a revolver.
Yet when they sleep, the images of home
Ride wishing horses of escape
Which herd the plain in a mass unspoken poem.

Finally, they cease to hate: for although hate   20
Bursts from the air and whips the earth like hail
Or pours it up in fountains to marvel at,
And although hundreds fall, who can connect
The inexhaustible anger of the guns
With the dumb patience of these tormented animals?   25

Clean silence drops at night when a little walk
Divides the sleeping armies, each
Huddled in linen woven by remote hands.
When the machines are stilled, a common suffering
Whitens the air with breath and makes both one   30
As though these enemies slept in each other's arms.

Only the lucid friend to aerial raiders,
The brilliant pilot moon, stares down
Upon the plain she makes a shining bone
Cut by the shadow of many thousand bones.   35
Where amber clouds scatter on No-Man's-Land
She regards death and time throw up
The furious words and minerals which destroy.

STEPHEN SPENDER

Eighth Air Force

If, in an odd angle of the hutment,
A puppy laps the water from a can
Of flowers, and the drunk sergeant shaving
Whistles *O Paradiso!*—shall I say that man
Is not as men have said: a wolf to man?   5

The other murderers troop in yawning;
Three of them play Pitch, one sleeps, and one
Lies counting missions, lies there sweating
Till even his heart beats: One; One; One.
O murderers! . . . Still, this is how it's done: 10

This is a war. . . . But since these play, before they die,
Like puppies with their puppy; since, a man,
I did as these have done, but did not die—
I will content the people as I can
And give up these to them: Behold the man!   15

I have suffered, in a dream, because of him,
Many things; for this last saviour, man,
I have lied as I lie now. But what is lying?
Men wash their hands, in blood, as best they can:
I find no fault in this just man.   20

RANDALL JARRELL

The Death of the Ball Turret Gunner

From my mother's sleep I fell into the State,
And I hunched in its belly till my wet fur froze.
Six miles from earth, loosed from its dream of life,
I woke to black flak and the nightmare fighters.
When I died they washed me out of the turret with a hose.   5

RANDALL JARRELL

Kilroy
(for John H. Finley, Jr.)

1

Also Ulysses once—that other war.
  (Is it because we find his scrawl
  Today on every privy door
  That we forget his ancient rôle?)
Also was there—he did it for the wages—   5
When a Cathay-drunk Genoese set sail.
Whenever "longen folk to goon on pilgrimages,"
Kilroy is there;
              he tells The Miller's Tale.

2

At times he seems a paranoiac king   10
Who stamps his crest on walls and says, "My own!"
But in the end he fades like a lost tune,
Tossed here and there, whom all the breezes sing.
"Kilroy was here"; these words sound wanly gay,
  Haughty yet tired with long marching.   15
He is Orestes—guilty of what crime?—
  For whom the Furies still are searching;
  When they arrive, they find their prey
(Leaving his name to mock them) went away.
Sometimes he does not flee from them in time: 20
"Kilroy was——"
              (*with his blood a dying man*
Wrote half the phrase out in Bataan.)

3

Kilroy beware. "HOME" is the final trap
That lurks for you in many a wily shape: 25
In pipe-and-slippers plus a Loyal Hound
  Or fooling around, just fooling around.
Kind to the old (their warm Penelope)
But fierce to boys,

                thus "home" becomes that sea,   30
Horribly disguised, where you were always drowned,—
  (How could suburban Crete condone
The yarns you would have V-mailed from the sun?)—
And folksy fishes sip Icarian tea.

One stab of hopeless wings imprinted your   35
  Exultant Kilroy-signature
Upon sheer sky for all the world to stare:
    "I was there! I was there! I was there!"

4

God is like Kilroy; He, too, sees it all;
That's how He knows of every sparrow's fall;   40
That's why we prayed each time the tightropes cracked
On which our loveliest clowns contrived their act.
The G. I. Faustus who was

            everywhere
Strolled home again. "What was it like outside?"   45
Asked Can't, with his good neighbors Ought and But
And pale Perhaps and grave-eyed Better Not;
For "Kilroy" means: the world is very wide.
  He was there, he was there, he was there!

And in the suburbs Can't sat down and cried.   50

PETER VIERECK

6
Society and Social Injustice

Discussing both society and social injustice under one heading may seem misleading, for some of the poems in this section make no mention of injustice. Yet there is a kind of injustice that grows out of man's social nature and that perhaps is inherent in all social relationships. Ulysses in *Troilus and Cressida* speaks of the order of society that must exist if harmony is to be the result; of course, the order that he speaks of will cause injustice for some, as Rousseau and others have pointed out. All men have recognized that living together socially requires the individual to adjust his rights and desires to those of the larger group.

Most of the poems in this section have to do, directly more often than not, with man's social restrictions and the injustice which sometimes results from those restrictions. The Rousseauistic idea that man's natural goodness is corrupted by society lies behind a number of the poems. The idea that society almost automatically limits and mistreats its members (irrespective of their goodness or lack of goodness) is a theme in several selections. Also present in most of the selections ("West London," "London," and "Sonnet on Chillon" are representative) is a cry to alleviate the sufferings of man at the hands of his fellows.

"The world is too much with us," cries Wordsworth; and even when it does not try to harm us, society, with its stratifications, is painfully anti-individualistic. Poverty, regimentation, and social stagnation occur and reoccur in these poems. The ladies who live in "furnished souls" have sold themselves to society; the "mind-forged manacles" they wear are as bad as the real manacles of the prisoner in Byron's "Sonnet on Chillon."

The novel, which has developed concurrently with modern ideas of equality, has found its chief theme in social questions. There are hundreds of novels in English that are mainly concerned with the compartmentalized and restrictive life of society. Paralleling the novelist's interest, playwrights too have become increasingly concerned with society.

READINGS IN OTHER GENRES

PLAYS

Edward Albee, *The American Dream*
Maxwell Anderson, *Winterset*
Anton Chekhov, *The Cherry Orchard*
Henrik Ibsen, *An Enemy of the People, Pillars of Society*
Eugene Ionesco, *The Bald Soprano*
Ben Jonson, *Volpone*
Arthur Miller, *All My Sons, The Crucible*
Molière, *Tartuffe*
Clifford Odets, *Awake and Sing!*
John Osborne, *Look Back in Anger*
Arthur Wing Pinero, *The Second Mrs. Tanqueray*
George Bernard Shaw, *Mrs. Warren's Profession*
Richard Brinsley Sheridan, *The School for Scandal*

NOVELS

Jane Austen, *Emma, Pride and Prejudice*
Honoré Balzac, *Père Goriot*
Theodore Dreiser, *An American Tragedy*
Charles Dickens, *Bleak House, Oliver Twist*
John Dos Passos, *U.S.A.*
William Faulkner, *The Sound and the Fury*
Gustave Flaubert, *Madame Bovary*
Ford Madox Ford, *Parade's End*
E. M. Forster, *A Passage to India, Howard's End*
Aldous Huxley, *Antic Hay, Point Counter Point*
Henry James, *The Ambassadors, The American, The Portrait of a Lady*
Sinclair Lewis, *Babbitt, Main Street*
George Orwell, *Animal Farm*
Anthony Powell, *The Music of Time*
Marcel Proust, *Remembrance of Things Past*
Stendhal, *The Red and the Black*
William Makepeace Thackeray, *Vanity Fair*
Anthony Trollope, *Barchester Towers*
Evelyn Waugh, *Decline and Fall*

SHORT STORIES

John Berryman, "The Imaginary Jew"
Stephen Crane, "The Bride Comes to Yellow Sky"

James T. Farrell, "The Benefits of American Life"
William Faulkner, "That Evening Sun"
Graham Greene, "The Brother"
Ernest Hemingway, "Ten Indians"
William Plomer, "A Child of Queen Victoria"
Ruth Suckow, "A Start in Life"
Virginia Woolf, "The Duchess and the Jeweller"

The Lie

Go, soul, the body's guest,
  Upon a thankless arrant;[1]
Fear not to touch the best;
  The truth shall be thy warrant.
    Go, since I needs must die,   5
    And give the world the lie.

Say to the court, it glows
  And shines like rotten wood;
Say to the church, it shows
  What's good, and doth no good: 10
    If church and court reply,
    Then give them both the lie.

Tell potentates, they live
  Acting by others' action,
Not loved unless they give,   15
  Not strong but by a faction:
    If potentates reply,
    Give potentates the lie.

Tell men of high condition
  That manage the estate,   20
Their purpose is ambition,
  Their practice only hate:
    And if they once reply,
    Then give them all the lie.

Tell them that brave it most,   25
  They beg for more by spending,
Who, in their greatest cost,

[1] Errand.

    Seek nothing but commending:
      And if they make reply,
        Then give them all the lie.   30

Tell zeal it wants devotion;
    Tell love it is but lust;
Tell time it is but motion;
    Tell flesh it is but dust:
      And wish them not reply,   35
      For thou must give the lie.

Tell age it daily wasteth;
    Tell honor how it alters;
Tell beauty how she blasteth;
    Tell favor how it falters: 40
      And as they shall reply,
      Give every one the lie.

Tell wit how much it wrangles
    In tickle points of niceness;
Tell wisdom she entangles   45
    Herself in over-wiseness:
      And when they do reply,
      Straight give them both the lie.

Tell physic of her boldness;
    Tell skill it is prevention;   50
Tell charity of coldness;
    Tell law it is contention:
      And as they do reply,
      So give them still the lie.

Tell fortune of her blindness;   55
    Tell nature of decay;
Tell friendship of unkindness;
    Tell justice of delay:
      And if they will reply,
      Then give them all the lie.   60

Tell arts they have no soundness,
    But vary by esteeming;
Tell schools they want profoundness,
    And stand too much on seeming:
      If arts and schools reply,   65
      Give arts and schools the lie.

Tell faith it's fled the city;
  Tell how the country erreth;
Tell, manhood shakes off pity;
  Tell, virtue least preferreth: 70
    And if they do reply,
    Spare not to give the lie.

So when thou hast, as I
  Commanded thee, done blabbing,
Although to give the lie   75
  Deserves no less than stabbing,
    Stab at thee he that will,
    No stab the soul can kill.

SIR WALTER RALEIGH

A Satirical Elegy on the Death of a Late Famous General, 1722

His Grace! impossible! what, dead!
Of old age, too, and in his bed!
And could that mighty warrior fall?
And so inglorious, after all!
Well, since he's gone, no matter how,   5
The last loud trump must wake him now:
And, trust me, as the noise grows stronger,
He'd wish to sleep a little longer.
And could he be indeed so old
As by the newspapers we're told?   10
Threescore, I think, is pretty high;
'Twas time, in conscience, he should die!
This world he cumbered long enough;
He burnt his candle to the snuff;
And that's the reason, some folks think,   15
He left behind so great a stink.
Behold his funeral appears,
Nor widow's sighs, nor orphan's tears,
Wont at such times each heart to pierce,
Attend the progress of his hearse.   20
And what of that? his friends may say,
He had those honors in his day.
True to his profit and his pride,
He made them weep before he died.
  Come hither, all ye empty things,   25
Ye bubbles raised by breath of kings;

Who float upon the tide of state;
Come hither, and behold your fate.
Let Pride be taught by this rebuke,
How very mean a thing's a duke;   30
From all his ill-got honors flung,
   Turned to that dirt from whence he sprung.

JONATHAN SWIFT

A Description of the Morning

Now hardly here and there an hackney-coach
Appearing, showed the ruddy morn's approach.
Now Betty from her master's bed had flown,
And softly stole to discompose her own.
The slip-shod 'prentice from his master's door   5
Had pared the dirt, and sprinkled round the floor;
Now Moll had whirled her mop with dextrous airs,
Prepared to scrub the entry and the stairs.
The youth with broomy stumps began to trace
The kennel-edge, where wheels had worn the place.   10
The small-coal man was heard with cadence deep;
Till drowned in shriller notes of chimney-sweep.
Duns at his lordship's gate began to meet;
And brick-dust Moll had screamed through half the street.
The turnkey now his flock returning sees,   15
Duly let out a-nights to steal for fees.
The watchful bailiffs take their silent stands;
And schoolboys lag with satchels in their hands.

JONATHAN SWIFT

To Sir Toby
A Sugar Planter in the Interior Parts of Jamaica

If there exists a hell—the case is clear—
Sir Toby's slaves enjoy that portion here:
Here are no blazing brimstone lakes, 'tis true;
But kindled rum too often burns as blue,
In which some fiend, whom nature must detest,   5
Steeps Toby's brand and marks poor Cudjoe's breast.
   Here whips on whips excite perpetual fears,
And mingled howlings vibrate on my ears;

Here nature's plagues abound, to fret and tease,
Snakes, scorpions, despots, lizards, centipedes.   10
No art, no care escapes the busy lash;
All have their dues—and all are paid in cash.
The eternal driver keeps a steady eye
On a black herd, who would his vengeance fly,
But chained, imprisoned, on a burning soil,   15
For the mean avarice of a tyrant, toil!
The lengthy cart-whip guards this monster's reign,
And cracks, like pistols, from the fields of cane.
    Ye powers who formed these wretched tribes, relate,
What had they done, to merit such a fate!   20
Why were they brought from Eboe's[1] sultry waste,
To see that plenty which they must not taste—
Food, which they cannot buy, and dare not steal,
Yams and potatoes—many a scanty meal!
    One, with a gibbet wakes his negro's fears,   25
One to the windmill nails him by the ears;
One keeps his slave in darkened dens, unfed,
One puts the wretch in pickle ere he's dead:
This, from a tree suspends him by the thumbs,
That, from his table grudges even the crumbs!   30
    O'er yond' rough hills a tribe of females go,
Each with her gourd, her infant, and her hoe;
Scorched by a sun that has no mercy here,
Driven by a devil, whom men call overseer;
In chains, twelve wretches to their labors haste;   35
Twice twelve I saw, with iron collars graced!
    Are such the fruits that spring from vast domains?
Is wealth, thus got, Sir Toby, worth your pains!
Who would your wealth on terms like these possess,
Where all we see is pregnant with distress;   40
Angola's natives scourged by ruffian hands,
And toil's hard product shipped to foreign lands.
    Talk not of blossoms and your endless spring;
What joy, what smile, can scenes of misery bring?
Though Nature here has every blessing spread,   45
Poor is the laborer—and how meanly fed!
    Here Stygian paintings light and shade renew,
Pictures of hell, that Virgil's pencil drew:
Here, surly Charons make their annual trip,
And ghosts arrive in every Guinea ship,   50
To find what beasts these western isles afford,
Plutonian scourges, and despotic lords:

---

[1] Africa, lower Niger.

Here, they, of stuff determined to be free,
Must climb the rude cliffs of the Liguanee;
Beyond the clouds, in skulking haste repair,   55
And hardly safe from brother traitors there.

PHILIP FRENEAU

Holy Thursday

Is this a holy thing to see
In a rich and fruitful land,
Babes reduced to misery,
Fed with cold and usurous hand?

Is that trembling cry a song?   5
Can it be a song of joy?
And so many children poor?
It is a land of poverty!

And their sun does never shine,
And their fields are bleak and bare,   10
And their ways are filled with thorns:
It is eternal winter there.

For where'er the sun does shine,
And where'er the rain does fall,
Babe can never hunger there,   15
Nor poverty the mind appall.

WILLIAM BLAKE
(From *Songs of Experience*)

London[1]

I wander through each chartered street,
Near where the chartered Thames does flow,
And mark in every face I meet
Marks of weakness, marks of woe.

In every cry of every man,   5
In every infant's cry of fear,
In every voice, in every ban,
The mind-forged manacles I hear.

How the chimney-sweeper's cry
Every blackening church appalls;   10

[1] See the student explication following Arnold's "West London," page 160.

And the hapless soldier's sigh
Runs in blood down palace walls.

But most through midnight streets I hear
How the youthful harlot's curse
Blasts the new-born infant's tear, 15
And blights with plagues the marriage hearse.

WILLIAM BLAKE

The World Is Too Much with Us

The world is too much with us; late and soon,
Getting and spending, we lay waste our powers:
Little we see in Nature that is ours;
We have given our hearts away, a sordid boon!
This Sea that bares her bosom to the moon; 5
The winds that will be howling at all hours,
And are up-gathered now like sleeping flowers;
For this, for everything, we are out of tune;
It moves us not.—Great God! I'd rather be
A Pagan suckled in a creed outworn; 10
So might I, standing on this pleasant lea,
Have glimpses that would make me less forlorn;
Have sight of Proteus rising from the sea;
Or hear old Triton blow his wreathèd horn.

WILLIAM WORDSWORTH

London, 1802

Milton! thou shouldst be living at this hour:
England hath need of thee: she is a fen
Of stagnant waters: altar, sword, and pen,
Fireside, the heroic wealth of hall and bower,
Have forfeited their ancient English dower 5
Of inward happiness. We are selfish men;
Oh! raise us up, return to us again;
And give us manners, virtue, freedom, power.
Thy soul was like a Star, and dwelt apart;
Thou hadst a voice whose sound was like the sea: 10
Pure as the naked heavens, majestic, free,
So didst thou travel on life's common way,
In cheerful godliness; and yet thy heart
The lowliest duties on herself did lay.

WILLIAM WORDSWORTH

Sonnet on Chillon

Eternal Spirit of the chainless Mind!
Brightest in dungeons, Liberty! thou art,
For there thy habitation is the heart—
The heart which love of thee alone can bind;
And when thy sons to fetters are consigned—   5
To fetters, and the damp vault's dayless gloom,
Their country conquers with their martyrdom,
And Freedom's fame finds wings on every wind.
Chillon! thy prison is a holy place,
And thy sad floor an altar—for 'twas trod,   10
Until his very steps have left a trace
Worn, as if thy cold pavement were a sod,
By Bonnivard! May none those marks efface!
For they appeal from tyranny to God.

GEORGE GORDON, LORD BYRON

When a Man Hath No Freedom to Fight for at Home

When a man hath no freedom to fight for at home,
    Let him combat for that of his neighbors;
Let him think of the glories of Greece and of Rome,
    And get knocked on his head for his labors.

To do good to mankind is the chivalrous plan,   5
    And is always as nobly requited;
Then battle for freedom wherever you can,
    And, if not shot or hanged, you'll get knighted.

GEORGE GORDON, LORD BYRON

The Isles of Greece

1

The isles of Greece, the isles of Greece!
    Where burning Sappho loved and sung,
Where grew the arts of war and peace,
    Where Delos rose, and Phoebus sprung!
Eternal summer gilds them yet,   5
But all, except their sun, is set.

2

The Scian[1] and the Teian[2] muse,
   The hero's harp, the lover's lute,
Have found the fame your shores refuse:
   Their place of birth alone is mute   10
To sounds which echo further west
Than your sires' "Islands of the Blest."

3

The mountains look on Marathon—
   And Marathon looks on the sea;
And musing there an hour alone,   15
   I dreamed that Greece might still be free,
For standing on the Persians' grave,
I could not deem myself a slave.

4

A king sate on the rocky brow
   Which looks o'er sea-born Salamis;   20
And ships, by thousands, lay below,
   And men in nations; all were his!
He counted them at break of day—
And when the sun set where were they?

5

And where are they? and where art thou,   25
   My country? On thy voiceless shore
The heroic lay is tuneless now—
   The heroic bosom beats no more!
And must thy lyre, so long divine,
Degenerate into hands like mine?   30

6

'Tis something, in the dearth of fame,
   Though linked among a fettered race,
To feel at least a patriot's shame,
   Even as I sing, suffuse my face;
For what is left the poet here?   35
For Greeks a blush—for Greeks a tear.

7

Must *we* but weep o'er days more blest?
   Must *we* but blush?—Our fathers bled.

[1] Homer.   [2] Anacreon.

Earth! render back from out thy breast
 A remnant of our Spartan dead!   40
Of the three hundred grant but three,
To make a new Thermopylae!

8

What, silent still? and silent all?
 Ah! no;—the voices of the dead
Sound like a distant torrent's fall,   45
 And answer, "Let one living head,
But one arise,—we come, we come!"
'Tis but the living who are dumb.

9

In vain—in vain: strike other chords;
 Fill high the cup with Samian wine!   50
Leave battles to the Turkish hordes,
 And shed the blood of Scio's vine!
Hark! rising to the ignoble call—
How answers each bold Bacchanal!

10

You have the Pyrrhic dance as yet;   55
 Where is the Pyrrhic phalanx gone?
Of two such lessons, why forget
 The nobler and the manlier one?
You have the letters Cadmus gave—
Think ye he meant them for a slave?   60

11

Fill high the bowl with Samian wine!
 We will not think of themes like these!
It made Anacreon's song divine:
 He served—but served Polycrates—
A tyrant; but our masters then   65
Were still, at least, our countrymen.

12

The tyrant of the Chersonese
 Was freedom's best and bravest friend;
That tyrant was Miltiades![3]
 Oh! that the present hour would lend 70
Another despot of the kind!
Such chains as his were sure to bind.

[3] Athenian general.

13

Fill high the bowl with Samian wine!
  On Suli's[4] rock, and Parga's[5] shore,
Exists the remnant of a line   75
  Such as the Doric mothers bore;
And there, perhaps, some seed is sown,
The Heracleidan blood might own.

14

Trust not for freedom to the Franks—
  They have a king who buys and sells;   80
In native swords, and native ranks,
  The only hope of courage dwells;
But Turkish force, and Latin fraud,
Would break your shield, however broad.

15

Fill high the bowl with Samian wine!   85
  Our virgins danced beneath the shade—
I see their glorious black eyes shine;
  But gazing on each glowing maid,
My own the burning tear-drop laves,
To think such breasts must suckle slaves.   90

16

Place me on Sunium's[6] marbled steep,
  Where nothing, save the waves and I,
May hear our mutual murmurs sweep;
  There, swan-like, let me sing and die:
A land of slaves shall ne'er be mine—   95
Dash down yon cup of Samian wine!

GEORGE GORDON, LORD BYRON
(From *Don Juan*, Canto III)

---

[4] In Albania.   [5] In Turkey.   [6] High cliff near Athens.

England in 1819

An old, mad, blind, despised, and dying king;
Princes, the dregs of their dull race, who flow
Through public scorn—mud from a muddy spring;
Rulers who neither see, nor feel, nor know,
But leech-like to their fainting country cling   5

Till they drop, blind in blood, without a blow;
A people starved and stabbed in the untilled field;
An army, which liberticide and prey
Makes as a two-edged sword to all who wield;
Golden and sanguine laws which tempt and slay;   10
Religion Christless, Godless—a book sealed;
A Senate—Time's worst statute unrepealed,—
Are graves, from which a glorious Phantom may
Burst, to illumine our tempestuous day.

                         PERCY BYSSHE SHELLEY

A Dirge

     Rough wind, that moanest loud
       Grief too sad for song;
     Wild wind, when sullen cloud
       Knells all the night long;
     Sad storm, whose tears are vain,   5
     Bare woods, whose branches strain,
     Deep caves and dreary main,—
       Wail, for the world's wrong!

                         PERCY BYSSHE SHELLEY

The Patriot

It was roses, roses, all the way,
     With myrtle mixed in my path like mad;
The house-roofs seemed to heave and sway,
     The church-spires flamed, such flags they had,
A year ago on this very day.   5

The air broke into a mist with bells,
     The old walls rocked with the crowd and cries.
Had I said, "Good folk, mere noise repels—
     But give me your sun from yonder skies!"
They had answered, "And afterward, what else?"   10

Alack, it was I who leaped at the sun
     To give it my loving friends to keep!
Naught man could do, have I left undone;
     And you see my harvest, what I reap
This very day, now a year is run.   15

There's nobody on the house-tops now—
 Just a palsied few at the windows set;
For the best of the sight is, all allow,
 At the Shambles' Gate—or, better yet,
By the very scaffold's foot, I trow.   20

I go in the rain, and, more than needs,
 A rope cuts both my wrists behind;
And I think, by the feel, my forehead bleeds,
 For they fling, whoever has a mind,
Stones at me for my year's misdeeds.   25

Thus I entered, and thus I go!
 In triumphs, people have dropped down dead.
"Paid by the world, what dost thou owe
 Me?"—God might question; now instead,
'Tis God shall repay; I am safer so.   30

                                        ROBERT BROWNING

The Latest Decalogue

Thou shalt have one God only; who
Would be at the expense of two?
No graven images may be
Worshiped, except the currency.
Swear not at all; for, for thy curse   5
Thine enemy is none the worse.
At church on Sunday to attend
Will serve to keep the world thy friend.
Honor thy parents; that is, all
From whom advancement may befall.   10
Thou shalt not kill; but need'st not strive
Officiously to keep alive.
Do not adultery commit;
Advantage rarely comes of it.
Thou shalt not steal; an empty feat,   15
When it's so lucrative to cheat.
Bear not false witness; let the lie
Have time on its own wings to fly.
Thou shalt not covet, but tradition
Approves all forms of competition.   20

                        ARTHUR HUGH CLOUGH

West London

Crouched on the pavement, close by Belgrave Square,
A tramp I saw, ill, moody, and tongue-tied.
A babe was in her arms, and at her side
A girl; their clothes were rags, their feet were bare.

Some laboring men, whose work lay somewhere there,   5
Passed opposite; she touched her girl, who hied
Across, and begged, and came back satisfied.
The rich she had let pass with frozen stare.

Thought I: "Above her state this spirit towers;
She will not ask of aliens, but of friends,   10
Of sharers in a common human fate.

"She turns from that cold succor, which attends
The unknown little from the unknowing great,
And points us to a better time than ours."

                                                MATTHEW ARNOLD

Blake's "London" and Arnold's "West London"[1]

Steve Larner

A comparison of William Blake's "London" to Matthew Arnold's "West London" clearly indicates that the poems were written from different points of view by men with dissimilar attitudes toward the poor people of London. Blake, viciously charging London and all its institutions with the responsibility for the lot of the city's poor, has left a more perceptive and artistic comment on the city than Arnold, whose bemused reaction to London beggars constitutes an evasion of the complete truth and a reluctance to accept his environment at its face value.

By the second line of his poem it is apparent from the play on the word "chartered" that Blake is bitterly indignant. "Chartered," applied to all the streets and even the river Thames, connotes a pervasive, city-wide spirit of legal constraint. Among the possible interpretations of "chartered," the one which allows the poem's images to work together most coherently and efficiently is "licensed for exclusive use," for implicit in Blake's attack on London institutions is that they are certainly *not* accessible to the poor and hence are reserved in some way

---

[1] Student theme.

only for the rich. In this sense Blake's subsequent images come more sharply into focus: he sees the poor as social pawns who are excluded from the religious, political, and social life of London.

Blake's use of repetition, parallel structure, and alliteration gives intensity to his protest. Repetition of "chartered," "mark" (twice, l. 4), "cry" (twice, ll. 6, 9), the phrase "in every" (four times), "every" itself twice more, "I hear," and "infant's" all contribute to Blake's unity of tone. Throughout the poem alliteration promotes internal strength within and between the images and figures: "*m*ark," "*m*eet" (1.3); "*w*eakness," "*w*oe" (1.4); "*m*ind," "*m*anacles" (1.8); "*ch*imney," "*ch*urch" (ll. 9, 10); "haple*ss* *s*oldier'*s* *s*igh" (l. 11); "*bl*ackening," "*bl*ood" (ll. 10, 12); "*H*ow," "*h*arlot's" (1.14); "*Bl*asts," "-*b*orn," "*bl*ights," "*pl*agues" (ll. 15–16). The basic iambic tetrameter gives the poem an insistent rhythm, varied only by the standard device of making initial iambs trochee in lines four, nine, twelve, and fifteen. Blake has obviously designed his poem to build and maintain a momentum that firmly supports his tone. An oral reading of the poem cannot fail to communicate the force of Blake's invective.

By contrast, the rhythm of Arnold's "West London" conveys a mood of detached reflection. A variation on the Italian sonnet form, this poem's pentameter naturally produces a less staccato pace than the tetrameter of "London," and Arnold's deliberate musing further decelerates his poem's pace so that Blake, who is actually in a reflective mood himself, seems to race by comparison. Arnold disrupts his narrative (aside from natural stanza conclusions) six times by period, colon, or semi-colon, three of which stops occur in mid-line (ll. 4, 6, 9). Besides these stops, Arnold further retards the flow of his thought with numerous modifiers and phrases requiring commas. In line 2, the modifiers "ill" and "moody," with their accompanying commas, slow the line to a crawl, and a lesser *retard* is accomplished by the commas in the compound predicate of line 7. The most explicit and revealing indication of Arnold's frame of mind, however, is found in the Victorian pose suggested by his "Thought I: . . ." (l. 9). This phrase clearly signals Arnold's shift from narration to contemplation, which becomes in the last stanza a retreat into optimistic speculation and an evasion of the fact of the girl's condition.

This wide divergence of tone is a measure of the relative intellectual perception and poetic capacity of the two men. Blake's poem is a scathing indictment that strips the veneer of respectability from every level of London's pretentious municipal structure with an abrasive technique. Were London on trial for domestic neglect, Arnold's poem might serve as a snapshot of Exhibit "A," Blake's as the entire case for the prosecution. The image of an oppressive system of legal restriction, which Blake first evokes with "chartered," he supplements by his use of "ban" in line seven, with its connotations of official prohibition or condemnation. His designation of legal restriction of some sort as the cause or perpetuator of misery among London's poor is established by his implication that the "chartered streets" are somehow contributors to the "marks of woe" (l. 4) on the people who travel them; and by his association of "ban" with cries of fear and condemnation Blake makes his accusation more explicit in line eight when he names "mind-forged manacles" as the cause of the injustice. The scope and relevance of this phrase, the poem's most crucial, are best defined in terms of the three images that make up the two final stanzas. These images make it apparent that Blake is accusing London's religious, political, and social institutions (symbolized by "church," "palace," and "marriage hearse") of abusing a segment of the population for whose service they ostensibly exist. Summarized, Blake's thesis is this: man's manipulation of his society by means of political, social, and moral laws fails when it is contingent upon economics. For when laws can be made and executed to the advantage of those with money, a portion of society without money can be rendered socially impotent, and, by the resulting stigmas of bottom-class residence, can be kept mute pawns of those who have the money and power. In London's rigidly stratified society, the chimney-sweep and young prostitute were as permanently doomed to their social level as if they had been handcuffed to the curbstone. In defense of the "youthful harlot" it should be noted that exploitation of women of relatively lower classes by the men of higher classes is an inevitable fact of human culture long recognized by sociologists. Blake reserves his strongest attack for this last case ("But most . . . I hear," l. 13), and in this image evokes his sharpest poignancy. The "mind-forged manacle" he deplores here is the old double sexual standard, which gives the young harlot total social responsibility for her partnership in a pregnancy, and permits the child's father moral immunity if he has the money to stage a socially prestigious union with anyone of his own "class." Man's capacity for indifference to his fellow man has nowhere been more passionately delineated. Blake's infrequent forays from his hermit's rooms were opportunity enough for him to recognize the irony of a religious establishment whose churches represented nothing more than soot-blackened shells to a vast number of people, and the injustice of a political system which invested the whims of a single monarch with life-or-death power over his subjects.

Arnold, on the other hand, chooses to see only the single incident, which he views from the detached perspective of one of the residents of fashionable Belgrave Square. The closest Arnold's aloof viewpoint allows him to approach to the tramp's emotional plane is to say that she was "moody." Other than this, Arnold's honest analysis of the situation is confined to exterior narration. The poem's last two stanzas are not rational conclusions, but romanticized conjecture (subsequent history notwithstanding). As for the objectivity of Arnold's reasoning, it is fair to say that when better times really come, they will not be any more justly founded on the tramp's "frozen stares" than on the "cold succor" of the rich. Immersion in that "common human fate" should not preclude empathy with "aliens" to one's personal adventure, or moral progress is trampled in the haste for revenge.

Finally, Blake's poem reflects a more imaginative technique than Arnold's. Blake's portrait of the lower class is abstract, based on a continuing, random experience reflected by a present tense, as opposed to Arnold's single completed action. Where Arnold is specific and literal, Blake is metaphoric and symbolic. Blake's images are conceived in a vividly synaesthetic framework: he *hears* the manacles "in every voice," he *sees* the soldier's sigh run "in blood down palace walls," and *sees* the harlot's curse "blight . . . the marriage hearse."

These are the depths to which Blake's poetry is committed, which make his "London" so much more immediate a comment on that city than Arnold's "West London."

The Man with the Hoe[1]

Bowed by the weight of centuries he leans
Upon his hoe and gazes on the ground,
The emptiness of ages in his face,
And on his back the burden of the world.
Who made him dead to rapture and despair,   5
A thing that grieves not and that never hopes,
Stolid and stunned, a brother to the ox?
Who loosened and let down this brutal jaw?
Whose was the hand that slanted back this brow?
Whose breath blew out the light within this brain?   10

Is this the Thing the Lord God made and gave
To have dominion over sea and land;
To trace the stars and search the heavens for power;
To feel the passion of Eternity?
Is this the dream He dreamed who shaped the suns   15
And marked their ways upon the ancient deep?
Down all the caverns of Hell to their last gulf
There is no shape more terrible than this—
More tongued with censure of the world's blind greed—
More filled with signs and portents for the soul—   20
More packt with danger to the universe.

What gulfs between him and the seraphim!
Slave of the wheel of labor, what to him
Are Plato and the swing of Pleiades?
What the long reaches of the peaks of song,   25
The rift of dawn, the reddening of the rose?

[1] Inspired by Millet's famous painting.

Through this dread shape the suffering ages look;
Time's tragedy is in that aching stoop,
Through this dread shape humanity betrayed,
Plundered, profaned, and disinherited,   30
Cries protest to the Judges of the World,
A protest that is also prophecy.

O masters, lords and rulers in all lands,
Is this the handiwork you give to God,
This monstrous thing distorted and soul-quenched?   35
How will you ever straighten up this shape;
Touch it again with immortality;
Give back the upward looking and the light;
Rebuild in it the music and the dream;
Make right the immemorial infamies,   40
Perfidious wrongs, immedicable woes?

O masters, lords and rulers in all lands,
How will the Future reckon with this man?
How answer his brute question in that hour
When whirlwinds of rebellion shake all shores?   45
How will it be with kingdoms and with kings—
With those who shaped him to the thing he is—
When this dumb terror shall rise to judge the world,
After the silence of the centuries?

                              EDWIN MARKHAM

The Poor

It's the anarchy of poverty
delights me, the old
yellow wooden house indented
among the new brick tenements

Or a cast iron balcony   5
with panels showing oak branches
in full leaf. It fits
the dress of the children

reflecting every stage and
custom of necessity—   10
Chimneys, roofs, fences of
wood and metal in an unfenced

age and enclosing next to
nothing at all: the old man
in a sweater and soft black   15
hat who sweeps the sidewalk—

his own ten feet of it—
in a wind that fitfully
turning his corner has
overwhelmed the entire city   20

WILLIAM CARLOS WILLIAMS

City-Life

When I am in a great city, I know that I despair.
I know there is no hope for us, death waits, it is useless to care.

For oh the poor people, that are flesh of my flesh,
I, that am flesh of their flesh,
when I see the iron hooked into their faces   5
their poor, their fearful faces
I scream in my soul, for I know I cannot
take the iron hooks out of their faces, that make them so drawn,
nor cut the invisible wires of steel that pull them
back and forth, to work,   10
back and forth to work,
like fearful and corpse-like fishes hooked and being played
by some malignant fisherman on an unseen shore
where he does not choose to land them yet, hooked fishes of the
   factory world.

D. H. LAWRENCE

Portrait d'une Femme

Your mind and you are our Sargasso Sea,
London has swept about you this score years
And bright ships left you this or that in fee:
Ideas, old gossip, oddments of all things,
Strange spars of knowledge and dimmed wares of price.   5
Great minds have sought you—lacking someone else.
You have been second always. Tragical?
No. You preferred it to the usual thing:
One dull man, dulling and uxorious,

One average mind—with one thought less, each year.   10
Oh, you are patient. I have seen you sit
Hours, where something might have floated up.
And now you pay one. Yes, you richly pay.
You are a person of some interest, one comes to you
And takes strange gain away: 15
Trophies fished up; some curious suggestion;
Fact that leads nowhere; and a tale or two,
Pregnant with mandrakes, or with something else
That might prove useful and yet never proves,
That never fits a corner or shows use,   20
Or finds its hour upon the loom of days:
The tarnished, gaudy, wonderful old work;
Idols, and ambergris and rare inlays.
These are your riches, your great store; and yet
For all this sea-hoard of deciduous things,   25
Strange woods half sodden, and new brighter stuff:
In the slow float of differing light and deep,
No! there is nothing! In the whole and all,
Nothing that's quite your own.
                 Yet this is you.   30

EZRA POUND

Justice Denied in Massachusetts[1]

Let us abandon then our gardens and go home
And sit in the sitting-room.
Shall the larkspur blossom or the corn grow under this cloud?
Sour to the fruitful seed
Is the cold earth under this cloud,   5
Fostering quack and weed, we have marched upon but cannot
   conquer;
We have bent the blades of our hoes against the stalks of them.

Let us go home, and sit in the sitting-room.
Not in our day
Shall the cloud go over and the sun rise as before,   10
Beneficent upon us
Out of the glittering bay,
And the warm winds be blown inward from the sea
Moving the blades of corn
With a peaceful sound.   15

---

[1] Occasioned by the Sacco-Vanzetti trial.

Forlorn, forlorn,
Stands the blue hay-rack by the empty mow.
And the petals drop to the ground,
Leaving the tree unfruited.
The sun that warmed our stooping backs and withered the weed
  uprooted—   20
We shall not feel it again.
We shall die in darkness, and be buried in the rain.

What from the splendid dead
We have inherited—
Furrows sweet to the grain, and the weed subdued—   25
See now the slug and the mildew plunder.
Evil does overwhelm
The larkspur and the corn;
We have seen them go under.

Let us sit here, sit still,   30
Here in the sitting-room until we die;
At the step of Death on the walk, rise and go;
Leaving to our children's children this beautiful doorway,
And this elm,
And a blighted earth to till   35
With a broken hoe.

EDNA ST. VINCENT MILLAY

the Cambridge ladies

the Cambridge ladies who live in furnished souls
are unbeautiful and have comfortable minds
(also, with the church's protestant blessings
daughters, unscented shapeless spirited)
they believe in Christ and Longfellow, both dead,   5
are invariably interested in so many things—
at the present writing one still finds
delighted fingers knitting for the is it Poles?
perhaps. While permanent faces coyly bandy
scandal of Mrs. N and Professor D   10
. . . . the Cambridge ladies do not care, above
Cambridge if sometimes in its box of
sky lavender and cornerless, the
moon rattles like a fragment of angry candy

E. E. CUMMINGS

anyone lived in a pretty how town

anyone lived in a pretty how town
(with up so floating many bells down)
spring summer autumn winter
he sang his didn't he danced his did.

Women and men (both little and small)   5
cared for anyone not at all
they sowed their isn't they reaped their same
sun moon stars rain

children guessed (but only a few
and down they forgot as up they grew   10
autumn winter spring summer)
that noone loved him more by more

when by now and tree by leaf
she laughed his joy she cried his grief
bird by snow and stir by still   15
anyone's any was all to her

someones married their everyones
laughed their cryings and did their dance
(sleep wake hope and then) they
said their nevers they slept their dream   20

stars rain sun moon
(and only the snow can begin to explain
how children are apt to forget to remember
with up so floating many bells down)

one day anyone died i guess   25
(and noone stooped to kiss his face)
busy folk buried them side by side
little by little and was by was

all by all and deep by deep
and more by more they dream their sleep   30
noone and anyone earth by april
wish by spirit and if by yes.

Women and men (both dong and ding)
summer autumn winter spring
reaped their sowing and went their came   35
sun moon stars rain

E. E. CUMMINGS

The Use of Language in Cummings' "anyone lived in a pretty how town"[1]

Mary Parker

Language in "anyone lived in a pretty how town" is what makes the poem "mean" in a new and distinctive way. The theme, a simple and familiar one, is the contrast of the responses to life of two individuals with that of the other people of the world. But Cummings' careful and clever use of words makes the poem not only interesting and sufficiently complex to create curiosity, but also much more to the point than other treatments of the same theme might have been.

In an effort to demonstrate how Cummings' uses of language help in carrying out his central idea, the poem might be considered as a love story—the story of the lives of two lovers called "noone" and "anyone." "Anyone," the main character of the poem, is at once, by way of the ambiguity connected with his name, a particular individual and still anyone at all. His girl friend "noone" may be considered either as a specific person or as really no one at all. Thus there is from the very outset a double level of meaning to the whole poem. Now "anyone" lived in a "pretty how town." Actually this could be turned around to read, "in a how pretty town" to give one idea of its meaning, but it may also be interpreted in another way. One might say that "anyone" lived in, not a *really* "how" town, but rather in a *pretty* or *middling* "how" town. In the second line of the poem, the very words themselves give the illusion of the leisurely, harmonious passage of time. All people, it seems, are tolled in and out by the bells—there are bells for marriage, birth, and death. The essence of people is what they do as heralded by the bells. However, these particular bells are distorted to the mind's eye because bells cannot really "float" at all. It is as if those bells were moving back and forth (or up and down); that is "floating" but making no sound. The bells have no identity nor do they have even the basic ability to ring out loud and clear. In the third line of the poem the image is carried on by the tolling off of the seasons to indicate perhaps the natural passage of time. As one reads the fourth line, he begins to see something of the character of the hero of the story. "Anyone" is portrayed as a man who disregards institutions. By using a seemingly meaningless ambiguity (he sang his didn't he danced his did), Cummings shows that "anyone" follows his inclinations, dreaming of what he didn't and enjoying what he did. Somehow he does not seem to be the kind of person who would be simply tolled in and out by soundless bells.

In the second stanza, the women and men of the usual, outside world appear as "both little and small." Here Cummings seems to use two almost synonymous words to represent opposite meanings. All of ordinary humanity seems to be con-

[1] Student theme.

demned for its pettiness and littleness of character and experience. In daily life these people do not care for "anyone" as an individual, but they also do not care for anyone outside of themselves. The calculated ambiguity of Cummings' choice of names is again evident in this passage. In the third line of the second stanza the people of the town are characterized as reaping what they sow, as everyone must. The distinction here comes in what they sow. They sow their "isn't"; that is, they sow only negativeness or nothingness. The language here, as in the whole poem, allows the reader to add his own interpretations and connotations to ordinary words used in new and unusually creative ways. No one can really "sow" his "isn't" because "isn't" simply is not something "sowable," but the very use of this word in a new context surprises the reader into new ideas. Last in the stanza comes a reminder of the passage of time, seasons, and life—"sun moon stars rain."

"Children guessed," in the third stanza, "but only a few/and down they forgot as up they grew." The Wordsworthian concept of "the child as father of the man" or the "visionary gleam" is evident here. Although some children can guess at the love that "noone" and "anyone" share ("noone loved him more by more"), they forget as they grow up about what innocent, true love really is. As the charm of childhood is forgotten, so the man grows away from his first intuitional knowledge and appreciation of, and the ability to give, love. As Wordsworth says, man forgets more and more of what he knew at birth about God and love. On a second level of language, the children could be guessing at and forgetting, that no one really ever loves anyone anymore. Nobody cares what becomes of others—he has enough to do to worry about what happens to himself. The bells and the children seem to be closely linked because of word choice. Bells float "up" and "down" and children forget "down" as they grow "up."

The "more by more" of the third stanza starts a series of pairs linked with "by." The link consists of what the reader sees as a significant relationship between the two terms. "More *by* more" is used as a starting point perhaps because readers are used to hearing about love becoming "more *and* more." From here on the images spread out, in the fifth stanza, to perhaps the most difficult part of the poem to understand, principally because of the ambiguity of the pairs linked with "by." It has been interpreted by Robert C. Walsh to mean:

> Children love and want love at all times (when by now); in all particulars (tree by leaf); through joy and grief; in all seasons of the year (bird by snow); and under all conditions (stir by still). Love is their any in any, their all in all.[2]

This seems to be a logical explanation. There is here, as well as the "by" pairs, a clever double meaning to the last line of the stanza ("anyone's any was all to her"). Beyond what Mr. Marsh has said, there is the indication that "any," the

[2] Robert C. Walsh, "anyone lived in a pretty how town," *The Explicator*, XXII, Item 72.

essence of "anyone," is "all" or everything to "noone." The lovers are completely united so that anything "anyone" is, is all that matters to "noone."

"Someones" in the fifth stanza "married their everyones"; that is, people just marry other people because it seems the thing to do. They forget their troubles and do "their dance." Recalling the first stanza, it is clear that these people are conventional and live a routine life because "anyone" "danced his did." Routine for the "busy folk" consists of a cycle—"sleep wake hope and then." It appears to be the only existence of which they are capable. On retiring one can imagine the "busy folk" kneeling down to repeat their "nevers"—perhaps these are the words of the Lord's Prayer parroted from childhood and addressed to a God who does not really exist. Then they "slept their dream," again contrary to "anyone" and "noone" who "dream their sleep" in the eighth stanza. Time goes on passing, children go on forgetting, and those grotesque, silent bells go on ringing. And "only the snow can begin to explain" how children can forget the joy and love of childhood. Snow obviously cannot really explain anything because it cannot communicate in any way. However, Cummings uses the snow as an image perhaps of forgetfulness—snow covers everything with a sort of soft, cold, blurry, impenetrable, forgetful cloak which no one really wants to bother about throwing aside once it has fallen. Then too, it falls so softly and silently that it is hardly noticed.

In the seventh stanza "anyone" dies. Cummings says that he *guesses* that "anyone" died, but he must *know* that he did because that is what happens to everyone. Perhaps he is not sure or cannot remember exactly because he cannot recall hearing the bells tolling for "anyone's" death. Then "noone stooped to kiss his face," but "busy folk buried them side by side." Did "anyone" die first, leaving "noone" to die later, perhaps of a broken heart? Or did "anyone" really die without anyone to stoop and kiss his face at his funeral? Again the ambiguity of language is intriguing. The two lovers were buried "little by little" just as if they had been of the usual adult world of "women and men (both little and small)" because the "busy folk" never even guessed that "noone" and "anyone" were really any different from anybody else. Here too, there is a return to the "by" pairs to be interpreted, it seems, in any way the reader sees fit.

Buried "was by was/all by all and deep by deep/and more by more" to "dream their sleep," it is clear that death to "noone" and "anyone" represents a final merging of their hearts in eternal love and harmony, a culmination and final affirmation of love. They do not die with "hope" of some resurrection, as the "busy folk" do, but rather with a perpetual sleep and an everlasting dream (all by all). Although "earth by april/wish by spirit and if by yes" appear to be hopeful images, they seem rather to be what was sought and won, aspiration by aspiration between the lovers. Another way to interpret the hopeful images comes from Walsh, who would have the poem read as a loss-of-innocence story with "anyone" as a child who grows up (but really down) into the adult world.

"Anyone" is a happy child, but when he grows up, he dies to the world of children. He is missed by the others, and they have to stoop to kiss him because he has become "both little and small." Childhood recedes "little by little and was by was," but the dream of childhood lingers on. There is hope that it will again

> blossom in the new generation (earth by april). Childhood dreams (wish by spirit) are realized (if by yes) as possibility becomes reality. Thus there is a cycle of regeneration.[3]

Coming finally to the last stanza, the world of the "busy folk" goes on with its sexual activities as attempts to achieve the meaning of real love (dong and ding). This particular image may have been used to recall the distorted bells tolling for everything. Perhaps the "someones" only move back and forth like the bells with "nothing higher than hope or profounder than sleep."[4] Living a futile life, they reap the nothing which they have sowed cut off from love and life. Yet the natural universal order of things goes on—"sun moon stars rain."

Cummings displays great creativity in using everyday words in new ways. For instance, he uses verbs for nouns (sowed their *isn't*) and adverbs for adjectives (a pretty *how* town). Though he is a romantic and sentimental poet, his shifts of grammatical forms keep the reader from being bored with old themes. Here Cummings avoids sentimentality and romantic diction in his idea of the uselessness of life without love by using childlike twistings of language, contradictions, and wit.

[3] Walsh, "anyone lived in a pretty how town."
[4] Herbert C. Barrows, Jr. and William R. Steinhoff, *The Explicator*, IX, Item 1.

The Epilogue Spoken by a Tape Recorder

Though I am buried, I am on the air.
I was, in the strictest sense of the word, not there.
You would call me Eichmann, but I cannot bear
That appellation. . . . You may call me Zero.

I loved my children, I obeyed the laws,   5
I hailed the leader, joined in the applause,
I read the ads to see what I should wear
And bought the shirts approved for every hero.

I served the general and the general will,
Obeyed instructions, answered all my mail,   10
Killed only those whom I was told to kill.

I understood it all except the why;
They gave me names of those to put in jail;
They gave me orders for the ones to die;
I had my family to think of, I   15
Did not decide. . . .

                              If anyone's to blame,
It was the leaders, but what could I do?
There were at first a few, only a few.
When millions died, I thought it was a shame.   20

They want to label it, to find a name.

I was condemned not by the law, but fate.
I was the man who happened to be there
When one state sought to try another state.

I was told, of all men, I was one to dare.   25

And I can see it as a tragedy
So wide it took three continents to frame,
And all of it was there except the heart:
The villain and the hero were the same.

The world is listening, I am on the air.   30

But if I did not live, I should not die:
They did not try me, but they tried the laws
That I obeyed. . . .
                              There was a nobler art
Lost somewhere in the scenes I helped contrive.   35
There was a better way, a fresher start,
And I have glimpsed at times my tragic part.

I died in it, but I was not alive.

                                        ARTHUR M. SAMPLEY

An Elementary School Classroom in a Slum

Far far from gusty waves, these children's faces.
Like rootless weeds the torn hair round their paleness.
The tall girl with her weighed-down head. The paper-
seeming boy with rat's eyes. The stunted unlucky heir
Of twisted bones, reciting a father's gnarled disease,   5

His lesson from his desk. At back of the dim class
One unnoted, mild and young: his eyes live in a dream
Of squirrels' game, in tree room, other than this.

On sour cream walls, donations. Shakespeare's head
Cloudless at dawn, civilized dome riding all cities.   10
Belled, flowery, Tyrolese valley. Open-handed map
Awarding the world its world. And yet, for these
Children, these windows, not this world, are world,
Where all their future's painted with a fog,
A narrow street sealed in with a lead sky,   15
Far far from rivers, capes, and stars of words.

Surely Shakespeare is wicked, the map a bad example
With ships and sun and love tempting them to steal—
For lives that slyly turn in their cramped holes
From fog to endless night? On their slag heap, these children   20
Wear skins peeped through by bones, and spectacles of steel
With mended glass, like bottle bits in slag.
Tyrol is wicked; map's promising a fable:
All of their time and space are foggy slum,
So blot their maps with slums as big as doom.   25

Unless, governor, teacher, inspector, visitor,
This map becomes their window and these windows
That open on their lives like crouching tombs
Break, O break open, till they break the town
And show the children to the fields and all their world   30
Azure on their sands, to let their tongues
Run naked into books, the white and green leaves open
The history theirs whose language is the sun.

                              STEPHEN SPENDER

At the Executed Murderer's Grave
(for J. L. D.)

Why should we do this? What good is it to us?
Above all, how can we do such a thing? How can it possibly be done?
                                                              —Freud

1

My name is James A. Wright, and I was born
Twenty-five miles from this infected grave,

In Martins Ferry, Ohio, where one slave
To Hazel-Atlas Glass became my father.
He tried to teach me kindness. I return   5
Only in memory now, aloof, unhurried,
To dead Ohio, where I might lie buried,
Had I not run away before my time.
Ohio caught George Doty. Clean as lime,
His skull rots empty here. Dying's the best   10
Of all the arts men learn in a dead place.
I walked here once. I made my loud display,
Leaning for language on a dead man's voice.
Now sick of lies, I turn to face the past.
I add my easy grievance to the rest: 15

2

Doty, if I confess I do not love you,
Will you let me alone? I burn for my own lies.
The nights electrocute my fugitive,
My mind. I run like the bewildered mad
At St. Clair Sanitarium, who lurk,   20
Arch and cunning, under the maple trees,
Pleased to be playing guilty after dark.
Starting to bed, they croon self-lullabies.
Doty, you make me sick. I am not dead.
I croon my tears at fifty cents per line.   25

3

Idiot, he demanded love from girls,
And murdered one. Also, he was a thief.
He left two women, and a ghost with child.
The hair, foul as a dog's upon his head,
Made such revolting Ohio animals   30
Fitter for vomit than a kind man's grief.
I waste no pity on the dead that stink,
And no love's lost between me and the crying
Drunks of Belaire, Ohio, where police
Kick at their kidneys till they die of drink.   35
Christ may restore them whole, for all of me.
Alive and dead, those giggling muckers who
Saddled my nightmares thirty years ago
Can do without my widely printed sighing
Over their pains with paid sincerity.   40
I do not pity the dead, I pity the dying.

4

I pity myself, because a man is dead.
If Belmont County killed him, what of me?
His victims never loved him. Why should we?
And yet, nobody had to kill him either.   45
It does no good to woo the grass, to veil
The quicklime hole of a man's defeat and shame.
Nature-lovers are gone. To hell with them.
I kick the clods away, and speak my name.

5

This grave's gash festers. Maybe it will heal,   50
When all are caught with what they had to do
In fear of love, when every man stands still
By the last sea,
And the princes of the sea come down
To lay away their robes, to judge the earth   55
And its dead, and we dead stand undefended everywhere,
And my bodies—father and child and unskilled criminal—
Ridiculously kneel to bare my scars,
My sneaking crimes, to God's unpitying stars.

6

Staring politely, they will not mark my face   60
From any murderer's, buried in this place.
Why should they? We are nothing but a man.

7

Doty, the rapist and the murderer,
Sleeps in a ditch of fire, and cannot hear;
And where, in earth or hell's unholy peace,   65
Men's suicides will stop, God knows, not I.
Angels and pebbles mock me under trees.
Earth is a door I cannot even face.
Order be damned, I do not want to die,
Even to keep Belaire, Ohio, safe.   70
The hackles on my neck are fear, not grief.
(Open, dungeon! Open, roof of the ground!)
I hear the last sea in the Ohio grass,
Heaving a tide of gray disastrousness.
Wrinkles of winter ditch the rotted face   75
Of Doty, killer, imbecile, and thief:
Dirt of my flesh, defeated, underground.

                              JAMES WRIGHT

7
Art and Aesthetics

Poems on the theme of art and aesthetics often seem to be of less interest to the general reader than to the poet or the artist, primarily because many such poems seem limited to matters of style and artistic craftsmanship. But most of the best poems on art and aesthetics also concern themselves with broader concepts, such as the nature of art and beauty or the relationship of art to life. Marianne Moore's "Poetry" and Archibald MacLeish's "Ars Poetica," for example, are important not only for their analysis of the craft of poetry but also for the philosophical concept of beauty which they convey.

The poems in this section reflect many attitudes toward art. Some poets consider art a vital social instrument; others insist that art exists for its own sake. Many of the poems reflect the poet's concern for the particular role of the artist in society. They reveal that poets have often taken a rather high-minded view of the role of the artist and the nature of art. Many subscribe to the view that life is short but art is long, to paraphrase the Latin proverb. Some insist that there is a special kind of "truth" in art.

Some works of long fiction have also dealt successfully with the theme of art and the artist. Among the best are Hawthorne's *The Marble Faun*, Joyce's *A Portrait of the Artist as a Young Man*, and Cary's *The Horse's Mouth*. Sometimes, as in Durrell's *Alexandria Quartet*, the theme is developed along with other related themes. Short stories that develop the theme are numerous, as the suggestions below indicate, but the theme has not been handled with signal success on the stage.

READINGS IN OTHER GENRES

PLAYS

Maxwell Anderson, *Joan of Lorraine*
S. N. Behrman, *No Time for Comedy*
Anton Chekhov, *The Sea Gull*
William Schwenck Gilbert and Sir Arthur Sullivan, *Patience*

Henrik Ibsen, *The Master Builder*
Clifford Odets, *Golden Boy*
Arthur Wing Pinero, *Trelawney of the "Wells"*
Luigi Pirandello, *Six Characters in Search of an Author*
William Saroyan, *My Heart's in the Highlands*
George Bernard Shaw, *The Doctor's Dilemma*

NOVELS

Joyce Cary, *The Horse's Mouth*
Willa Cather, *The Song of the Lark*
Theodore Dreiser, *The Genius*
Lawrence Durrell, *The Alexandria Quartet*
E. M. Forster, *The Longest Journey*
Nathaniel Hawthorne, *The Marble Faun*
James Gibbons Huneker, *Painted Veils*
Henry James, *The Tragic Muse*
James Joyce, *A Portrait of the Artist as a Young Man*
Rudyard Kipling, *The Light That Failed*
D. H. Lawrence, *Sons and Lovers*
Romain Rolland, *Jean Christophe*
Thomas Wolfe, *You Can't Go Home Again, The Web and the Rock*

SHORT STORIES

Isaac Babel, "The Awakening"
Anton Chekhov, "The Dance Pianist"
E. M. Forster, "The Celestial Omnibus"
Nathaniel Hawthorne, "The Artist of the Beautiful"
Hermann Hesse, "The Poet"
E. T. A. Hoffman, "The Ritter Gluck"
Henry James, "The Figure in the Carpet"
Franz Kafka, "A Hunger Artist," "In the Penal Colony"
William Saroyan, "There Was a Young Lady of Perth"
Leo Tolstoy, "The Kreutzer Sonata"

Not Marble, nor the Gilded Monuments

Not marble, nor the gilded monuments
Of princes, shall outlive this powerful rhyme;
But you shall shine more bright in these contents
Than unswept stone besmeared with sluttish time.
When wasteful war shall statues overturn,   5

And broils root out the work of masonry,
Nor Mars his sword nor war's quick fire shall burn
The living record of your memory.
'Gainst death and all-oblivious enmity
Shall you pace forth; your praise shall still find room   10
Even in the eyes of all posterity
That wear this world out to the ending doom.
   So, till the judgment that yourself arise,
    You live in this, and dwell in lovers' eyes.

WILLIAM SHAKESPEARE

At a Solemn Music

Blest pair of Sirens, pledges of Heaven's joy,
Sphere-born harmonious sisters, Voice and Verse,
Wed your divine sounds, and mixed power employ,
Dead things with inbreathed sense able to pierce;
And to our high-raised fantasy present   5
That undisturbed song of pure consent,
Aye sung before the sapphire-colored throne
To him that sits thereon
With saintly shout and solemn jubilee;
Where the bright Seraphim in burning row   10
Their loud uplifted angel trumpets blow,
And the Cherubic host in thousand quires
Touch their immortal harps of golden wires,
With those just spirits that wear victorious palms,
Hymns devout and holy psalms   15
Singing everlastingly:
That we on Earth, with undiscording voice,
May rightly answer that melodious noise;
As once we did, till disproportioned sin
Jarred against nature's chime, and with harsh din   20
Broke the fair music that all creatures made
To their great lord, whose love their motion swayed
In perfect diapason, whilst they stood
In first obedience, and their state of good.
O may we soon again renew that song,   25
And keep in tune with Heaven, till God ere long
To his celestial consort us unite,
To live with him, and sing in endless morn of light.

JOHN MILTON

A Song for St. Cecilia's Day

1

From harmony, from heavenly harmony
    This universal frame began;
    When Nature underneath a heap
      Of jarring atoms lay,
    And could not heave her head,   5
The tuneful Voice was heard from high,
    "Arise, ye more than dead."
Then cold, and hot, and moist, and dry,
    In order to their stations leap,
      And Music's power obey.   10
From harmony, from heavenly harmony
    This universal frame began:
    From harmony to harmony
Through all the compass of the notes it ran,
The diapason closing full in Man.   15

2

What passion cannot Music raise and quell?
    When Jubal struck the corded shell,
    His listening brethren stood around,
      And, wondering, on their faces fell
    To worship that celestial sound: 20
Less than a God they thought there could not dwell
    Within the hollow of that shell,
    That spoke so sweetly and so well.
What passion cannot Music raise and quell?

3

The trumpet's loud clangor   25
    Excites us to arms
With shrill notes of anger
    And mortal alarms.
The double, double, double beat
    Of the thundering drum   30
    Cries: "Hark! the foes come;
Charge, charge, 'tis too late to retreat."

4

    The soft complaining flute
    In dying notes discovers
    The woes of hopeless lovers,   35
Whose dirge is whispered by the warbling lute.

5

Sharp violins proclaim
Their jealous pangs, and desperation,
Fury, frantic indignation,
Depth of pains, and height of passion,   40
    For the fair, disdainful dame.

6

But Oh! What art can teach,
What human voice can reach,
    The sacred organ's praise?
Notes inspiring holy love,   45
Notes that wing their heavenly ways
    To mend the choirs above.

7

Orpheus could lead the savage race;
And trees unrooted left their place,
    Sequaceous of the lyre;   50
But bright Cecilia raised the wonder higher:
When to her organ vocal breath was given,
An angel heard, and straight appeared,
    Mistaking earth for heaven.

Grand Chorus

As from the power of sacred lays   55
    The spheres began to move,
And sung the great Creator's praise
    To all the blest above;
So when the last and dreadful hour
This crumbling pageant shall devour,   60
The trumpet shall be heard on high,
The dead shall live, the living die,
And Music shall untune the sky.

                                        JOHN DRYDEN

Kubla Khan: Or, A Vision in a Dream
A Fragment

In Xanadu did Kubla Khan
A stately pleasure-dome decree:
Where Alph, the sacred river, ran
Through caverns measureless to man
    Down to a sunless sea.   5

So twice five miles of fertile ground
With walls and towers were girdled round:
And there were gardens bright with sinuous rills,
Where blossomed many an incense-bearing tree;
And here were forests ancient as the hills,   10
Enfolding sunny spots of greenery.

But oh! that deep romantic chasm which slanted
Down the green hill athwart a cedarn cover!
A savage place! as holy and enchanted
As e'er beneath a waning moon was haunted   15
By woman wailing for her demon-lover!
And from this chasm, with ceaseless turmoil seething,
As if this earth in fast thick pants were breathing,
A mighty fountain momently was forced:
Amid whose swift half-intermitted burst   20
Huge fragments vaulted like rebounding hail,
Or chaffy grain beneath the thresher's flail:
And 'mid these dancing rocks at once and ever
It flung up momently the sacred river.
Five miles meandering with a mazy motion   25
Through wood and dale the sacred river ran,
Then reached the caverns measureless to man,
And sank in tumult to a lifeless ocean:
And 'mid this tumult Kubla heard from far
Ancestral voices prophesying war!   30

          The shadow of the dome of pleasure
          Floated midway on the waves;
          Where was heard the mingled measure
          From the fountain and the caves.
It was a miracle of rare device,   35
A sunny pleasure-dome with caves of ice!
          A damsel with a dulcimer
          In a vision once I saw:
          It was an Abyssinian maid,
          And on her dulcimer she played,   40
          Singing of Mount Abora.
          Could I revive within me
          Her symphony and song,
          To such a deep delight 'twould win me,
That with music loud and long,   45
I would build that dome in air,
That sunny dome! those caves of ice!
And all who heard should see them there,
And all should cry, Beware! Beware!

His flashing eyes, his floating hair!   50
Weave a circle round him thrice,
And close your eyes with holy dread,
For he on honey-dew hath fed,
And drunk the milk of Paradise.

SAMUEL TAYLOR COLERIDGE

Ode on a Grecian Urn

1

Thou still unravished bride of quietness,
　Thou foster-child of silence and slow time,
Sylvan historian, who canst thus express
　A flowery tale more sweetly than our rhyme:
What leaf-fringed legend haunts about thy shape   5
　Of deities or mortals, or of both,
　　In Tempe or the dales of Arcady?
What men or gods are these? What maidens loth?
　What mad pursuit? What struggle to escape?
　　What pipes and timbrels? What wild ecstasy?   10

2

Heard melodies are sweet, but those unheard
　Are sweeter; therefore, ye soft pipes, play on;
Not to the sensual ear, but, more endeared,
　Pipe to the spirit ditties of no tone:
Fair youth, beneath the trees, thou canst not leave   15
　Thy song, nor ever can those trees be bare;
　　Bold Lover, never, never canst thou kiss,
Though winning near the goal—yet, do not grieve;
　She cannot fade, though thou hast not thy bliss,
　　For ever wilt thou love, and she be fair!   20

3

Ah, happy, happy boughs! that cannot shed
　Your leaves, nor ever bid the Spring adieu;
And, happy melodist, unwearièd,
　For ever piping songs for ever new;
More happy love! more happy, happy love!   25
　For ever warm and still to be enjoyed,
　　For ever panting, and for ever young;
All breathing human passion far above,
　That leaves a heart high-sorrowful and cloyed,
　　A burning forehead, and a parching tongue.   30

4

Who are these coming to the sacrifice?
   To what green altar, O mysterious priest,
Lead'st thou that heifer lowing at the skies,
   And all her silken flanks with garlands drest?
What little town by river or sea shore,   35
   Or mountain-built with peaceful citadel,
      Is emptied of this folk, this pious morn?
And, little town, thy streets for evermore
   Will silent be; and not a soul to tell
      Why thou art desolate, can e'er return.   40

5

O Attic shape! Fair attitude! with brede
   Of marble men and maidens overwrought,
With forest branches and the trodden weed;
   Thou, silent form, dost tease us out of thought
As doth eternity: Cold Pastoral!   45
   When old age shall this generation waste,
      Thou shalt remain, in midst of other woe
Than ours, a friend to man, to whom thou say'st,
   "Beauty is truth, truth beauty,"—that is all
      Ye know on earth, and all ye need to know.   50

JOHN KEATS

Lines on the Mermaid Tavern

Souls of Poets dead and gone,
What Elysium have ye known,
Happy field or mossy cavern,
Choicer than the Mermaid Tavern?
Have ye tippled drink more fine   5
Than mine host's Canary wine?
Or are fruits of Paradise
Sweeter than those dainty pies
Of venison? O generous food!
Dressed as though bold Robin Hood   10
Would, with his maid Marian,
Sup and bowse from horn and can.

   I have heard that on a day
Mine host's signboard flew away,

Nobody knew whither, till 15
An astrologer's old quill
To a sheepskin gave the story,
Said he saw you in your glory,
Underneath a new old-sign
Sipping beverage divine, 20
And pledging with contented smack
The Mermaid in the Zodiac.

Souls of Poets dead and gone,
What Elysium have ye known,
Happy field or mossy cavern, 25
Choicer than the Mermaid Tavern?

JOHN KEATS

A Toccata of Galuppi's

I

Oh Galuppi, Baldassare, this is very sad to find!
I can hardly misconceive you; it would prove me deaf and blind;
But although I take your meaning, 'tis with such a heavy mind!

II

Here you come with your old music, and here's all the good it
brings.
What, they lived once thus at Venice where the merchants were the
kings, 5
Where St. Mark's is, where the Doges used to wed the sea with
rings?

III

Ay, because the sea's the street there; and 'tis arched by . . . what
you call
. . . Shylock's bridge with houses on it, where they kept the carnival:
I was never out of England—it's as if I saw it all.

IV

Did young people take their pleasure when the sea was warm in
May? 10
Balls and masks begun at midnight, burning ever to mid-day,
When they made up fresh adventures for the morrow, do you say?

V

Was a lady such a lady, cheeks so round and lips so red,—
On her neck the small face buoyant, like a bell-flower on its bed,
O'er the breast's superb abundance where a man might base his
    head?   15

VI

Well, and it was graceful of them—they'd break talk off and afford—
—She, to bite her mask's black velvet—he, to finger on his sword,
While you sat and played Toccatas, stately at the clavichord?

VII

What? Those lesser thirds so plaintive, sixths diminished, sigh on
    sigh,
Told them something? Those suspensions, those solutions,—"Must
    we die?"   20
Those commiserating sevenths—"Life might last! we can but try!"

VIII

"Were you happy?"—"Yes."—"And are you still as happy?"—
    "Yes. And you?"
—"Then, more kisses!"—"Did *I* stop them, when a million seemed
    so few?"
Hark, the dominant's persistence, till it must be answered to!

IX

So, an octave struck the answer. Oh, they praised you, I dare say!   25
"Brave Galuppi! that was music! good alike at grave and gay!
I can always leave off talking when I hear a master play!"

X

Then they left you for their pleasure: till in due time, one by one,
Some with lives that came to nothing, some with deeds as well
    undone,
Death stepped tacitly and took them where they never see the sun.   30

XI

But when I sit down to reason, think to take my stand nor swerve,
While I triumph o'er a secret wrung from nature's close reserve,
In you come with your cold music till I creep thro' every nerve.

XII

Yes, you, like a ghostly cricket, creaking where a house was burned:
"Dust and ashes, dead and done with, Venice spent what Venice
    earned.   35
The soul, doubtless, is immortal—where a soul can be discerned.

XIII

"Yours for instance: you know physics, something of geology,
Mathematics are your pastime; souls shall rise in their degree;
Butterflies may dread extinction,—you'll not die, it cannot be!

XIV

"As for Venice and her people, merely born to bloom and drop,   40
Here on earth they bore their fruitage, mirth and folly were the crop;
What of soul was left, I wonder, when the kissing had to stop?

XV

"Dust and ashes!" So you creak it, and I want the heart to scold.
Dear dead women, with such hair, too—what's become of all the
  gold
Used to hang and brush their bosoms? I feel chilly and grown old.   45

ROBERT BROWNING

Art

In placid hours well-pleased we dream
Of many a brave unbodied scheme.
But form to lend, pulsed life create,
What unlike things must meet and mate:
A flame to melt—a wind to freeze;   5
Sad patience—joyous energies;
Humility—yet pride and scorn;
Instinct and study; love and hate;
Audacity—reverence. These must mate,
And fuse with Jacob's mystic heart,   10
To wrestle with the angel—Art.

HERMAN MELVILLE

I Died for Beauty

I died for beauty, but was scarce
Adjusted in the tomb,
When one who died for truth was lain
In an adjoining room.

He questioned softly why I failed?   5
"For beauty," I replied.
"And I for truth—themself are one—

We brethren are," he said.
And so, as kinsmen met a-night,
We talked between the rooms,   10
Until the moss had reached our lips,
And covered up our names.

                    EMILY DICKINSON

I Hoed and Trenched and Weeded

I hoed and trenched and weeded,
   And took the flowers to fair:
I brought them home unheeded;
   The hue was not the wear.

So up and down I sow them   5
   For lads like me to find,
When I shall lie below them,
   A dead man out of mind.

Some seed the birds devour,
   And some the season mars,   10
But here and there will flower
   The solitary stars,

And fields will yearly bear them
   As light-leaved spring comes on,
And luckless lads will wear them   15
   When I am dead and gone.

                    A. E. HOUSMAN

Sailing to Byzantium

I

That is no country for old men. The young
In one another's arms, birds in the trees
—Those dying generations—at their song,
The salmon-falls, the mackerel-crowded seas,
Fish, flesh, or fowl, commend all summer long   5
Whatever is begotten, born, and dies.
Caught in that sensual music all neglect
Monuments of unageing intellect.

II

An aged man is but a paltry thing,
A tattered coat upon a stick, unless   10
Soul clap its hands and sing, and louder sing
For every tatter in its mortal dress,
Nor is there singing school but studying
Monuments of its own magnificence;
And therefore I have sailed the seas and come   15
To the holy city of Byzantium.

III

O sages standing in God's holy fire
As in the gold mosaic of a wall,
Come from the holy fire, perne[1] in a gyre,[2]
And be the singing-masters of my soul.   20
Consume my heart away; sick with desire
And fastened to a dying animal
It knows not what it is; and gather me
Into the artifice of eternity.

IV

Once out of nature I shall never take   25
My bodily form from any natural thing,
But such a form as Grecian goldsmiths make
Of hammered gold and gold enamelling
To keep a drowsy Emperor awake;
Or set upon a golden bough to sing   30
To lords and ladies of Byzantium
Of what is past, or passing, or to come.

WILLIAM BUTLER YEATS

[1] Turn or whirl.   [2] A whirling cone.

Byzantium

The unpurged images of day recede;
The Emperor's drunken soldiery are abed;
Night resonance recedes, night-walkers' song
After great cathedral gong;
A starlit or a moonlit dome disdains   5
All that man is,
All mere complexities,
The fury and the mire of human veins.

Before me floats an image, man or shade,
Shade more than man, more image than a shade;   10
For Hades' bobbin bound in mummy-cloth
May unwind the winding path;
A mouth that has no moisture and no breath
Breathless mouths may summon;
I hail the superhuman;   15
I call it death-in-life and life-in-death.

Miracle, bird or golden handiwork,
More miracle than bird or handiwork,
Planted on the star-lit golden bough,
Can like the cocks of Hades crow,   20
Or, by the moon embittered, scorn aloud
In glory of changeless metal
Common bird or petal
And all complexities of mire or blood.

At midnight on the Emperor's pavement flit   25
Flames that no faggot feeds, nor steel has lit,
Nor storm disturbs, flames begotten of flame,
Where blood-begotten spirits come
And all complexities of fury leave,
Dying into a dance,   30
An agony of trance,
An agony of flame that cannot singe a sleeve.

Astraddle on the dolphin's mire and blood,
Spirit after spirit! The smithies break the flood,
The golden smithies of the Emperor!   35
Marbles of the dancing floor
Break bitter furies of complexity,
Those images that yet
Fresh images beget,
That dolphin-torn, that gong-tormented sea.   40

WILLIAM BUTLER YEATS

Ten Definitions of Poetry

1   Poetry is a projection across silence of cadences arranged to break the
    silence with definite intentions of echoes, syllables, wave lengths.

2   Poetry is the journal of a sea animal living on land, wanting to fly the
    air.

3 Poetry is a series of explanations of life, fading off into horizons too swift for explanations.

4 Poetry is a search for syllables to shoot at the barriers of the unknown and the unknowable.

5 Poetry is a theorem of a yellow-silk handkerchief knotted with riddles, sealed in a balloon tied to the tail of a kite flying in a white wind against a blue sky in spring.

6 Poetry is the silence and speech between a wet struggling root of a flower and a sunlit blossom of that flower.

7 Poetry is the harnessing of the paradox of earth cradling life and then entombing it.

8 Poetry is a phantom script telling how rainbows are made and why they go away.

9 Poetry is the synthesis of hyacinths and biscuits.

10 Poetry is the opening and closing of a door, leaving those who look through to guess about what is seen during a moment.

CARL SANDBURG

Anecdote of the Jar

I placed a jar in Tennessee,
And round it was, upon a hill.
It made the slovenly wilderness
Surround that hill.

The wilderness rose up to it,   5
And sprawled around, no longer wild.
The jar was round upon the ground
And tall and of a port in air.

It took dominion everywhere.
The jar was gray and bare.   10
It did not give of bird or bush,
Like nothing else in Tennessee.

WALLACE STEVENS

Peter Quince at the Clavier

I

Just as my fingers on these keys
Make music, so the self-same sounds
On my spirit make a music, too.

Music is feeling, then, not sound;
And thus it is that what I feel,   5
Here in this room, desiring you,

Thinking of your blue-shadowed silk,
Is music. It is like the strain
Waked in the elders by Susanna:

Of a green evening, clear and warm,   10
She bathed in her still garden, while
The red-eyed elders, watching, felt

The basses of their beings throb
In witching chords, and their thin blood
Pulse pizzicati of Hosanna.   15

II

In the green water, clear and warm,
Susanna lay.
She searched
The touch of springs,
And found   20
Concealed imaginings.
She sighed,
For so much melody.

Upon the bank, she stood
In the cool   25
Of spent emotions.
She felt, among the leaves,
The dew
Of old devotions.

She walked upon the grass,   30
Still quavering.
The winds were like her maids,

On timid feet,
Fetching her woven scarves,
Yet wavering.   35

A breath upon her hand
Muted the night.
She turned—
A cymbal crashed,
And roaring horns.   40

III

Soon, with a noise like tambourines,
Came her attendant Byzantines.

They wondered why Susanna cried
Against the elders by her side;

And as they whispered, the refrain   45
Was like a willow swept by rain.

Anon, their lamps' uplifted flame
Revealed Susanna and her shame.

And then, the simpering Byzantines
Fled, with a noise like tambourines.   50

IV

Beauty is momentary in the mind—
The fitful tracing of a portal;
But in the flesh it is immortal.

The body dies; the body's beauty lives.
So evenings die, in their green going,   55
A wave, interminably flowing.
So gardens die, their meek breath scenting
The cowl of Winter, done repenting.
So maidens die, to the auroral
Celebration of a maiden's choral.   60

Susanna's music touched the bawdy strings
Of those white elders; but, escaping,
Left only Death's ironic scraping.
Now, in its immortality, it plays
On the clear viol of her memory,   65
And makes a constant sacrament of praise.

WALLACE STEVENS

Poetry

I, too, dislike it: there are things that are important beyond all this fiddle.
  Reading it, however, with a perfect contempt for it, one discovers in
  it after all, a place for the genuine.
    Hands that can grasp, eyes
    that can dilate, hair that can rise   5
      if it must, these things are important not because a

high-sounding interpretation can be put upon them but because they are
  useful. When they become so derivative as to become unintelligible,
  the same thing may be said for all of us, that we
    do not admire what   10
    we cannot understand: the bat
      holding on upside down or in quest of something to

eat, elephants pushing, a wild horse taking a roll, a tireless wolf under
  a tree, the immovable critic twitching his skin like a horse that feels a
    flea, the base ball fan, the statistician—   15
    nor is it valid
      to discriminate against "business documents and

school-books"; all these phenomena are important. One must make a
    distinction
  however: when dragged into prominence by half poets, the result is not
    poetry,
  nor till the poets among us can be   20
    "literalists of
    the imagination"—above
      insolence and triviality and can present

for inspection, imaginary gardens with real toads in them, shall we have
  it. In the meantime, if you demand on the one hand,   25
  the raw material of poetry in
    all its rawness and
    that which is on the other hand
      genuine, then you are interested in poetry.

MARIANNE MOORE

Euclid Alone Has Looked on Beauty Bare

    Euclid alone has looked on Beauty bare.
    Let all who prate of Beauty hold their peace,

And lay them prone upon the earth and cease
To ponder on themselves, the while they stare
At nothing, intricately drawn nowhere   5
In shapes of shifting lineage; let geese
Gabble and hiss, but heroes seek release
From dusty bondage into luminous air.
O blinding hour, O holy, terrible day,
When first the shaft into his vision shone   10
Of light anatomized! Euclid alone
Has looked on Beauty bare. Fortunate they
Who, though once only and then but far away,
Have heard her massive sandal set on stone.

EDNA ST. VINCENT MILLAY

Ars Poetica

A poem should be palpable and mute
As a globed fruit

Dumb
As old medallions to the thumb

Silent as the sleeve-worn stone   5
Of casement ledges where the moss has grown—

A poem should be wordless
As the flight of birds

A poem should be motionless in time
As the moon climbs   10

Leaving, as the moon releases
Twig by twig the night-entangled trees,

Leaving, as the moon behind the winter leaves,
Memory by memory the mind—

A poem should be motionless in time   15
As the moon climbs

A poem should be equal to:
Not true

For all the history of grief
An empty doorway and a maple leaf   20

For love
The leaning grasses and two lights above the sea—

A poem should not mean
But be.

ARCHIBALD MACLEISH

A Pinch of Salt

When a dream is born in you
   With a sudden clamorous pain,
When you know the dream is true
   And lovely, with no flaw nor stain,
O then, be careful, or with sudden clutch   5
You'll hurt the delicate thing you prize so much.

Dreams are like a bird that mocks,
   Flirting the feathers of his tail.
When you seize at the salt box,
   Over the hedge you'll see him sail.   10
Old birds are neither caught with salt nor chaff:
They watch you from the apple bough and laugh.

Poet, never chase the dream.
   Laugh yourself, and turn away.
Mask your hunger; let it seem   15
   Small matter if he come or stay;
But when he nestles in your hand at last,
Close up your fingers tight and hold him fast.

ROBERT GRAVES

Musée des Beaux Arts

About suffering they were never wrong,
The Old Masters: how well they understood
Its human position; how it takes place
While someone else is eating or opening a window or just
   walking dully along;
How, when the aged are reverently, passionately waiting   5
For the miraculous birth, there always must be

Children who did not specially want it to happen, skating
On a pond at the edge of the wood:
They never forgot
That even the dreadful martyrdom must run its course   10
Anyhow in a corner, some untidy spot
Where the dogs go on with their doggy life and the tor-
    turer's horse
Scratches its innocent behind on a tree.

In Brueghel's *Icarus,* for instance: how everything turns
    away
Quite leisurely from the disaster; the ploughman may   15
Have heard the splash, the forsaken cry,
But for him it was not an important failure; the sun shone
As it had to on the white legs disappearing into the green
Water; and the expensive delicate ship that must have seen
Something amazing, a boy falling out of the sky,   20
Had somewhere to get to and sailed calmly on.

W. H. AUDEN

Poet

Il arrive que l'esprit demande la poesié[1]

Left leg flung out, head cocked to the right,
Tweed coat or army uniform, with book,
Beautiful eyes, who is this walking down?
Who, glancing at the pane of glass looks sharp
And thinks it is not he—as when a poet   5
Comes swiftly on some half-forgotten poem
And loosely holds the page, steady of mind,
    Thinking it is not his?

And when will *you* exist?—Oh, it is I,
Incredibly skinny, stooped, and neat as pie,   10
Ignorant as dirt, erotic as an ape,
Dreamy as puberty—with dirty hair!
Into the room like kangaroo he bounds,
Ears flopping like the most expensive hound's;
His chin receives all questions as he bows   15
    Mouthing a green bon-bon.

[1] It so happens that the soul demands poetry.

Has no more memory than rubber. Stands
Waist-deep in heavy mud of thought and broods
At his own wetness. When he would get out,
To his surprise he lifts in air a phrase   20
As whole and clean and silvery as a fish.
Which jumps and dangles on his damned hooked grin,
But like a name-card on a man's lapel
    Calls him a conscious fool.

And childlike he remembers all his life   25
And cannily constructs it, fact by fact,
As boys paste postage stamps in careful books,
Denoting pence and legends and profiles,
Nothing more valuable.—And like a thief,
His eyes glassed over and concealed with guilt,   30
Fondles his secrets like a case of tools,
    And waits in empty doors.

By men despised for knowing what he is,
And by himself. But he exists for women.
As dolls to girls, as perfect wives to men,   35
So he to women. And to himself a thing,
All ages, epicene, without a trade.
To girls and wives always alive and fated;
To men and scholars always dead like Greek
    And always mistranslated.   40

Towards exile and towards shame he lures himself,
Tongue winding on his arm, and thinks like Eve
By biting apple will become most wise.
Sentio ergo sum: he feels his way
And words themselves stand up for him like Braille   45
And punch and perforate his parchment ear.
All language falls like Chinese on his soul,
    Image of song unsounded.

This is the coward's coward that in his dreams
Sees shapes of pain grow tall. Awake at night   50
He peers at sounds and stumbles at a breeze.
And none holds life less dear. For as a youth
Who by some accident observes his love
Naked and in some natural ugly act,
He turns with loathing and with flaming hands,   55
    Seared and betrayed by sight.

He is the business man, on beauty trades,
Dealer in arts and thoughts who, like the Jew,

Shall rise from slums and hated dialects
A tower of bitterness. Shall be always strange,   60
Hunted and then sought after. Shall be sat
Like an ambassador from another race
At tables rich with music. He shall eat flowers,
Chew honey and spit out gall. They shall all smile
    And love and pity him.   65

His death shall be by drowning. In that hour
When the last bubble of pure heaven's air
Hovers within his throat, safe on his bed,
A small eternal figurehead in terror,
He shall cry out and clutch his days of straw   70
Before the blackest wave. Lastly, his tomb
Shall list and founder in the troughs of grass.
    And none shall speak his name.

KARL SHAPIRO

Poet

"Toute forme créée, même par l'homme, est immortelle. Car la forme est indépendante de la matière, et ce ne sont pas les molécules qui constituent la forme."[1]

(Baudelaire: Mon Coeur Mis à Nu)

The night he died, earth's images all came
To gloat in liberation round his tomb.
Now vengeful colors, stones, and faces dare
    To argue with his metaphor;
And stars his fancy painted on the skies   5
Drop down like swords
            to pierce his too wide eyes.

Words that begged favor at his court in vain—
Lush adverbs, senile rhymes in tattered gowns—
    Send notes to certain exiled nouns   10
And mutter openly against his reign.
While rouged clichés hang out red lights again.
Hoarse refugees report from far-flung towns
That exclamation-marks are running wild
And prowling half-truths carried off a child.   15

But he lives on in Form, and Form shall shatter
    This tuneless mutiny of Matter.

[1] Any created form, even that created by man, is immortal. For the form is independent of the materials, and it is not the molecules that constitute form.

His bones are dead; his voice is horribly strong
Those famed vibrations of life's dancing dust,
Whose thrice-named pangs are "birth" and "death" and lust,"   20
Are but the split iambics of his song.
Scansion of flesh in endless ebb and flow,
Mere grace-notes of that living thousand-year
Tyrannic metronome whose every gear
Is some shy craftsman buried long ago.   25
What terror crowns the sweetness of all song?

What hardness leaps at us from each soft tune
And hammers us to shapes we never planned?
This was a different dying from our own.
        Call every wizard in the land—   30
Bell, book, and test tube; let the dark be rife
With every exorcism we command.
In vain. This death is stronger than our life.

In vain we drive stakes through such a haunter
Or woo with spiced applaudings such a heart.   35
His news of April do but mock our Winter
Like maps of heaven breathed on window-frost
By cruel clowns in codes whose key is lost.
Yet some sereneness in our rage has guessed
That we are being blessed and blessed and blessed   40
When least we know it and when coldest art
    Seems hostile
        useless,
            or apart.

    Not worms, not worms in such a skull   45
But rhythms, rhythms writhe and sting and crawl.
He sings the seasons round, from bud to snow.
And all things are because he willed them so.

                        PETER VIERECK

8
Illusion and Escape

For many people the word "illusion" has distinctly unattractive overtones of the false, the deceptive, and the unreal. In their minds, a person who cherishes illusions shows weakness and will inevitably be disillusioned. These "anti-illusionists," however, are themselves laboring under an illusion. For illusions (that is, dreams and beliefs about things unseen) can be the driving force behind much human endeavor; and illusions can be just as real for those who hold them as more tangible reality.

There is some truth, however, in the common indictment of illusions. There is pathos in the case of the girl who tries to construct a world out of the tinsel of Hollywood, where "Alice and Cinderella are most real." There is pathos in the dilemma of a Miniver Cheevy and a Mr. Flood. There is something approaching the tragic in the false illusions of Browning's Duke.

Many illusions offer a means of escape. When the pressures and complexities of the world become too great, a man tends to fly, either in dream or in reality, to something better. He may remove himself physically to some other environment, a house in the country or an exotic land. More likely he will enter a movie house or a library for a couple of hours. He may take to drink or drugs. When he cannot escape and the pressures become too great, he may, like Richard Cory, go home and put a bullet through his head.

The list below indicates that the theme of illusion and escape can be adequately treated in any of the major genres.

READINGS IN OTHER GENRES

PLAYS

Maxwell Anderson, *High Tor*
Jean Anouilh, *The Madwoman of Chaillot*
Mary Chase, *Harvey*
Anton Chekhov, *The Sea Gull*
Lillian Hellman, *The Autumn Garden*

Henrik Ibsen, *The Wild Duck*
Eugene O'Neill, *The Iceman Cometh*
Luigi Pirandello, *Right You Are If You Think You Are, Henry IV*
William Saroyan, *The Time of Your Life*
William Shakespeare, *A Midsummer Night's Dream, As You Like It, The Tempest*
August Strindberg, *A Dream Play, The Ghost Sonata*
Tennessee Williams, *The Glass Menagerie*

NOVELS

James Branch Cabel, *Jurgen, The Cream of the Jest*
François René Chateaubriand, *René*
Joseph Conrad, *Heart of Darkness, Lord Jim*
Daniel Defoe, *Robinson Crusoe*
Nigel Denis, *The Cards of Identity*
Ralph Ellison, *The Invisible Man*
James Hilton, *Lost Horizon*
Thomas Mann, *The Magic Mountain*
John P. Marquand, *The Late George Apley*
Iris Murdoch, *The Unicorn*
Walker Percy, *The Moviegoer*
J. D. Salinger, *The Catcher in the Rye*
Mark Twain, *A Connecticut Yankee in King Arthur's Court*

SHORT STORIES

Stephen Vincent Benét, "By the Waters of Babylon"
Ambrose Bierce, "An Occurrence at Owl Creek Bridge"
Anton Chekhov, "The New Villa"
Gustave Flaubert, "A Simple Heart"
E. M. Forster, "The Other Side of the Hedge," "The Story of the Siren"
Henry James, "Maud-Evelyn"
D. H. Lawrence, "The Man Who Loved Islands"
Thomas Mann, "Mario and the Magician"
Katherine Mansfield, "Miss Brill"
Somerset Maugham, "The Outstation"
Herman Melville, "Bartleby the Scrivener"
Christopher Morley, "Where the Blue Begins"
Jean Stafford, "A Country Love Story"

The Silver Swan

The silver swan, who living had no note,
When death approached unlocked her silent throat;
Leaning her breast against the reedy shore,
Thus sung her first and last, and sung no more:
Farewell, all joys: O death, come close mine eyes;   5
More geese than swans now live, more fools than wise.

ANONYMOUS
(Seventeenth Century)

The Passionate Shepherd to His Love

Come live with me, and be my love,
And we will all the pleasures prove,
That valleys, groves, hills, and fields,
Woods, or steepy mountain yields.

And we will sit upon the rocks,   5
Seeing the shepherds feed their flocks
By shallow rivers, to whose falls
Melodious birds sing madrigals.

And I will make thee beds of roses,
And a thousand fragrant posies,   10
A cap of flowers, and a kirtle,
Embroidered all with leaves of myrtle;

A gown made of the finest wool,
Which from our pretty lambs we pull,
Fair linèd slippers for the cold,   15
With buckles of the purest gold;

A belt of straw and ivy buds,
With coral clasps and amber studs.
And if these pleasures may thee move,
Come live with me, and be my love.   20

The shepherds' swains shall dance and sing
For thy delight each May morning.
If these delights thy mind may move,
Then live with me, and be my love.

CHRISTOPHER MARLOWE

The Nymph's Reply to the Shepherd

If all the world and love were young,
And truth in every shepherd's tongue,
These pretty pleasures might me move,
To live with thee, and be thy love.

Time drives the flocks from field to fold,   5
When rivers rage and rocks grow cold,
And Philomel becometh dumb,
The rest complains of cares to come.

The flowers do fade, and wanton fields
To wayward winter reckoning yields;   10
A honey tongue, a heart of gall,
Is fancy's spring, but sorrow's fall.

Thy gowns, thy shoes, thy beds of roses,
Thy cap, thy kirtle, and thy posies,
Soon break, soon wither, soon forgotten: 15
In folly ripe, in reason rotten.

Thy belt of straw and ivy buds,
Thy coral clasps and amber studs,
All these in me no means can move,
To come to thee, and be thy love.   20

But could youth last, and love still breed,
Had joys no date, nor age no need,
Then these delights my mind might move,
To live with thee, and be thy love.

                              SIR WALTER RALEIGH

Farewell! Thou Art Too Dear

Farewell! thou art too dear for my possessing,
And like enough thou know'st thy estimate:
The charter of thy worth gives thee releasing;
My bonds in thee are all determinate.
For how do I hold thee but by thy granting?   5
And for that riches where is my deserving?
The cause of this fair gift in me is wanting,

And so my patent back again is swerving.
Thyself thou gav'st, thy own worth then not knowing,
Or me, to whom thou gav'st it, else mistaking;   10
So thy great gift, upon misprision growing,
Comes home again, on better judgment making.
    Thus have I had thee as a dream doth flatter,
    In sleep a king, but waking no such matter.

WILLIAM SHAKESPEARE

Are They Shadows That We See?

    Are they shadows that we see?
    And can shadows pleasure give?
    Pleasures only shadows be
    Cast by bodies we conceive,
      And are made the things we deem,   5
      In those figures which they seem.
But these pleasures vanish fast,
Which by shadows are expressed:
    Pleasures are not, if they last,
      In their passing, is their best.   10
      Glory is most bright and gay
      In a flash, and so away.
Feed apace then, greedy eyes,
On the wonder you behold.
    Take it sudden as it flies   15
    Though you take it not to hold:
When your eyes have done their part,
Thought must length it in the heart.

SAMUEL DANIEL

The Garden

How vainly men themselves amaze
To win the palm, the oak, or bays;
And their incessant labors see
Crowned from some single herb or tree,
Whose short and narrow-vergèd shade   5
Does prudently their toils upbraid;
While all flowers and all trees do close
To weave the garlands of repose.

Fair Quiet, have I found thee here,
And Innocence thy sister dear!   10
Mistaken long, I sought you then
In busy companies of men.
Your sacred plants, if here below,
Only among the plants will grow.
Society is all but rude,   15
To this delicious solitude.

No white nor red was ever seen
So amorous as this lovely green.
Fond lovers, cruel as their flame,
Cut in these trees their mistress' name.   20
Little, alas, they know, or heed,
How far these beauties hers exceed!
Fair trees! whereso'er your barks I wound,
No name shall but your own be found.

When we have run our passion's heat,   25
Love hither makes his best retreat.
The gods, that mortal beauty chase,
Still in a tree did end their race.
Apollo hunted Daphne so,
Only that she might laurel grow.   30
And Pan did after Syrinx speed,
Not as a nymph, but for a reed.

What wondrous life in this I lead!
Ripe apples drop about my head;
The luscious clusters of the vine   35
Upon my mouth do crush their wine;
The nectaren, and curious peach,
Into my hands themselves do reach;
Stumbling on melons, as I pass,
Ensnared with flowers, I fall on grass.   40

Meanwhile the mind, from pleasure less,
Withdraws into its happiness:
The mind, that ocean where each kind
Does straight its own resemblance find;
Yet it creates, transcending these,   45
Far other worlds, and other seas;
Annihilating all that's made
To a green thought in a green shade.

Here at the fountain's sliding foot,
Or at some fruit tree's mossy root,   50

Casting the body's vest aside,
My soul into the boughs does glide;
There like a bird it sits, and sings,
Then whets, and combs its silver wings;
And till prepared for longer flight,   55
Waves in its plumes the various light.

Such was that happy garden-state,
While man there walked without a mate;
After a place so pure, and sweet,
What other help could yet be meet!   60
But 'twas beyond a mortal's share
To wander solitary there;
Two paradises 'twere in one,
To live in paradise alone.

How well the skillful gardener drew   65
Of flowers and herbs this dial new,
Where, from above, the milder sun
Does through a fragrant zodiac run;
And, as it works, the industrious bee
Computes its time as well as we.   70
How could such sweet and wholesome hours
Be reckoned but with herbs and flowers!

ANDREW MARVELL

Ode on Solitude

Happy the man, whose wish and care
    A few paternal acres bound,
Content to breathe his native air,
        In his own ground.

Whose herds with milk, whose fields with bread,   5
    Whose flocks supply him with attire,
Whose trees in summer yield him shade,
        In winter fire.

Blest, who can unconcern'dly find
    Hours, days, and years slide soft away,   10
In health of body, peace of mind,
        Quiet by day;

Sound sleep by night; study and ease
    Together mixed; sweet recreation,

And innocence, which most does please,   15
    With meditation.

Thus let me live, unseen, unknown,
    Thus unlamented let me die,
Steal from the world, and not a stone
    Tell where I lie.   20

ALEXANDER POPE

To the Honourable Charles Montague, Esq.

Howe'er, 'tis well, that while mankind
    Through Fate's perverse meander errs,
He can imagined pleasures find,
    To combat against real cares.

Fancies and notions he pursues,   5
    Which ne'er had being but in thought;
Each, like the Grecian artist, woos
    The image he himself has wrought.

Against experience he believes;
    He argues against demonstration;   10
Pleased, when his reason he deceives;
    And sets his judgment by his passion.

The hoary fool, who many days
    Has struggled with continued sorrow,
Renews his hope, and blindly lays   15
    The desperate bet upon to-morrow.

To-morrow comes: 'tis noon, 'tis night;
    This day like all the former flies:
Yet on he runs, to seek delight
    To-morrow, till to-night he dies.   20

Our hopes, like towering falcons, aim
    At objects in an airy height:
The little pleasure of the game
    Is from afar to view the flight.

Our anxious pains we, all the day,   25
    In search of what we like, employ:
Scorning at night the worthless prey,
    We find the labor gave the joy.

> At distance through an artful glass
>> To the mind's eye things well appear: 30
> They lose their forms, and make a mass
>> Confused and black, if brought too near.

> If we see right, we see our woes:
>> Then what avails it to have eyes?
> From ignorance our comfort flows.   35
>> The only wretched are the wise.

> We wearied should lie down in death:
>> This cheat of life would take no more,
> If you thought fame but empty breath;
>> I, Phyllis, but a perjured whore.   40

MATTHEW PRIOR

"To the Honourable Charles Montague, Esq.": An Explication
Gerald A. Kirk

"To the Honourable Charles Montague, Esq." was written by Prior during the early years of his career as secretary to the English ambassador to The Hague. He had known Charles Montague, who was three years older than he, for about fifteen years, and a close friendship existed between the two despite the fact that Montague, though poor, was the grandson of an earl and Prior merely the son of a joiner. At the time the poem was written, Montague was a rising young politician in England who had recently made an unusual but advantageous marriage. These elementary biographical facts help define the dramatic situation of the poem and add to its texture the dimension of the busy political world in which the two men, and particularly Montague, are engaged.

The tone of the poem—conversational, familiar—suggests that it be read as a letter, a communication from Prior in Holland to his more successful friend in England. The first word of the poem, "Howe'er," further suggests that the poem is only part of the communication; it stands perhaps as a conclusion to a lengthy discussion, or perhaps is a poetic summation of the prose contents of the letter. Indeed, in Prior's first authorized poetic collection, *Poems on Several Occasions* (1709), the title is lengthened to "In a Letter to the Honourable Mr. Charles Montague."

The characters of the two young men, and especially that of the writer, emerge as the poem develops. They are educated, urbane, and philosophically skeptical, apparently having no illusions about the world. The role through which Prior speaks is one found often in his work; it is that of the clear-eyed observer of this distracted world, one who is capable of seeing his own folly as well as that of others and one whose philosophical roots are more classical than Christian. When the poem was published for the second time, in the third Dryden Miscellany (1693), it was titled "Heraclitus," a reference which can serve as a gloss to the speaker's attitude. The Heraclitean doctrines of change, strife, contradiction, and disillusionment echo throughout the poem and particularly in Prior's seventh stanza.

The emphasis upon the ephemeral nature of things and the paradoxical fact that to achieve one's desire is only to discover that it was merely "worthless prey" help determine the strategy of the poem. Since the poem has the form of personal communication, the abstract themes are given concrete form by focusing upon the predominant concern of each of the two friends: the political ambitions of Montague and the emotional and sexual involvement of Prior. Biographical relevance aside, ambition and love are two of the basic drives in the lives of men, and in the poem they establish a spectrum for the multiple hopes and desires of all men. The startling, bitter final stanza thus is a philosophic commitment extending to every ambition and passion.

The revelation in the final stanza is anticipated in the reference to Pygmalion in the second stanza. The myth, of course, is about a man who created an illusion that came to life. But that, after all, is myth. The purity of the nonexistent Galatea is in effective contrast to the faithlessness of the all too real Phyllis, "the perjured whore." But in a very real sense Phyllis is a worldly Galatea, a work of art that is lovely only to the imagination that created her, that believes her lies, and is blind to her behavior. For the aspiring politician, Galatea is the career he wishes to carve, which, because of the realities of political life, will possess only those imaginary charms he will create. Biographically, there is another ironic dimension. Three years before the writing of this poem, Montague had married the Countess Dowager of Manchester. She was a wealthy, elderly widow who had had nine children by her first husband, whom she had married six years before Charles Montague was born. Prior wrote a poem celebrating the marriage, in which he wished for Montague "Successive Hopes of thy great Progeny." In a sense this was a prophetic request. Montague's political rise quickened appreciably after the marriage, a rise however that permits the reader to see Montague's career as a creation of the Countess' wealth, a subtle reversal of the Pygmalion myth.

The reference to the "hoary fool" would have been recognized by the reader of the 1690's, with his classically oriented education, as an allusion to the third book of *On the Nature of the Universe*. Lucretius is concerned with the folly of fearing death when one is aged but, having long experienced the deceptions of life, is still clinging to existence, foolishly desiring to be "only a prey to future misfortunes" (1. 942). Prior's use of the allusion reenforces the fact that man's capacity to deceive himself does not diminish with experience ("Against experience he believes"), that one of the conditions of human existence is perpetual and futile hope, which leads to the kind of frenzied, aimless pursuit described in stanza five—also an echo of a subsequent passage in Lucretius (ll. 1080–84).

The images of continual search, of pursuit, are refined in the simile of the falcons. Ambition and love are transformed into activities that make men into predators. The reference to "delight" in stanza five can be particularized in that the ceaseless search for love, for example, can degenerate into satyriasis, a condition in which women become merely prey for an insatiable appetite, the male equivalent of "whore" at the end of the poem. This kind of obsession is also reflected in the gambling image in line 16, which adds to the poem the sense of the great waste exacted by illusion, the prodigality and energy expended so vainly. These images are also applicable to political ambition, for in the jungle of English politics one could rise only through preferment, only by stalking the wealthy and powerful and, through trick and stratagem, trapping them into promises they could not evade keeping.

This is the world that the poem presents. It is a world that cannot bear close scrutiny, as stanzas eight and nine point out, and for this reason distance is required. The world can be tolerated only if one stands back from it, viewing it but dimly and finding escape by a deliberate, an almost Oedipus-like, blinding of oneself.

The Lucretian passages alluded to in stanzas four and five are separated in *On the Nature of the Universe* by nearly fifty lines in which Lucretius maintains that hell does not exist and that its supposed torments are merely allegories describing what men suffer on earth. In particular, he describes the punishments of Tityus, the lustful sinner, and Sisyphus, whom he unaccountably portrays as the ambitious politician. The vultures that eternally eat the heart of Tityus, he says, are symbols of the emotions and sexual desires that rend the lover on earth; the boulder Sisyphus eternally pushes symbolizes the futile pursuit of political power.

The appropriateness of Lucretius' allegory for Prior's poem is undeniable: in both the map of the world is the geography of hell. The rapid movement, the confusion, and the anxiety stressed in much of the poem also suggest the endlessly futile activity of Dante's landscape. There is, of course, no evidence that Prior intended this identification with Tityus and Sisyphus, but the identification helps to explain why "we wearied should lie down in death" and points to the ultimate meaning of the poem. Men flee from death and cling to life because in their blindness they do not know the final secret. Death is the escape from illusion, the salvation from hell.

Ode on the Death of a Favorite Cat, Drowned in a Tub of Gold Fishes

'Twas on a lofty vase's side,
Where China's gayest art had dyed
    The azure flowers that blow;

Demurest of the tabby kind,
The pensive Selima reclined,   5
   Gazed on the lake below.

Her conscious tail her joy declared;
The fair round face, the snowy beard,
   The velvet of her paws,
Her coat, that with the tortoise vies;   10
Her ears of jet, and emerald eyes,
   She saw; and purred applause.

Still had she gazed; but 'midst the tide
Two angel forms were seen to glide,
   The Genii of the stream: 15
Their scaly armour's Tyrian hue
Through richest purple to the view
   Betrayed a golden gleam.

The hapless Nymph with wonder saw:
A whisker first and then a claw,   20
   With many an ardent wish,
She stretched in vain to reach the prize.
What female heart can gold despise?
   What cat's averse to fish?

Presumptuous maid! with looks intent   25
Again she stretched, again she bent,
   Nor knew the gulf between.
(Malignant Fate sat by, and smiled)
The slippery verge her feet beguiled,
   She tumbled headlong in.   30

Eight times emerging from the flood
She mewed to every watery God,
   Some speedy aid to send.
No dolphin came, no Nereid stirred
Nor cruel Tom, nor Susan heard.   35
   A favorite has no friend!

From hence, ye beauties, undeceived,
Know, one false step is ne'er retrieved,
   And be with caution bold.
Not all that tempts your wandering eyes   40
And heedless hearts, is lawful prize:
   Nor all that glisters gold.

THOMAS GRAY

Ode to a Nightingale

My heart aches, and a drowsy numbness pains
  My sense, as though of hemlock I had drunk,
Or emptied some dull opiate to the drains
  One minute past, and Lethe-wards had sunk:
'Tis not through envy of thy happy lot,   5
  But being too happy in thy happiness,—
    That thou, light-wingèd Dryad of the trees,
      In some melodious plot
  Of beechen green, and shadows numberless,
    Singest of summer in full-throated ease.   10

O for a draught of vintage! that hath been
  Cooled a long age in the deep-delvèd earth,
Tasting of Flora and the country green,
  Dance, and Provençal song, and sunburnt mirth!
O for a beaker full of the warm South,   15
  Full of the true, the blushful Hippocrene,
    With beaded bubbles winking at the brim,
      And purple-stainèd mouth;
  That I might drink, and leave the world unseen,
    And with thee fade away into the forest dim: 20

Fade far away, dissolve, and quite forget
  What thou among the leaves hast never known,
The weariness, the fever, and the fret
  Here, where men sit and hear each other groan;
Where palsy shakes a few, sad, last grey hairs,   25
  Where youth grows pale, and spectre-thin, and dies;
    Where but to think is to be full of sorrow
      And leaden-eyed despairs,
  Where Beauty cannot keep her lustrous eyes,
    Or new Love pine at them beyond to-morrow.   30

Away! away! for I will fly to thee,
  Not charioted by Bacchus and his pards,
But on the viewless wings of Poesy,
  Though the dull brain perplexes and retards;
Already with thee! tender is the night,   35
  And haply the Queen-Moon is on her throne,
    Clustered around by all her starry Fays;
      But here there is no light,
  Save what from heaven is with the breezes blown
    Through verdurous glooms and winding mossy ways.   40

I cannot see what flowers are at my feet,
 Nor what soft incense hangs upon the boughs,
But, in embalmèd darkness, guess each sweet
 Wherewith the seasonable month endows
The grass, the thicket, and the fruit tree wild;   45
 White hawthorn, and the pastoral eglantine;
  Fast fading violets covered up in leaves;
   And mid-May's eldest child,
 The coming musk-rose, full of dewy wine,
  The murmurous haunt of flies on summer eves. 50

Darkling I listen; and, for many a time
 I have been half in love with easeful Death,
Called him soft names in many a musèd rhyme,
 To take into the air my quiet breath;
Now more than ever seems it rich to die,   55
 To cease upon the midnight with no pain
  While thou art pouring forth thy soul abroad
   In such an ecstacy!
 Still wouldst thou sing, and I have ears in vain—
  To thy high requiem become a sod.   60

Thou wast not born for death, immortal Bird!
 No hungry generations tread thee down;
The voice I hear this passing night was heard
 In ancient days by emperor and clown:
Perhaps the self-same song that found a path 65
 Through the sad heart of Ruth, when, sick for home,
  She stood in tears amid the alien corn;
   The same that oft-times hath
 Charmed magic casements, opening on the foam
  Of perilous seas, in faery lands forlorn. 70

Forlorn! the very word is like a bell
 To toll me back from thee to my sole self!
Adieu! the fancy cannot cheat so well
 As she is famed to do, deceiving elf.
Adieu! adieu! thy plaintive anthem fades 75
 Past the near meadows, over the still stream,
  Up the hillside; and now 'tis buried deep
   In the next valley glades:
 Was it a vision, or a waking dream?
  Fled is that music:—Do I wake or sleep? 80

JOHN KEATS

Ode on Melancholy

No, no, go not to Lethe, neither twist
    Wolfsbane, tight-rooted, for its poisonous wine;
Nor suffer thy pale forehead to be kissed
    By nightshade, ruby grape of Proserpine;
Make not your rosary of yew-berries,   5
    Nor let the beetle, nor the death-moth be
        Your mournful Psyche, nor the downy owl
A partner in your sorrow's mysteries;
    For shade to shade will come too drowsily,
        And drown the wakeful anguish of the soul.   10

But when the melancholy fit shall fall
    Sudden from heaven like a weeping cloud,
That fosters the droop-headed flowers all,
    And hides the green hill in an April shroud;
Then glut thy sorrow on a morning rose,   15
    Or on the rainbow of the salt sand-wave,
        Or on the wealth of globèd peonies;
Or if thy mistress some rich anger shows,
    Emprison her soft hand, and let her rave,
        And feed deep, deep upon her peerless eyes.   20

She dwells with Beauty—Beauty that must die;
    And Joy, whose hand is ever at his lips
Bidding adieu; and aching Pleasure nigh,
    Turning to poison while the bee-mouth sips;
Aye, in the very temple of Delight   25
    Veiled Melancholy has her sovereign shrine,
        Though seen of none save him whose strenuous tongue
Can burst Joy's grape against his palate fine;
His soul shall taste the sadness of her might,
    And be among her cloudy trophies hung.   30

JOHN KEATS

A Subterranean City

I followed once a fleet and mighty serpent
Into a cavern in a mountain's side;
And, wading many lakes, descending gulfs,
At last I reached the ruins of a city,

Built not like ours but of another world,   5
As if the aged earth had loved in youth
The mightiest city of a perished planet,
And kept the image of it in her heart,
So dream-like, shadowy, and spectral was it.
Nought seemed alive there, and the very dead   10
Were of another world the skeletons.
The mammoth, ribbed like to an arched cathedral,
Lay there, and ruins of great creatures else
More like a shipwrecked fleet, too great they seemed
For all the life that is to animate: 15
And vegetable rocks, tall, sculptured palms,
Pine grown, not hewn, in stone; and giant ferns
Whose earthquake-shaken leaves bore graves for nests.

THOMAS LOVELL BEDDOES

from *The Rubáiyát of Omar Khayyám*

2

Before the phantom of False morning died,
Methought a Voice within the Tavern cried,
    "When all the Temple is prepared within,
Why nods the drowsy Worshiper outside?"

54

Waste not your Hour, nor in the vain pursuit   5
Of This and That endeavor and dispute;
    Better be jocund with the fruitful Grape
Than sadden after none, or bitter, Fruit.

58

And lately, by the Tavern Door agape,
Came shining through the Dusk an Angel Shape   10
    Bearing a Vessel on his Shoulder; and
He bid me taste of it; and 'twas—the Grape!

59

The Grape that can with Logic absolute
The Two-and-Seventy jarring Sects confute;
    The sovereign Alchemist that in a trice   15
Life's leaden metal into Gold transmute;

91

Ah, with the Grape my fading Life provide,
And wash the Body whence the Life has died,
   And lay me, shrouded in the living Leaf,
By some not unfrequented Garden-side— 20

94

Indeed, indeed, Repentance oft before
I swore—but was I sober when I swore?
   And then and then came Spring, and Rose-in-hand
My threadbare Penitence apieces tore.

95

And much as Wine has played the Infidel, 25
And robbed me of my Robe of Honor—Well,
   I wonder often what the Vintners buy
One-half so precious as the stuff they sell.

EDWARD FITZGERALD

The City in the Sea

Lo! Death has reared himself a throne
In a strange city lying alone
Far down within the dim West,
Where the good and the bad and the worst and the best
Have gone to their eternal rest. 5
There shrines and palaces and towers
(Time-eaten towers that tremble not!)
Resemble nothing that is ours.
Around, by lifting winds forgot,
Resignedly beneath the sky 10
The melancholy waters lie.

No rays from the holy heaven come down
On the long night-time of that town;
But light from out the lurid sea
Streams up the turrets silently— 15
Gleams up the pinnacles far and free—
Up domes—up spires—up kingly halls—
Up fanes—up Babylon-like walls—
Up shadowy long-forgotten bowers
Of sculptured ivy and stone flowers— 20

Up many and many a marvellous shrine
Whose wreathed friezes intertwine
The viol, the violet, and the vine.

Resignedly beneath the sky
The melancholy waters lie.   25
So blend the turrets and shadows there
That all seem pendulous in air,
While from a proud tower in the town
Death looks gigantically down.

There open fanes and gaping graves   30
Yawn level with the luminous waves;
But not the riches there that lie
In each idol's diamond eye—
Not the gaily-jewelled dead
Tempt the waters from their bed;   35
For no ripples curl, alas!
Along that wilderness of glass—
No swellings tell that winds may be
Upon some far-off happier sea—
No heavings hint that winds have been   40
On seas less hideously serene.

But lo, a stir is in the air!
The wave—there is a movement there!
As if the towers had thrust aside,
In slightly sinking, the dull tide—   45
As if their tops had feebly given
A void within the filmy Heaven.
The waves have now a redder glow—
The hours are breathing faint and low—
And when, amid no earthly moans,   50
Down, down that town shall settle hence,
Hell, rising from a thousand thrones,
Shall do it reverence.

EDGAR ALLAN POE

My Last Duchess

That's my last Duchess painted on the wall,
Looking as if she were alive. I call
That piece a wonder, now: Frà Pandolf's hands
Worked busily a day, and there she stands.
Will't please you sit and look at her? I said   5
"Frà Pandolf" by design, for never read

Strangers like you that pictured countenance,
The depth and passion of its earnest glance,
But to myself they turned (since none puts by
The curtain I have drawn for you, but I)   10
And seemed as they would ask me, if they durst,
How such a glance came there; so, not the first
Are you to turn and ask thus. Sir, 'twas not
Her husband's presence only, called that spot
Of joy into the Duchess' cheek; perhaps   15
Frà Pandolf chanced to say, "Her mantle laps
Over my lady's wrist too much," or "Paint
Must never hope to reproduce the faint
Half-flush that dies along her throat": such stuff
Was courtesy, she thought, and cause enough   20
For calling up that spot of joy. She had
A heart—how shall I say?—too soon made glad,
Too easily impressed: she liked whate'er
She looked on, and her looks went everywhere.
Sir, 'twas all one! My favor at her breast,   25
The dropping of the daylight in the West,
The bough of cherries some officious fool
Broke in the orchard for her, the white mule
She rode with round the terrace—all and each
Would draw from her alike the approving speech,   30
Or blush, at least. She thanked men,—good! but thanked
Somehow—I know not how—as if she ranked
My gift of a nine-hundred-years-old name
With anybody's gift. Who'd stoop to blame
This sort of trifling? Even had you skill   35
In speech—which I have not—to make your will
Quite clear to such an one, and say, "Just this
Or that in you disgusts me; here you miss,
Or there exceed the mark"—and if she let
Herself be lessoned so, nor plainly set   40
Her wits to yours, forsooth, and made excuse,
—E'en then would be some stooping; and I choose
Never to stoop. Oh sir, she smiled, no doubt,
Whene'er I passed her; but who passed without
Much the same smile? This grew; I gave commands;   45
Then all smiles stopped together. There she stands
As if alive. Will't please you rise? We'll meet
The company below, then. I repeat,
The Count your master's known munificence
Is ample warrant that no just pretence   50
Of mine for dowry will be disallowed;
Though his fair daughter's self, as I avowed
At starting, is my object. Nay, we'll go

> Together down, sir. Notice Neptune, though,
> Taming a sea-horse, thought a rarity,   55
> Which Claus of Innsbruck cast in bronze for me!

ROBERT BROWNING

Explication of Robert Browning's "My Last Duchess"[1]
Carol Vaughan

Robert Browning's "My Last Duchess" is important not only as a poignant psychological study, but also as a statement of the purpose of art. In the fifty-six lines of the dramatic monologue, the reader learns a great deal about the deceased Duchess of the poem's title, and even more about the speaker, the Duke of Ferrara. It is postulated that Browning modeled his Renaissance Duke after Alfonso II, who lived in Italy during the 1500's;[2] however, Browning so masterfully created the character of the Duke that historical verification of his actual existence seems irrelevant.

The poem opens as the proud Duke is showing his art collection on an upper floor of his mansion to an envoy sent by a count whose daughter is about to marry the Duke. The dowry has been set, and the Duke concludes the business by subtly letting the envoy know what he expects from his new duchess by talking about a portrait of his late wife. He begins:

> That's my last Duchess painted on the wall,
> Looking as if she were alive; I call
> That piece a wonder, now: Frà Pandolf's hands
> Worked busily a day, and there she stands.
> Will't please you sit and look at her?

The Duke admits that he said Frà Pandolf "by design" because the envoy obviously is amazed by the depth of feeling the monk has captured. The Duke further reveals that none draws back the curtain covering the portrait but himself: the first indication that the Duke regards his dead wife as his own private art object.

Apparently the envoy has a puzzled look on his face, for the Duke says that he is not the first to ask how "such a glance" came on his wife's countenance. Snidely the Duke explains:

> Sir, 'twas not
> Her husband's presence only, called that spot
> Of joy into the Duchess' cheek.

He suggests that Frà Pandolf flattered the duchess, easily swayed by such courtesy, by saying:

---

[1] Student theme.

[2] Laurence Perrine, "Browning's Shrewd Duke," *PMLA*, LXXIV (March 1959), 158.

> "Her mantle laps
> Over my Lady's wrist too much," or "Paint
> Must never hope to reproduce the faint
> Half-flush that dies along her throat."

The Duke continues his critical remarks by commenting that

> She had
> A heart—how shall I say?—too soon made glad,
> Too easily impressed: she liked whate'er
> She looked on, and her looks went everywhere.

It is here that his nonchalant façade wears thin and his jealousy fully emerges. It is evident that the Duke abhors the Duchess' spontaneous response to life. He can talk freely about her beauty now that she is far removed, but her presence was unbearable. Most of all, the Duke cannot bear the fact that she ranked his gift of a nine-hundred-years-old name with

> The dropping of the daylight in the West,
> The bough of cherries some officious fool
> Broke in the orchard for her, the white mule
> She rode with round the terrace.

Each would bring the Duchess' "approving speech." The tyrannical Duke resents her overt display of democracy, for he is an aristocrat who demands deference solely on the basis of his title.

To correct the situation, the Duke says he would have to stoop—"and I choose/ Never to stoop." He states his recourse in line 45: "I gave commands;/ Then all smiles stopped together." Having made it perfectly clear to the envoy that he will tolerate no less than worshipful loyalty from his forthcoming bride, the arrogant Duke invites his guest to descend the stairs. He calls attention to one last art treasure:

> Notice Neptune, though,
> Taming a sea-horse, thought a rarity,
> Which Claus of Innsbruck cast in bronze for me!

These closing lines reinforce a number of the Duke's characteristics that have been suggested throughout the poem. First, one gets the impression that the painting he has been appraising is just one more beautiful thing he owns, like the statue of Neptune. Secondly, while "thought a rarity" may be considered an antecedent to Neptune, it could also be that the Duke is suggesting that "taming a sea-horse" is "thought a rarity." He probably identifies his subjugation of his wife with the taming of a sea-horse—especially since the statue was commissioned by him and he almost certainly chose the topic of the work. Lastly, we are reminded that the Duke is a name dropper when he mentions the artist—Claus of Innsbruck—much as he called attention to Frà Pandolf's name in the opening of his speech.

What began as an indictment of "my last Duchess" turns out to be an unfavorable picture of a man totally committed to art, but cursed with an eye for beauty that has blinded his ethical insight. Writing in *Victorian Poetry*, Professor Robert Stevens has said of the Duke: "his love of art is estimable; but it is not adequate . . . to compensate for his insufficiencies as a man."[3] The Duke loves beauty, but in the course of his appreciation, he has lost his humanity. His cold eye cannot perceive the warmth—the joy of life—enjoyed by his last Duchess. His response is twice removed, for he looks to artificial forms to provide the stimulus of experience.

The implication for the artist is this: when creative genius is not channelled toward ethical ends, it loses its value. It is as if Browning (as early as 1842 when the poem was written) foresaw the terrible turn the art for art's sake creed would take in the latter years of the nineteenth century. In *The Picture of Dorian Gray*, Oscar Wilde fully develops the idea—introduced by Browning—that art devoid of ethics is destructive.

Browning's themes are curiously modern. Perhaps his choice of form—the dramatic monologue—enhanced this development. Using this form, he could maintain his artistic distance and let the character speak for himself. One never feels that Browning is manipulating his creation. Rather, the empirical method is applied: the facts are presented, and the reader is left to draw his own conclusions about the character. Browning challenges his reader to make a judgment after examining the evidence. In the end, one concludes that the Duke's view of art is unfulfilling, his life immoral, and his contribution negligible. All of this is realized without one word of interference from the poet.

Technically, Browning's language is intriguing. His word choice in "My Last Duchess" is that of a duke. The use of a conversational tone creates the effect of believability. One feels this familiarity with the Duke because Browning packs each word of his speech with implications. The reader does not have to be told that the Duke's entire speech, despite its eloquence, is a veiled threat.

In "My Last Duchess" Browning has achieved two purposes: he has created a memorable character, and perhaps more importantly, by illustrating to what extent aestheticism can be debased, he has implied that art for its own sake is incomplete. For Browning, poetry is not fulfilling unless it says something of importance about the human condition. One critic has commented that "by revealing the minds, hearts, and souls of many different men and women, he provide[s] a gallery of portraits in which readers of every age and time can recognize all humanity."[4] In "My Last Duchess" Browning combines a talent for characterization with a keen insight into human experience and distinguishes himself as a man of acute sensibilities and a poet of rare genius.

---

[3] Robert Stevens, "Aestheticism in Browning's Early Renaissance Monologues," *Victorian Poetry*, III (Winter 1965), 20.

[4] Rosemary Sprague, *Poems of Robert Browning* (New York, 1964), p. 11.

Longing

Come to me in my dreams, and then
By day I shall be well again!
For then the night will more than pay
The hopeless longing of the day.

Come, as thou cam'st a thousand times,   5
A messenger from radiant climes,
And smile on thy new world, and be
As kind to others as to me!

Or, as thou never cam'st in sooth,
Come now, and let me dream it truth;   10
And part my hair, and kiss my brow,
And say: *My love! why sufferest thou?*

Come to me in my dreams, and then
By day I shall be well again!
For then the night will more than pay   15
The hopeless longing of the day.

MATTHEW ARNOLD

Echo

Come to me in the silence of the night;
  Come in the speaking silence of a dream;
Come with soft rounded cheeks and eyes as bright
  As sunlight on a stream;
    Come back in tears,   5
O memory, hope, love of finished years.

O dream how sweet, too sweet, too bitter sweet,
  Whose wakening should have been in Paradise,
Where souls brimful of love abide and meet;
    Where thirsty longing eyes   10
      Watch the slow door
That opening, letting in, lets out no more.

Yet come to me in dreams, that I may live
  My very life again though cold in death:
Come back to me in dreams, that I may give   15
    Pulse for pulse, breath for breath:

Speak low, lean low,
As long ago, my love, how long ago!

CHRISTINA ROSSETTI

To Make a Prairie

To make a prairie it takes a clover and one bee,
One clover, and a bee,
And revery.
The revery alone will do,
If bees are few.   5

EMILY DICKINSON

Heaven-Haven
A nun takes the veil

I have desired to go
    Where springs not fail,
To fields where flies no sharp and sided hail
    And a few lilies blow.

And I have asked to be   5
    Where no storms come,
Where the green swell is in the havens dumb,
    And out of the swing of the sea.

GERARD MANLEY HOPKINS

Politics

In our time the destiny of man presents its meaning in political terms.—
Thomas Mann

How can I, that girl standing there,
 My attention fix
On Roman or on Russian
Or on Spanish politics?
Yet here's a travelled man that knows   5
What he talks about,
And there's a politician
That has read and thought,

And maybe what they say is true
Of war and war's alarms,   10
But O that I were young again
And held her in my arms!

WILLIAM BUTLER YEATS

Cynara

Last night, ah, yesternight, betwixt her lips and mine
There fell thy shadow, Cynara! thy breath was shed
Upon my soul between the kisses and the wine;
And I was desolate and sick of an old passion,
    Yea, I was desolate and bowed my head: 5
I have been faithful to thee, Cynara! in my fashion.

All night upon mine heart I felt her warm heart beat,
Night-long within mine arms in love and sleep she lay;
Surely the kisses of her bought red mouth were sweet;
But I was desolate and sick of an old passion,   10
    When I awoke and found the dawn was gray:
I have been faithful to thee, Cynara! in my fashion.

I have forgot much, Cynara! gone with the wind,
Flung roses, roses, riotously with the throng,
Dancing, to put thy pale, lost lilies out of mind;   15
But I was desolate and sick of an old passion,
    Yea, all the time, because the dance was long:
I have been faithful to thee, Cynara! in my fashion.

I cried for madder music and for stronger wine,
But when the feast is finished and the lamps expire,   20
Then falls thy shadow, Cynara! the night is thine;
And I am desolate and sick of an old passion,
    Yea, hungry for the lips of my desire:
I have been faithful to thee, Cynara! in my fashion.

ERNEST DOWSON

Mr. Flood's Party

Old Eben Flood, climbing alone one night
Over the hill between the town below
And the forsaken upland hermitage
That held as much as he should ever know
On earth again of home, paused warily.   5

The road was his with not a native near;
And Eben, having leisure, said aloud,
For no man else in Tilbury Town to hear:

"Well, Mr. Flood, we have the harvest moon
Again, and we may not have many more;   10
The bird is on the wing, the poet says,
And you and I have said it here before.
Drink to the bird." He raised up to the light
The jug that he had gone so far to fill,
And answered huskily: "Well, Mr. Flood,   15
Since you propose it, I believe I will."

Alone, as if enduring to the end
A valiant armor of scarred hopes outworn,
He stood there in the middle of the road
Like Roland's ghost winding a silent horn.   20
Below him, in the town among the trees,
Where friends of other days had honored him,
A phantom salutation of the dead
Rang thinly till old Eben's eyes were dim.

Then, as a mother lays her sleeping child   25
Down tenderly, fearing it may awake,
He set the jug down slowly at his feet
With trembling care, knowing that most things break;
And only when assured that on firm earth
It stood, as the uncertain lives of men   30
Assuredly did not, he paced away,
And with his hand extended paused again:

"Well, Mr. Flood, we have not met like this
In a long time; and many a change has come
To both of us, I fear, since last it was   35
We had a drop together. Welcome home!"
Convivially returning with himself,
Again he raised the jug up to the light;
And with an acquiescent quaver said:
"Well, Mr. Flood, if you insist, I might.   40

"Only a very little, Mr. Flood—
For auld lang syne. No more, sir; that will do."
So, for the time, apparently it did,
And Eben evidently thought so too;
For soon amid the silver loneliness   45
Of night he lifted up his voice and sang,

Secure, with only two moons listening,
Until the whole harmonious landscape rang—

"For auld lang syne." The weary throat gave out,
The last word wavered; and the song being done,   50
He raised again the jug regretfully
And shook his head, and was again alone.
There was not much that was ahead of him,
And there was nothing in the town below—
Where strangers would have shut the many doors   55
That many friends had opened long ago.

                                        EDWIN ARLINGTON ROBINSON

Miniver Cheevy

Miniver Cheevy, child of scorn,
    Grew lean while he assailed the seasons;
He wept that he was ever born,
    And he had reasons.

Miniver loved the days of old   5
    When swords were bright and steeds were prancing;
The vision of a warrior bold
    Would set him dancing.

Miniver sighed for what was not,
    And dreamed, and rested from his labors;   10
He dreamed of Thebes and Camelot,
    And Priam's neighbors.

Miniver mourned the ripe renown
    That made so many a name so fragrant;
He mourned Romance, now on the town,   15
    And Art, a vagrant.

Miniver loved the Medici,
    Albeit he had never seen one;
He would have sinned incessantly
    Could he have been one.   20

Miniver cursed the commonplace
    And eyed a khaki suit with loathing;
He missed the medieval grace
    Of iron clothing.

Miniver scorned the gold he sought,   25
    But sore annoyed was he without it;
Miniver thought, and thought, and thought,
    And thought about it.

Miniver Cheevy, born too late,
    Scratched his head and kept on thinking;   30
Miniver coughed, and called it fate,
    And kept on drinking.

EDWIN ARLINGTON ROBINSON

Richard Cory

Whenever Richard Cory went down town,
    We people on the pavement looked at him:
He was a gentleman from sole to crown,
    Clean favored, and imperially slim.

And he was always quietly arrayed,   5
    And he was always human when he talked;
But still he fluttered pulses when he said,
    "Good-morning," and he glittered when he walked.

And he was rich—yes, richer than a king—
    And admirably schooled in every grace: 10
In fine, we thought that he was everything
    To make us wish that we were in his place.

So on we worked, and waited for the light,
    And went without the meat, and cursed the bread;
And Richard Cory, one calm summer night,   15
    Went home and put a bullet through his head.

EDWIN ARLINGTON ROBINSON

Sanctuary

This is the bricklayer; hear the thud
Of his heavy load dumped down on stone.
His lustrous bricks are brighter than blood,
His smoking mortar whiter than bone.

Set each sharp-edged, fire-bitten brick   5
Straight by the plumb-line's shivering length;

Make my marvelous wall so thick,
Dead nor living may shake its strength.

Full as a crystal cup with drink
Is my cell with dreams, and quiet, and cool.   10
Stop, old man! You must leave a chink;
How can I breathe? *You can't, you fool!*

ELINOR WYLIE

Two Realities

A waggon passed with scarlet wheels
    And a yellow body, shining new.
"Splendid!" said I. "How fine it feels
To be alive, when beauty peels
    The grimy husk from life." And you   5

Said, "Splendid!" and I thought you'd seen
    That waggon blazing down the street;
But I looked and saw that your gaze had been
On a child that was kicking an obscene
    Brown ordure with his feet.   10

Our souls are elephants, thought I,
    Remote behind a prisoning grill,
With trunks thrust out to peer and pry
And pounce upon reality;
    And each at his own sweet will   15
Seizes the bun that he likes best
And passes over all the rest.

ALDOUS HUXLEY

The Leg in the Subway

When I saw the woman's leg on the floor of the subway train,
Protrude beyond the panel (while her body overflowed my mind's
    eye),
When I saw the pink stocking, black shoe, curve bulging with
    warmth,
The delicate etching of the hair behind the flesh-colored gauze,
When I saw the ankle of Mrs. Nobody going nowhere for a nickel,   5

When I saw this foot motionless on the moving motionless floor,
My mind caught on a nail of a distant star, I was wrenched out
Of the reality of the subway ride, I hung in a socket of distance:
And this is what I saw:

The long tongue of the earth's speed was licking the leg,   10
Upward and under and around went the long tongue of speed:
It was made of a flesh invisible, it dripped the saliva of miles:
It drank moment, lit shivers of insecurity in niches between bones:
It was full of eyes, it stopped licking to look at the passengers:
It was as alive as a worm, and busier than anybody in the train: 15

It spoke saying: To whom does this leg belong? Is it a bonus leg
For the rush hour? Is it a forgotten leg? Among the many
Myriads of legs did an extra leg fall in from the Out There?
O Woman, sliced off bodily by the line of the panel, shall I roll
Your leg into the abdominal nothing, among the digestive teeth?   20
Or shall I fit it in with the pillars that hold up the headlines?
But nobody spoke, though all the faces were talking silently,
As the train zoomed, a zipper closing up swiftly the seam of time.

Alas, said the long tongue of the speed of the earth quite faintly,
What is one to do with an incorrigible leg that will not melt—   25
But everybody stopped to listen to the train vomiting cauldrons
Of silence, while somebody's jolted-out after-thought trickled down
The blazing shirt-front solid with light bulbs, and just then
The planetary approach of the next station exploded atoms of light,
And when the train stopped, the leg had grown a surprising mate,   30
And the long tongue had slipped hurriedly out through the window:

I perceived through the hole left by the nail of the star in my mind
How civilization was as dark as a wood and dimensional with things
And how birds dipped in chromium sang in the crevices of our
    deeds.

OSCAR WILLIAMS

Readings, Forecasts, Personal Guidance

It is not—I swear it by every fiery omen to be seen these nights in
    every quarter of the heavens, I affirm it by all the monstrous
    portents of the earth and of the sea—
It is not that my belief in the true and mystic science is shaken,
    nor that I have lost faith in the magic of the cards, or in the
    augury of dreams, or in the great and good divinity of the stars.

No, I know still whose science fits the promise to the inquirer's
   need, invariably, for a change: Mine. My science foretells the
   wished-for journey, the business adjustment, the handsome
   stranger. (Each of these is considered a decided change.)
And I know whose skill weighs matrimony, risks a flyer in steel or
   wheat against the vagaries of the moon.
(Planet of dreams, of mothers and of children, goddess of sailors and
   of all adventurers, forgive the liberty. But a man must eat.) My
   skill,   5
Mine, and the cunning and the patience. (Two dollars for the horo-
   scope in brief and five for a twelve months' forecast in detail.)

No, it is this: The wonders that I have seen with my own eyes.

It is this: That still these people know, as I do not, that what has
   never been on earth before may still well come to pass,
That always, always there are new and brighter things beneath the
   sun,
That surely, in bargain basements or in walk-up flats, it must be so
   that still from time to time they hear wild angel voices speak.   10
It is this: That I have known them for what they are,
Seen thievery written plainly in their planets, found greed and
   murder and worse in their birth dates and their numbers, guilt
   etched in every line of every palm;
But still a light burns through the eyes they turn to me, a need more
   moving than the damned and dirty dollars (which I must take)
   that form the pattern of their larger hopes and deeper fears.

And it comes to this: That always I feel another hand, not mine,
   has drawn and turned the card to find some incredible ace,
Always another word I did not write appears in the spirit parchment
   prepared by me,   15
Always another face I do not know shows in the dream, the crystal
   globe, or the flame.

And finally, this: Corrupt, in a world bankrupt and corrupt, what
   have I got to do with these miracles?
If they want miracles, let them consult someone else.
Would they, in extremity, ask them of a physician? Or expect them,
   in desperation, of an attorney? Or of a priest? Or of a poet?

Nevertheless, a man must eat.   20
Mrs. Raeburn is expected at five. She will communicate with a number of friends and relatives long deceased.

KENNETH FEARING

Museums

Museums offer us, running from among the buses,
A centrally heated refuge, parquet floors and sarcophaguses,
Into whose tall fake porches we hurry without a sound
Like a beetle under a brick that lies, useless, on the ground.
Warmed and cajoled by the silence the cowed cypher revives,   5
Mirrors himself in the cases of pots, paces himself by marble lives,
Makes believe it was he that was the glory that was Rome,
Soft on his cheek the nimbus of other people's martyrdom,
And then returns to the street, his mind an arena where sprawls
Any number of consumptive Keatses and dying Gauls.   10

                    LOUIS MACNEICE

The British Museum Reading Room

Under the hive-like dome the stooping haunted readers
Go up and down the alleys, tap the cells of knowledge—
    Honey and wax, the accumulation of years—
Some on commission, some for the love of learning,
Some because they have nothing better to do   5
Or because they hope these walls of books will deaden
    The drumming of the demon in their ears.

Cranks, hacks, poverty-stricken scholars,
In pince-nez, period hats or romantic beards
    And cherishing their hobby or their doom.   10
Some are too much alive and some are asleep
Hanging like bats in a world of inverted values,
Folded up in themselves in a world which is safe and silent:
    This is the British Museum Reading Room.

Out on the steps in the sun the pigeons are courting,   15
Puffing their ruffs and sweeping their tails or taking
    A sun-bath at their ease
And under the totem poles—the ancient terror—
Between the enormous fluted Ionic columns
There seeps from heavily jowled or hawk-like foreign faces   20
    The guttural sorrow of the refugees.

                    LOUIS MACNEICE

Hollywood

Farthest from any war, unique in time
Like Athens or Baghdad, this city lies
Between dry purple mountains and the sea.
The air is clear and famous, every day
Bright as a postcard, bringing bungalows   5
   And sights. The broad nights advertise
For love and music and astronomy.

Heart of a continent, the hearts converge
On open boulevards where palms are nursed
With flare-pots like a grove, on villa roads   10
Where castles cultivated like a style
Breed fabulous metaphors in foreign stone,
   And on enormous movie lots
Where history repeats its vivid blunders.

Alice and Cinderella are most real.   15
Here may the tourist, quite sincere at last,
Rest from his dream of travels. All is new,
No ruins claim his awe, and permanence,
Despised like customs, fails at every turn.
   Here where the eccentric thrives,   20
Laughter and love are leading industries.

Luck is another. Here the body-guard,
The parasite, the scholar are well paid,
The quack erects his alabaster office,
The moron and the genius are enshrined,   25
And the mystic makes a fortune quietly;
   Here all superlatives come true
And beauty is marketed like a basic food.

O can we understand it? Is it ours,
A crude whim of a beginning people,   30
A private orgy in a secluded spot?
Or alien like the word *harem,* or true
Like hideous Pittsburgh or depraved Atlanta?
   Is adolescence just as vile
As this its architecture and its talk?   35

Or are they parvenus, like boys and girls?
Or ours and happy, cleverest of all?

Yes. Yes. Though glamorous to the ignorant
This is the simplest city, a new school.
What is more nearly ours? If soul can mean   40
    The civilization of the brain,
This is a soul, a possibly proud Florence.

KARL SHAPIRO

9
Mutability

The lives of some men are devoted to a search for order and permanence in a world that is unstable. It is disconcerting when one is forced to admit that there is very little in life that is permanent, and that about the only thing in life that is certain is change itself. Man has tested his power and ingenuity through the years in an effort to slow down the inexorable pace of time. It is some comfort to the average man to realize that even those who wield power and authority are powerless to overcome "time's fell hand." The frowning visage of the tyrant Ozymandias, lying half buried in the sand, is mute evidence of the futility of man's effort to preserve the ephemeral.

The poets have done as well as mere man can to counter the effects of time. That poetry can preserve a man's fame or a woman's beauty is not an idle boast, as Shakespeare reminds us in several sonnets. The poets never tire of reminding us of the passage of time. The *carpe diem* theme has an ancient and illustrious heritage. As the poems in this section reveal, "Time's wingèd chariot" makes ominous sounds, especially to the young and to the lover. When Herrick reminds the ladies that "this same flower that smiles today,/ Tomorrow will be dying," his argument is not entirely academic. The implied "wisdom" in the *carpe diem* theme is, to borrow the phrase of another poet, that the young should "take the cash, and let the credit go."

Even the few works listed below indicate the extent of the theme of mutability in other genres. The range and sweep of such novels as Proust's *Remembrance of Things Past*, Powell's *The Music of Time*, and Durrell's *Alexandria Quartet* offer striking evidence that the theme lends itself especially well to development in the novel. Plays such as Wilder's *Our Town* and Williams's *The Glass Menagerie* show that the theme of mutability can be effectively developed despite the limitations of the stage.

READINGS IN OTHER GENRES

PLAYS

Anton Chekhov, *The Cherry Orchard, The Three Sisters*
Lillian Hellman, *Another Part of the Forest, The Little Foxes*

Eugene O'Neill, *Strange Interlude*
George Bernard Shaw, *Heartbreak House*
Thornton Wilder, *Our Town*
Tennessee Williams, *Summer and Smoke, The Glass Menagerie*

NOVELS

Heinrich Böll, *Billiards at Half-Past Nine*
Miguel de Cervantes, *Don Quixote*
Lawrence Durrell, *The Alexandria Quartet*
William Faulkner, *Absalom, Absalom!*
E. M. Forster, *Howard's End*
Thomas Mann, *Buddenbrooks*
Anthony Powell, *The Music of Time*
Marcel Proust, *Remembrance of Things Past*
Muriel Spark, *Memento Mori*
Evelyn Waugh, *Brideshead Revisited*
Oscar Wilde, *The Picture of Dorian Gray*
Virginia Woolf, *Orlando*

SHORT STORIES

Anton Chekhov, "The New Villa"
William Faulkner, "A Rose for Emily"
Thomas Mann, "Disorder and Early Sorrow"
Katherine Mansfield, "A Dill Pickle"
Seán O'Faoláin, "A Touch of Autumn in the Air"
Katherine Anne Porter, "Old Mortality"
John Steinbeck, "The Leader of the People"
Ivan Turgenev, "A Living Relic"

That Time of Year Thou Mayst in Me Behold

That time of year thou mayst in me behold
When yellow leaves, or none, or few, do hang
Upon those boughs which shake against the cold,
Bare ruined choirs, where late the sweet birds sang.
In me thou see'st the twilight of such day   5
As after sunset fadeth in the west;
Which by and by black night doth take away,
Death's second self, that seals up all in rest.
In me thou see'st the glowing of such fire
That on the ashes of his youth doth lie,   10

As the death-bed whereon it must expire,
Consumed with that which it was nourished by.
   This thou perceiv'st, which makes thy love more strong,
   To love that well which thou must leave ere long.

WILLIAM SHAKESPEARE

When I Have Seen by Time's Fell Hand Defaced

When I have seen by Time's fell hand defaced
The rich proud cost of outworn buried age;
When sometime lofty towers I see down-razed,
And brass eternal slave to mortal rage;
When I have seen the hungry ocean gain   5
Advantage on the kingdom of the shore,
And the firm soil win of the watery main,
Increasing store with loss and loss with store;
When I have seen such interchange of state,
Or state itself confounded to decay;   10
Ruin hath taught me thus to ruminate,
That Time will come and take my love away.
   This thought is as a death, which cannot choose
   But weep to have that which it fears to lose.

WILLIAM SHAKESPEARE

Song: To Celia

Come, my Celia, let us prove,
While we may, the sports of love;
Time will not be ours for ever:
He at length our good will sever.
Spend not then his gifts in vain: 5
Suns that set, may rise again;
But if once we lose this light,
'Tis with us perpetual night.
Why should we defer our joys?
Fame and rumor are but toys.   10
Cannot we delude the eyes
Of a few poor household spies?
Or his easier ears beguile,
Thus removèd by our wile?
'Tis no sin love's fruits to steal;   15
But the sweet theft to reveal:

To be taken, to be seen,
These have crimes accounted been.

BEN JONSON

To the Virgins, to Make Much of Time

Gather ye rosebuds while ye may,
   Old time is still a-flying;
And this same flower that smiles today,
   Tomorrow will be dying.

The glorious lamp of heaven, the sun,   5
   The higher he's a-getting
The sooner will his race be run,
   And nearer he's to setting.

That age is best which is the first,
   When youth and blood are warmer;   10
But being spent, the worse, and worst
   Times still succeed the former.

Then be not coy, but use your time,
   And while ye may, go marry;
For having lost but once your prime,   15
   You may for ever tarry.

ROBERT HERRICK

Go, Lovely Rose

Go, lovely rose!
Tell her that wastes her time and me,
   That now she knows,
When I resemble her to thee,
   How sweet and fair she seems to be.   5

Tell her that's young,
And shuns to have her graces spied,
   That hadst thou sprung
In deserts, where no men abide,
   Thou must have uncommended died.   10

Small is the worth
Of beauty from the light retired;
   Bid her come forth,

Suffer her self to be desired,
      And not blush so to be admired.   15

Then die! that she,
The common fate of all things rare,
      May read in thee;
How small a part of time they share,
      That are so wondrous sweet and fair!   20

                                        EDMUND WALLER

How Soon Hath Time

How soon hath Time, the subtle thief of youth,
      Stol'n on his wing my three-and-twentieth year!
      My hasting days fly on with full career,
      But my late spring no bud or blossom shew'th.
Perhaps my semblance might deceive the truth,   5
      That I to manhood am arrived so near,
      And inward ripeness doth much less appear,
      That some more timely-happy spirits indu'th.[1]
Yet it be less or more, or soon or slow,
      It shall be still in strictest measure even,   10
      To that same lot, however mean or high,
Toward which Time leads me, and the will of Heaven;
      All is, if I have grace to use it so,
      As ever in my great Taskmaster's eye.

                                        JOHN MILTON

[1] Endoweth.

To His Coy Mistress

Had we but world enough, and time,
This coyness, lady, were no crime.
We would sit down, and think which way
To walk, and pass our long love's day.
Thou by the Indian Ganges' side   5
Should'st rubies find; I by the tide
Of Humber would complain. I would
Love you ten years before the flood:
And you should, if you please, refuse
Till the conversion of the Jews.   10
My vegetable love should grow
Vaster than empires, and more slow;
An hundred years should go to praise

Thine eyes, and on thy forehead gaze;
Two hundred to adore each breast;   15
But thirty thousand to the rest.
An age at least to every part,
And the last age should show your heart.
For, lady, you deserve this state;
Nor would I love at lower rate.   20
   But at my back I always hear
Time's wingèd chariot hurrying near;
And yonder all before us lie
Deserts of vast eternity.
Thy beauty shall no more be found,   25
Nor in thy marble vault shall sound
My echoing song; then worms shall try
That long-preserved virginity,
And your quaint honor turn to dust,
And into ashes all my lust.   30
The grave's a fine and private place,
But none I think do there embrace.
   Now therefore, while the youthful hue
Sits on thy skin like morning dew,
And while thy willing soul transpires   35
At every pore with instant fires,
Now let us sport us while we may;
And now, like amorous birds of prey,
Rather at once our time devour,
Than languish in his slow-chapped power.   40
Let us roll all our strength, and all
Our sweetness, up into one ball,
And tear our pleasures with rough strife,
Through the iron gates of life.
Thus, though we cannot make our sun   45
Stand still, yet we will make him run.

                  ANDREW MARVELL

John Anderson, My Jo

John Anderson, my jo,[1] John,
   When we were first acquent,
Your locks were like the raven,
   Your bonnie brow was brent;[2]
But now your brow is beld,[3] John,   5
   Your locks are like the snaw;

---

[1] Sweetheart.   [2] Smooth.   [3] Bald.

But blessings on your frosty pow,[4]
  John Anderson, my jo!

John Anderson, my jo, John,
  We clamb the hill thegither;   10
And mony a canty[5] day, John,
  We've had wi' ane anither:
Now we maun totter down, John,
  And hand in hand we'll go,
And sleep thegither at the foot,   15
  John Anderson, my jo!

ROBERT BURNS

[4] Head.   [5] Happy.

Oft, in the Stilly Night

Oft, in the stilly night,
  Ere Slumber's chain has bound me,
Fond Memory brings the light
  Of other days around me;
    The smiles, the tears,   5
    Of boyhood's years,
The words of love then spoken;
    The eyes that shone,
    Now dimmed and gone,
  The cheerful hearts now broken!   10
Thus, in the stilly night,
  Ere Slumber's chain has bound me,
Sad Memory brings the light
  Of other days around me.

When I remember all   15
  The friends, so linked together,
I've seen around me fall,
  Like leaves in wintry weather;
    I feel like one
    Who treads alone   20
Some banquet-hall deserted,
    Whose lights are fled,
    Whose garlands dead,
  And all but he departed!
Thus, in the stilly night,   25
  Ere Slumber's chain has bound me,
Sad Memory brings the light
  Of other days around me.

THOMAS MOORE

The Harp That Once through Tara's Halls

The harp that once through Tara's halls
   The soul of music shed,
Now hangs as mute on Tara's walls
   As if that soul were fled.—
So sleeps the pride of former days,   5
   So glory's thrill is o'er.
And hearts, that once beat high for praise,
   Now feel that pulse no more!
No more to chiefs and ladies bright
   The harp of Tara swells;   10
The chord alone, that breaks at night,
   Its tale of ruin tells.
Thus Freedom now so seldom wakes,
   The only throb she gives,
Is when some heart indignant breaks,   15
   To show that still she lives.

THOMAS MOORE

Rondeau

Jenny kissed me when we met,
   Jumping from the chair she sat in;
Time, you thief, who love to get
   Sweets into your list, put that in:
Say I'm weary, say I'm sad,   5
   Say that health and wealth have missed me,
Say I'm growing old, but add,
   Jenny kissed me.

LEIGH HUNT

Mutability

I

The flower that smiles to-day
   Tomorrow dies;
All that we wish to stay
   Tempts and then flies.
What is this world's delight?   5

Lightning that mocks the night,
   Brief even as bright.

II

Virtue, how frail it is!
   Friendship how rare!
Love, how it sells poor bliss   10
   For proud despair!
But we, though soon they fall,
Survive their joy, and all
   Which ours we call.

III

Whilst skies are blue and bright,   15
   Whilst flowers are gay,
Whilst eyes that change ere night
   Make glad the day;
Whilst yet the calm hours creep,
Dream thou—and from thy sleep   20
   Then wake to weep.

PERCY BYSSHE SHELLEY

Lines

I

When the lamp is shattered
The light in the dust lies dead—
   When the cloud is scattered
The rainbow's glory is shed.
   When the lute is broken,   5
Sweet tones are remembered not;
   When the lips have spoken,
Loved accents are soon forgot.

II

   As music and splendor
Survive not the lamp and the lute,   10
   The heart's echoes render
No song when the spirit is mute,—
   No song but sad dirges,
Like the wind through a ruined cell,

Or the mournful surges   15
That ring the dead seaman's knell.

III

When hearts have once mingled
Love first leaves the well-built nest,—
    The weak one is singled
To endure what it once possessed.   20
    O, Love! who bewailest
The frailty of all things here,
    Why choose you the frailest
For your cradle, your home and your bier?

IV

Its passions will rock thee   25
As the storms rock the ravens on high:
    Bright reason will mock thee,
Like the sun from a wintry sky.
    From thy nest every rafter
Will rot, and thine eagle home   30
    Leave thee naked to laughter,
When leaves fall and cold winds come.

PERCY BYSSHE SHELLEY

Ozymandias

I met a traveller from an antique land
Who said: Two vast and trunkless legs of stone
Stand in the desert. Near them, on the sand,
Half sunk, a shattered visage lies, whose frown,
And wrinkled lip, and sneer of cold command,   5
Tell that its sculptor well those passions read
Which yet survive, stamped on these lifeless things,
The hand that mocked them, and the heart that fed:
And on the pedestal these words appear:
"My name is Ozymandias, king of kings: 10
Look on my works, ye Mighty, and despair!"
Nothing beside remains. Round the decay
Of that colossal wreck, boundless and bare
The lone and level sands stretch far away.

PERCY BYSSHE SHELLEY

On Seeing the Elgin Marbles

My spirit is too weak—mortality
  Weighs heavily on me like unwilling sleep,
  And each imagined pinnacle and steep
Of godlike hardship, tells me I must die
Like a sick eagle looking at the sky.   5
  Yet 'tis a gentle luxury to weep
  That I have not the cloudy winds to keep,
Fresh for the opening of the morning's eye.
Such dim conceivèd glories of the brain
  Bring round the heart an indescribable feud;   10
So do these wonders a most dizzy pain,
  That mingles Grecian grandeur with the rude
Wasting of old Time—with a billowy main—
  A sun—a shadow of a magnitude.

JOHN KEATS

Tears, Idle Tears

  Tears, idle tears, I know not what they mean,
Tears from the depth of some divine despair
Rise in the heart, and gather to the eyes,
In looking on the happy autumn-fields,
And thinking of the days that are no more.   5

  Fresh as the first beam glittering on a sail,
That brings our friends up from the underworld,
Sad as the last which reddens over one
That sinks with all we love below the verge;
So sad, so fresh, the days that are no more.   10

  Ah, sad and strange as in dark summer dawns
The earliest pipe of half-awakened birds
To dying ears, when unto dying eyes
The casement slowly grows a glimmering square;
So sad, so strange, the days that are no more.   15

  Dear as remembered kisses after death,
And sweet as those by hopeless fancy feigned
On lips that are for others; deep as love,
Deep as first love, and wild with all regret;
O Death in Life, the days that are no more!   20

ALFRED, LORD TENNYSON

from *The Rubáiyát of Omar Khayyám*

3

And, as the Cock crew, those who stood before
The Tavern shouted—"Open, then, the Door!
   You know how little while we have to stay,
And, once departed, may return no more."

7

Come, fill the Cup, and in the fire of Spring   5
Your Winter-garment of Repentance fling;
   The Bird of Time has but a little way
To flutter—and the Bird is on the Wing.

8

Whether at Naishápúr or Babylon,
Whether the Cup with sweet or bitter run,   10
   The Wine of Life keeps oozing drop by drop,
The Leaves of Life keep falling one by one.

13

Some for the Glories of This World; and some
Sigh for the Prophet's Paradise to come;
   Ah, take the Cash, and let the Credit go,   15
Nor heed the rumble of a distant Drum!

15

And those who husbanded the Golden Grain,
And those who flung it to the winds like Rain,
   Alike to no such aureate Earth are turned
As, buried once, Men want dug up again.   20

16

The Worldly Hope men set their Hearts upon
Turns Ashes—or it prospers; and anon,
   Like Snow upon the Desert's dusty Face,
Lighting a little hour or two—is gone.

19

I sometimes think that never blows so red   25
The Rose as where some buried Caesar bled;

That every Hyacinth the Garden wears
Dropped in her Lap from some once lovely Head.

24

Ah, make the most of what we yet may spend,
Before we too into the Dust descend;   30
   Dust into Dust, and under Dust to lie,
Sans Wine, sans Song, sans Singer, and—sans End!

47

When You and I behind the Veil are past,
Oh, but the long, long while the World shall last,
   Which of our Coming and Departure heeds   35
As the Sea's self should heed a pebble-cast.

63

Oh threats of Hell and Hopes of Paradise!
One thing at least is certain—*This* Life flies;
   One thing is certain and the rest is Lies—
The Flower that once has blown forever dies.   40

71

The Moving Finger writes, and, having writ,
Moves on; nor all your Piety nor Wit
   Shall lure it back to cancel half a Line,
Nor all your Tears wash out a Word of it.

93

Indeed the Idols I have loved so long   45
Have done my credit in this World much wrong,
   Have drowned my Glory in a shallow Cup,
And sold my Reputation for a Song.

96

Yet Ah, that Spring should vanish with the Rose!
That Youth's sweet-scented manuscript should close!   50
   The Nightingale that in the branches sang,
Ah whence, and whither flown again, who knows!

100

Yon rising Moon that looks for us again—
How oft hereafter will she wax and wane;

How oft hereafter rising look for us   55
Through this same Garden—and for *one* in vain!

101

And when like her, O Sákí, you shall pass
Among the Guests Star-scattered on the Grass,
    And in your joyous errand reach the spot
Where I made One—turn down an empty Glass!   60

EDWARD FITZGERALD

The Ballad of Dead Ladies
(From François Villon)[1]

Tell me now in what hidden way is
    Lady Flora the lovely Roman?
Where's Hipparchia, and where is Thais,
    Neither of them the fairer woman?
    Where is Echo, beheld of no man,   5
Only heard on river and mere—
    She whose beauty was more than human? . . .
But where are the snows of yester-year?

Where's Héloise, the learned nun,
    For whose sake Abeillard, I ween,   10
Lost manhood and put priesthood on?
    (From Love he won such dule and teen!)
    And where, I pray you, is the Queen
Who willed that Buridan should steer
    Sewed in a sack's mouth down the Seine? . . .   15
But where are the snows of yester-year?

White Queen Blanche, like a queen of lilies,
    With a voice like any mermaiden—
Bertha Broadfoot, Beatrice, Alice,
    And Ermengarde the lady of Maine—   20
    And that good Joan whom Englishmen
At Rouen doomed and burned her there—
    Mother of God, where are they then? . . .
    But where are the snows of yester-year?

---

[1] Rossetti's poem is a translation of "Ballade des Dames du Temps Jadis," by François Villon, the medieval French poet.

Nay, never ask this week, fair lord,   25
    Where they are gone, nor yet this year,
Except with this for an overword—
    But where are the snows of yester-year?

DANTE GABRIEL ROSSETTI

With Rue My Heart Is Laden

With rue my heart is laden
    For golden friends I had,
For many a rose-lipt maiden
    And many a lightfoot lad.

By brooks too broad for leaping   5
    The lightfoot boys are laid;
The rose-lipt girls are sleeping
    In fields where roses fade.

A. E. HOUSMAN

Why Should Not Old Men Be Mad?

Why should not old men be mad?
Some have known a likely lad
That had a sound fly-fisher's wrist
Turn to a drunken journalist;
A girl that knew all Dante once   5
Live to bear children to a dunce;
A Helen of social welfare dream,
Climb on a wagonette to scream.
Some think it a matter of course that chance
Should starve good men and bad advance,   10
That if their neighbours figured plain,
As though upon a lighted screen,
No single story would they find
Of an unbroken happy mind,
A finish worthy of the start.   15
Young men know nothing of this sort,
Observant old men know it well;
And when they know what old books tell,
And that no better can be had,
Know why an old man should be mad.   20

WILLIAM BUTLER YEATS

Time, You Old Gypsy Man

Time, you old gypsy man,
   Will you not stay,
Put up your caravan
   Just for one day?

All things I'll give you   5
Will you be my guest,
Bells for your jennet
Of silver the best,
Goldsmiths shall beat you
A great golden ring,   10
Peacocks shall bow to you,
Little boys sing,
Oh, and sweet girls will
Festoon you with may.
Time, you old gypsy,   15
Why hasten away?

Last week in Babylon,
Last night in Rome,
Morning, and in the crush
Under Paul's dome;   20
Under Paul's dial
You tighten your rein—
Only a moment,
And off once again;
Off to some city   25
Now blind in the womb,
Off to another
Ere that's in the tomb.

Time, you old gypsy man,
   Will you not stay,   30
Put up your caravan
   Just for one day?

RALPH HODGSON

Blue Girls

Twirling your blue skirts, traveling the sward
Under the towers of your seminary,
Go listen to your teachers old and contrary
Without believing a word.

Tie the white fillets then about your lustrous hair   5
And think no more of what will come to pass
Than bluebirds that go walking on the grass
And chattering on the air.

Practice your beauty, blue girls, before it fail;
And I will cry with my loud lips and publish   10
Beauty which all our power shall never establish,
It is so frail.

For I could tell you a story which is true:
I know a lady with a terrible tongue,
Blear eyes fallen from blue,   15
All her perfections tarnished—and yet it is not long
Since she was lovelier than any of you.

                              JOHN CROWE RANSOM

You, Andrew Marvell

And here face down beneath the sun
And here upon earth's noonward height
To feel the always coming on
The always rising of the night

To feel creep up the curving east   5
The earthly chill of dusk and slow
Upon those under lands the vast
And ever-climbing shadow grow

And strange at Ecbatan the trees
Take leaf by leaf the evening strange   10
The flooding dark about their knees
The mountains over Persia change

And now at Kermanshah the gate
Dark empty and the withered grass
And through the twilight now the late   15
Few travelers in the westward pass

And Baghdad darken and the bridge
Across the silent river gone
And through Arabia the edge
Of evening widen and steal on   20

And deepen on Palmyra's street
The wheel rut in the ruined stone
And Lebanon fade out and Crete
High through the clouds and overblown

And over Sicily the air   25
Still flashing with the landward gulls
And loom and slowly disappear
The sails above the shadowy hulls

And Spain go under and the shore
Of Africa the gilded sand   30
And evening vanish and no more
The low pale light across that land

Nor now the long light on the sea—

And here face downward in the sun
To feel how swift how secretly   35
The shadow of the night comes on . . .

ARCHIBALD MACLEISH

Moo!

Summer is over, the old cow said,
And they'll shut me up in a draughty shed
To milk me by lamplight in the cold,
But I won't give much for I am old.
It's long ago that I came here   5
Gay and slim as a woodland deer;
It's long ago that I heard the roar
Of Smith's white bull by the sycamore.
And now there are bones where my flesh should be;
My backbone sags like an old roof tree.   10
And an apple snatched in a moment's frolic
Is just so many days of colic.
I'm neither a Jersey nor Holstein now
But only a faded sort of cow.
My calves are veal and I had as lief   15
That I could lay me down as beef;
Somehow, they always kill by halves,—
Why not take me when they take my calves?
Birch turns yellow and sumac red,
I've seen this all before, she said.   20
I'm tired of the field and tired of the shed.
There's no more grass, there's no more clover;
Summer is over, summer is over.

ROBERT HILLYER

10
Reconciliation and Acceptance

There comes a time when everyone must reconcile himself to life's vicissitudes and accept its consequences to achieve maturity. Such reconciliation takes many forms: Job says, "The Lord giveth and the Lord taketh away, blessed be the name of the Lord"; Housman has one of his desperate youths say that the troubles of life will inevitably occur, and "bear them we can, and if we can we must." Milton considers that he is serving God even in the adversity of his blindness and seems to achieve a calm happiness. Donne asks God to seize and capture him to make him accept and thus be free. Emily Dickinson accepts heaven with an act of faith.

Whatever the circumstances, the mature man has observed, and has often rejected, but has finally come to some sort of acceptance either of God or of a godless universe. When the world is accepted without God, a substitute such as Arnold's is frequently found—"Ah, love, let us be true to one another." Housman says that one must learn to "train for ill," and Hemingway, in stories and novels, counsels the reader to set himself standards to live by in a godless world.

The theme is more often treated as a central idea by the poet than by the dramatist, novelist, or short-story writer. It does come up again and again in genres other than poetry, but usually as a collateral theme.

READINGS IN OTHER GENRES

PLAYS

James M. Barrie, *What Every Woman Knows*
Samuel Beckett, *Endgame, Waiting for Godot*
Robert Bolt, *A Man for All Seasons*
Anton Chekhov, *Uncle Vanya*
T. S. Eliot, *The Cocktail Party*
Lillian Hellman, *The Autumn Garden*
Sidney Howard, *They Knew What They Wanted*

Sean O'Casey, *Juno and the Paycock*
Eugene O'Neill, *Beyond the Horizon*
Arthur Wing Pinero, *The Thunderbolt*
William Shakespeare, *The Tempest, The Winter's Tale*
Leo Tolstoy, *The Power of Darkness*

NOVELS

Joseph Conrad, *Under Western Eyes*
Graham Greene, *The Heart of the Matter*
Nathaniel Hawthorne, *The Scarlet Letter*
Ernest Hemingway, *The Old Man and the Sea*
John Knowles, *A Separate Peace*
Selma Lagerlof, *The Story of Gosta Berling*
Anthony Trollope, *The Last Chronicle of Barset*
Robert Penn Warren, *All the King's Men*

SHORT STORIES

Elizabeth Bowen, "A Queer Heart"
E. M. Forster, "The Story of the Siren"
J. F. Powers, "The Valiant Woman"
John Steinbeck, "The Leader of the People"

No, Time, Thou Shalt Not Boast That I Do Change

No, Time, thou shalt not boast that I do change;
Thy pyramids built up with newer might
To me are nothing novel, nothing strange;
They are but dressings of a former sight.
Our dates are brief, and therefore we admire   5
What thou dost foist upon us that is old;
And rather make them born to our desire
Than think that we before have heard them told.
Thy registers and thee I both defy,
Not wondering at the present nor the past,   10
For thy records and what we see doth lie,
Made more or less by thy continual haste.
    This I do vow, and this shall ever be:
    I will be true, despite thy scythe and thee.

WILLIAM SHAKESPEARE

To Heaven

Good and great God! can I not think of thee,
    But it must straight my melancholy be?
Is it interpreted in me disease,
    That, laden with my sins, I seek for ease?
O be thou witness, that the reins[1] dost know   5
    And hearts of all, if I be sad for show;
And judge me after, if I dare pretend
    To aught but grace, or aim at other end.
As thou art all, so be thou all to me,
    First, midst, and last, converted One and Three!   10
My faith, my hope, my love; and, in this state,
    My judge, my witness, and my advocate!
Where have I been this while exiled from thee,
    And whither rapt, now thou but stoop'st to me?
Dwell, dwell here still! O, being everywhere,   15
    How can I doubt to find thee ever here?
I know my state, both full of shame and scorn,
    Conceived in sin, and unto labor born,
Standing with fear, and must with horror fall,
    And destined unto judgment, after all.   20
I feel my griefs too, and there scarce is ground
    Upon my flesh t' inflict another wound;
Yet dare I not complain or wish for death
    With holy Paul, lest it be thought the breath
Of discontent; or that these prayers be   25
    For weariness of life, not love of thee.

BEN JONSON

[1] The region of the kidneys or loins, as the seat of the affections.

At the Round Earth's Imagined Corners

At the round earth's imagined corners, blow
Your trumpets, angels; and arise, arise
From death, you numberless infinities
Of souls, and to your scattered bodies go;
All whom the flood did, and fire shall, o'erthrow,   5
All whom war, dearth, age, agues, tyrannies,
Despair, law, chance hath slain, and you whose eyes
Shall behold God, and never taste death's woe.
But let them sleep, Lord, and me mourn a space;

For if, above all these, my sins abound,   10
'Tis late to ask abundance of Thy grace
When we are there. Here on this lowly ground,
Teach me how to repent; for that's as good
As if Thou hadst sealed my pardon with Thy blood.

                              JOHN DONNE

Batter My Heart, Three-Personed God

Batter my heart, three-personed God; for you
As yet but knock, breathe, shine, and seek to mend;
That I may rise and stand, o'erthrow me and bend
Your force to break, blow, burn and make me new.
I, like an usurped town, to another due,   5
Labor to admit you, but Oh, to no end;
Reason, your viceroy in me, me should defend,
But is captived and proves weak or untrue.
Yet dearly I love you and would be lovèd fain,
But am betrothed unto your enemy;   10
Divorce me, untie or break that knot again,
Take me to you, imprison me, for I
Except you enthrall me, never shall be free,
Nor ever chaste, except you ravish me.

                              JOHN DONNE

No. 14 of Donne's *Holy Sonnets*

John E. Parish

Within the last ten years four critics have published articles about No. 14 of Donne's *Holy Sonnets*. In the first (*Explicator*, March 1953), J. C. Levenson suggested that in the opening quatrain God is compared to a tinker and sinful man to a damaged pewter vessel. Later in the same year (*Explicator*, December 1953) George Herman expressed doubt that the image of a tinker is implied. More likely, he felt, the sonnet is unified by a single extended metaphor which (if it could be realized) would demonstrate the part each Person of the Trinity plays in saving the penitent, since (according to Herman) in the first quatrain God the Father is implored to *break* rather than merely *knock*, the Holy Ghost to *blow* rather than simply *breathe*, and God the Son (Sun) to *burn* rather than gently *shine* on the sinner's heart, "which is also the town and a woman." In the words *make me new* Herman believed that all three Persons are beseeched to act on the heart-town-woman and that, as applied to the woman, *make me* is a plea (like that in the sestet) to be violated. "Clearly, *make* had the appropriate popular meaning in Donne's day that it has today, and it seems to me likely that Donne here consciously employed the pun."

After three years George Knox replied to Herman (*Explicator,* October 1956), whom he wished to spare "the strain of trying to imagine the poet in the role of woman." According to Knox, "the traditions of Christian mysticism allow such symbolism of ravishment as a kind of 'as if.'" (One must infer that in Knox's opinion such symbolism shares nothing with metaphor in its effect on the imagination.) Describing the interpretations of both Levenson and Herman as "somewhat oblivious of the obvious," Knox claimed to see the unifying conceit that had eluded Herman: "It seems very clear to me that the very first line invites contemplation of the Trinity and that this concept determines the structure of the whole sonnet. . . . The first quatrain calls on God the Father's omnipotence to batter the heart. The second envisions the admission of God through the medium or agency of Rectified Reason, Reason rectified through love [the Son]. The third exemplifies the reborn understanding (en*light*ened through the Son) conceiving the consubstantiality of man and God through imagery of interpenetration [the Holy Ghost]."

Then in 1961 Arthur L. Clements (*Modern Language Notes,* June 1961)—by citing biblical passages associating each of the verbs *knock, breathe* and *shine* with all three Persons of the Trinity—proved beyond doubt (in my opinion) that "the sonnet's structure cannot then be viewed as the development of three quatrains each separately assigned to each of the Three Persons." Contending that "the organizing principle of the poem . . . is the paradox of death and rebirth, the central paradox of Christianity," Clements pointed out further that to illustrate this paradox of destroying in order to revive or throwing down in order to raise Donne employs throughout the sonnet two kinds of figurative language: "one kind is warlike, military, destructive; the other is marital, sexual, or uniting." The two kinds of metaphor are fused in lines 11–14 and are "made to achieve between themselves what Donne wishes to achieve with God."

Like Clements, I must join those whom Knox considered "oblivious of the obvious," those who cannot perceive three divisions of the sonnet devoted respectively to the Father, the Son, and the Holy Ghost. I believe that the sinner's only reason for addressing God as "three-personed" is that he is imploring him to exert all his power, his triple power, to rescue him from Satan. I hope that my interpretation will show, even more clearly than Clements has shown, how the interlocking of the various metaphors and of the stanzaic divisions gives the sonnet its unity.

In the first quatrain, I believe, the repentant sinner compares his heart to a walled town, one of many over which God is the rightful King. Upon approaching, the King has found this particular town closed to him, a Usurper (Satan) having captured it. Now the King with his army is encamped outside the walls, knocking at the gates and asking to be re-admitted so that he can restore (*mend*) whatever has been demolished in the capture and whatever has deteriorated during the occupation. But, declares the sinner, such gentle overtures will not suffice. The King must burst open the gates with *a battering ram*. (On another level, God *is* the battering ram.) Beyond all mending, the town must be completely destroyed, after which a new one will *rise* in its place, built by the King to *stand* forever.

The verbs *batter, break,* and *burn* all suggest storming a citadel; and even *blow* may be intended to suggest the use of gunpowder to blow up the fortress or blow it into smithereens. One is reminded of the violent scenes described by Aeneas in telling Dido about the fall of Troy and (faintly) of the fact that a new Troy is fated to rise. Even richer and more apt, however, are the allusions to the destruction of Jerusalem by Nebuchadnezzar (God's unwitting agent) and to the many predictions by the Prophets of the New Jerusalem to rise when a chastened people come to deserve it. There are also echoes of "the name of the city of my God, which is new Jerusalem" and of "Behold, I stand at the door and knock: if any man hear my voice and open the door, I will come in to him" (Revelation iii:12, 20).

The sonnet as a whole is unified by a shifting viewpoint which produces the effect of God's boring from the outside into the very center of the human heart. In the first quatrain the perspective is mainly that of the King outside the walls, seeking admission. In the second, the reader is carried inside the usurped town and sees the lamentable state of affairs through the eyes of the populace, rightfully the subjects of the King and of the Princess whom he has appointed as his Viceroy (these subjects being all the forces of man that should be governed by reason, here identified with the soul). In the sestet the point of view is that of the captive Princess herself (Reason, or the Soul), who has entered into a shameful marriage with the Usurper and is held in solitary confinement deep within the citadel.

Still further to invigorate and unify the prayer, Donne personifies the fortified town of the first quatrain as a woman, a woman urging her suitor to take her by force rather than by courtship. (In the Psalms, fallen Jerusalem or Zion is often personified as a mourning woman.) This plea of the personified city for violent attack anticipates the similar plea which the dishonored Princess makes in the sestet.[1]

The phrase *usurped town* is deliberately ambiguous and transitional, connecting the first and second quatrains. It refers back to the walled town, of course; but

---

[1] This begging for violation is less shocking when the woman is a personified city than when she is the soul of the repentant sinner. Few readers will detect this imagery in the first quatrain until *after* discovering it in the sestet; but in a re-reading, awareness of its first employment will mollify the shock of the second.

simultaneously it designates the wretched people within the town, just as one might have said in 1944 "Paris awaits her deliverers," meaning that the *people* of Paris were hoping soon to be liberated. The complaint of the populace in the second quatrain is that though they acknowledge their duty to the King and labor to admit him, without the guidance of the Princess their efforts are futile. (It is not clear to me how the nonspiritual forces in man, unaided by the reason-soul, can labor at all to admit God.) Since the capture of the town, the Usurper has held the Princess incommunicado; and her unhappy people, while aware of her shameful marriage, are unable to pass fair judgment on it, not knowing whether it was forced on her or whether she has voluntarily shifted allegiance to the Usurper and is therefore guilty of treason (*untrue*).

After the prayers of the personified city and of the leaderless people, finally in the sestet the captive Princess is heard from her solitary confinement. In language of almost unendurable anguish, which gives the sonnet much of its tone of passionate sincerity, she beseeches the King to deliver her from shame, declaring paradoxically that she can never be free unless he enthralls her and can never be chaste again unless he ravishes her. Appropriately, since the subject of the sonnet is remorse,[2] Donne is alluding again to the third chapter of Revelation —this time to the nineteenth verse: "As many as I love, I rebuke and *chasten:* be zealous therefore, and repent," and he has in mind two meanings of the verb *chasten:* to castigate and to purify.

Readers like Knox, who find it a strain "to imagine the poet in the role of woman," should remember that with Donne (as with Shakespeare, Spenser and others) the soul is always feminine. For example, in No. 2 of the *Holy Sonnets,* in the first nine lines the penitent describes himself as (among other things) one of God's sons and then as a temple of God's spirit presently usurped by Satan; but in the last five lines the feminine soul urges God to rescue her from Satan, who has kidnaped and ravished her.

To represent man's body as a temple or a castle and his soul as the priestess or governess was conventional.[3] Alma within her beleaguered castle, in Book Two of *The Faerie Queene,* is the most celebrated example; but since Alma has managed to remain chaste, a passage from *The Rape of Lucrece* more closely resembles Donne's sonnet. Shakespeare attributes to Tarquin, after he has committed the crime, something indistinguishable from Christian remorse. He is "a

[2] Here I disagree with Helen Gardner, who regards this sonnet (No. 10 in her arrangement) as one of three "on the love man owes to God and to his neighbour." (*The Divine Poems* [Oxford, 1952], p. xli.) Donne's sonnet seems to me to be a sinner's plea that remorse enough be put into his heart to start him on the way to repentance. As such, it would serve admirably as the first of a sequence; but perhaps all the sonnets are what Grierson called them—"separate ejaculations."

[3] During Elizabeth's long reign, English poets must have found new value in the old conceit, since a flesh-and-blood Princess was God's viceroy over them and sole head (under God) of their church.

heavy convertite"; both his body (a temple) and his soul (a princess now as dishonored as Lucrece herself) have been polluted by his lustful will. Shakespeare's choice of words is remarkably like Donne's:

> Besides his soules faire temple is defaced,
>   To whose weake ruines muster troopes of cares,
>   To aske the spotted Princesse how she fares.
> Shee sayes her subiects with fowle insurrection,
> Haue batterd downe her consecrated wall,
> And by their mortall fault brought in subiection
> Her immortalitie, and made her thrall,
> To liuing death and payne perpetuall.
>   Which in her prescience shee controlled still,
>   But her foresight could not forestall their will. (719–728)

But if the exhausted metaphor of the castle-body and the princess-soul was anemic by the 1590's, until Donne wrote his *Holy Sonnets* no poet had thought of wedding it to the equally weary and thin-blooded convention of comparing a cold mistress to a castle and her lover to the general of an army besieging it. Miraculously, this marriage of two ancient weaklings produced an abnormally vigorous offspring, a sonnet in which Donne, with his accustomed daring, requires the reader to see God wearing (with a difference) the rue of a Petrarchan lover.

His Desire

> Give me a man that is not dull,
> When all the world with rifts is full;
> But unamazed dares clearly sing,
> Whenas the roof's a-tottering;
> And, though it falls, continues still   5
> Tickling the cittern with his quill.

ROBERT HERRICK

The Quip

> The merry World did on a day
> With his train-bands and mates agree
> To meet together where I lay,
> And all in sport to jeer at me.
>
> First Beauty crept into a rose,   5
> Which when I plucked not, "Sir," said she,
> "Tell me, I pray, whose hands are those?"
> But thou shalt answer, Lord, for me.

Then Money came, and chinking still,
"What tune is this, poor man?" said he;   10
"I heard in music you had skill";
But thou shalt answer, Lord, for me.

Then came brave Glory puffing by
In silks that whistled, who but he!
He scarce allowed me half an eye;   15
But thou shalt answer, Lord, for me.

Then came quick Wit and Conversation,
And he would needs a comfort be,
And, to be short, make an oration;
But thou shalt answer, Lord, for me.   20

Yet when the hour of thy design
To answer these fine things shall come,
Speak not at large, say, I am thine,
And then they have their answer home.

GEORGE HERBERT

Love

Love bade me welcome; yet my soul drew back,
  Guilty of dust and sin.
But quick-eyed Love, observing me grow slack
  From my first entrance in,
Drew nearer to me, sweetly questioning   5
  If I lacked anything.

A guest, I answered, worthy to be here.
  Love said, You shall be he.
I, the unkind, ungrateful? Ah, my dear,
  I cannot look on Thee.   10
Love took my hand, and smiling, did reply,
  Who made the eyes but I?

Truth, Lord, but I have marred them; let my shame
  Go where it doth deserve.
And know you not, says Love, who bore the blame?   15
  My dear, then I will serve.
You must sit down, says Love, and taste my meat;
  So I did sit and eat.

GEORGE HERBERT

The Pulley

When God at first made man,
Having a glass of blessings standing by,
"Let us," said he, "pour on him all we can;
Let the world's riches, which dispersèd lie,
  Contract into a span."   5

So strength first made a way,
Then beauty flowed, then wisdom, honor, pleasure;
When almost all was out, God made a stay,
Perceiving that, alone of all his treasure,
  Rest in the bottom lay.   10

"For if I should," said he,
"Bestow this jewel also on my creature,
He would adore my gifts instead of me,
And rest in Nature, not the God of Nature;
  So both should losers be.   15

"Yet let him keep the rest,
But keep them with repining restlessness;
Let him be rich and weary, that at least,
If goodness lead him not, yet weariness
  May toss him to my breast."   20

GEORGE HERBERT

The Collar

I struck the board and cried, "No more;
    I will abroad!
What? shall I ever sigh and pine?
My lines and life are free, free as the road,
  Loose as the wind, as large as store.   5
    Shall I be still in suit?
Have I no harvest but a thorn
To let me blood, and not restore
What I have lost with cordial fruit?
    Sure there was wine   10
Before my sighs did dry it; there was corn
  Before my tears did drown it.
Is the year only lost to me?

Have I no bays to crown it,
No flowers, no garlands gay? all blasted?   15
And wasted?
Not so, my heart; but there is fruit,
And thou hast hands.
Recover all thy sigh-blown age
On double pleasures: leave thy cold dispute   20
Of what is fit and not. Forsake thy cage,
Thy rope of sands,
Which petty thoughts have made, and made to thee
Good cable, to enforce and draw,
And be thy law,   25
While thou didst wink and wouldst not see.
Away! take heed;
I will abroad.
Call in thy death's-head there; tie up thy fears.
He that forbears   30
To suit and serve his need,
Deserves his load."
But as I raved and grew more fierce and wild
At every word,
Methought I heard one calling, *Child!*   35
And I replied, *My Lord*.

GEORGE HERBERT

When I Consider How My Light Is Spent

When I consider how my light is spent
Ere half my days in this dark world and wide,
And that one talent which is death to hide,
Lodged with me useless, though my soul more bent
To serve therewith my Maker, and present   5
My true account, lest he returning chide;
Doth God exact day-labor, light denied,
I fondly ask; but patience, to prevent
That murmur, soon replies, God doth not need
Either man's work or his own gifts; who best   10
Bear his mild yoke, they serve him best, his state
Is kingly. Thousands at his bidding speed
And post o'er land and ocean without rest;
They also serve who only stand and wait.

JOHN MILTON

Bermudas

Where the remote Bermudas ride
In the ocean's bosom unespied,
From a small boat that rowed along,
The listening winds received this song:

  "What should we do but sing His praise,   5
That led us through the watery maze,
Unto an isle so long unknown,
And yet far kinder than our own?
Where He the huge sea-monsters wracks,
That lift the deep upon their backs,   10
He lands us on a grassy stage,
Safe from the storms, and prelate's rage.
He gave us this eternal spring,
Which here enamels everything,
And sends the fowls to us in care,   15
On daily visits through the air.
He hangs in shades the orange bright,
Like golden lamps in a green night,
And does in the pomegranates close
Jewels more rich than Ormus[1] shows.   20
He makes the figs our mouths to meet,
And throws the melons at our feet.
But apples[2] plants of such a price,
No tree could ever bear them twice;
With cedars, chosen by His hand,   25
From Lebanon, he stores the land;
And makes the hollow seas, that roar
Proclaim the ambergris on shore;
He cast (of which we rather boast)
The Gospel's pearl upon our coast,   30
And in these rocks for us did frame
A temple, where to sound His name.
Oh! let our voice His praise exalt,
Till it arrive at Heaven's vault,
Which thence (perhaps) rebounding, may   35
Echo beyond the Mexique Bay."

  Thus sung they, in the English boat,
An holy and a cheerful note;

[1] Hormuz, on the Persian Gulf.   [2] Pineapples.

And all the way, to guide their chime,
With falling oars they kept the time.   40

ANDREW MARVELL

Huswifery

Make me, O Lord, Thy spinning-wheel complete.
  Thy holy word my distaff make for me.
Make mine affections Thy swift flyers neat
  And make my soul Thy holy spool to be.
  My conversation make to be Thy reel   5
  And reel the yarn thereon spun of Thy wheel.

Make me Thy loom then, knit therein this twine,
  And make Thy Holy Spirit, Lord, wind quills;
Then weave the web Thyself. The yarn is fine.
  Thine ordinances make my fulling-mills.   10
  Then dye the same in heavenly colors choice,
  All pinked with varnished flowers of paradise.

Then clothe therewith mine understanding, will,
  Affections, judgment, conscience, memory,
My words and actions, that their shine may fill   15
  My ways with glory and Thee glorify.
  Then mine apparel shall display before Ye
  That I am clothed in holy robes for glory.

EDWARD TAYLOR

Hymn to Adversity

Daughter of Jove, relentless Power,
Thou Tamer of the human breast,
Whose iron scourge and torturing hour,
The bad affright, afflict the best!
Bound in thy adamantine chain   5
The Proud are taught to taste of pain,
And purple Tyrants vainly groan
With pangs unfelt before, unpitied and alone.

When first thy Sire to send on earth
Virtue, his darling Child, designed,   10

To thee he gave the heavenly birth,
And bade to form her infant mind.
Stern rugged nurse! thy rigid lore
With patience many a year she bore:
What sorrow was, thou bad'st her know,   15
And from her own she learned to melt at other's woe.

Scared at thy frown terrific, fly
Self-pleasing Folly's idle brood,
Wild Laughter, Noise, and thoughtless Joy,
And leave us leisure to be good.   20
Light they disperse, and with them go
The summer friend, the flattering foe;
By vain Prosperity received,
To her they vow their truth, and are again believed.

Wisdom in sable garb arrayed,   25
Immersed in rapturous thought profound,
And Melancholy, silent maid
With leaden eye, that loves the ground,
Still on thy solemn steps attend:
Warm Charity, the genial Friend,   30
With Justice to herself severe,
And Pity, dropping soft the sadly-pleasing tear.

Oh, gently on thy suppliant's head,
Dread goddess, lay thy chastening hand!
Not in thy gorgon terrors clad,   35
Nor circled with the vengeful band
(As by the impious thou art seen)
With thundering voice, and threatening mien,
With screaming Horror's funeral cry,
Despair, and fell Disease, and ghastly Poverty: 40

Thy form benign, oh goddess, wear,
Thy milder influence impart,
Thy philosophic train be there
To soften, not to wound my heart,
The generous spark extinct revive,   45
Teach me to love and to forgive,
Exact my own defects to scan,
What others are, to feel, and know myself a man.

THOMAS GRAY

On His Seventy-Fifth Birthday

I strove with none; for none was worth my strife;
    Nature I loved, and next to Nature, Art;
I warmed both hands before the fire of life;
    It sinks, and I am ready to depart.

                                    WALTER SAVAGE LANDOR

from *The Rubáiyát of Omar Khayyám*

26

Why, all the Saints and Sages who discussed
Of the Two Worlds so wisely—they are thrust
    Like foolish Prophets forth; their Words to Scorn
Are scattered, and their Mouths are stopped with Dust.

27

Myself when young did eagerly frequent   5
Doctor and Saint, and heard great argument
    About it and about; but evermore
Came out by the same door where in I went.

28

With them the seed of Wisdom did I sow,
And with mine own hand wrought to make it grow;   10
    And this was all the Harvest that I reaped—
"I came like Water, and like Wind I go."

29

Into this Universe, and *Why* not knowing
Nor *Whence*, like Water willy-nilly flowing;
    And out of it, as Wind along the Waste,   15
I know not *Whither*, willy-nilly blowing.

30

What, without asking, hither hurried *Whence?*
And, without asking, *Whither* hurried hence!
    Oh, many a Cup of this forbidden Wine
Must drown the memory of that insolence!   20

31

Up from the Earth's Center through the Seventh Gate
I rose, and on the Throne of Saturn sate,
    And many a Knot unraveled by the Road;
But not the Master-knot of Human Fate.

32

There was the Door to which I found no Key;   25
There was the Veil through which I might not see;
    Some little talk awhile of Me and Thee
There was—and then no more of Thee and Me.

33

Earth could not answer; nor the Seas that mourn
In flowing Purple, of their Lord forlorn;   30
    Nor rolling Heaven, with all his Signs revealed
And hidden by the sleeve of Night and Morn.

34

Then of the Thee in Me who works behind
The Veil, I lifted up my hands to find
    A lamp amid the Darkness; and I heard,   35
As from Without—"The Me within Thee blind!"

35

Then to the Lip of this poor earthen Urn
I leaned, the Secret of my Life to learn;
    And Lip to Lip it murmured—"While you live,
Drink!—for, once dead, you never shall return."   40

48

A Moment's Halt—a momentary taste
Of Being from the Well amid the Waste—
    And Lo!—the phantom Caravan has reached
The Nothing it set out from—Oh, make haste!

52

A moment guessed—then back behind the Fold   45
Immersed of Darkness round the Drama rolled
    Which, for the Pastime of Eternity,
He doth Himself contrive, enact, behold.

64

Strange, is it not? that of the myriads who
Before us passed the door of Darkness through,   50
   Not one returns to tell us of the Road
Which to discover we must travel too.

66

I sent my Soul through the Invisible,
Some letter of that After-life to spell;
   And by and by my Soul returned to me,   55
And answered, "I Myself am Heaven and Hell"—

67

Heaven but the Vision of fulfilled Desire,
And Hell the Shadow from a Soul on fire
   Cast on the Darkness into which Ourselves,
So late emerged from, shall so soon expire.   60

68

We are no other than a moving row
Of Magic Shadow-shapes that come and go
   Round with the Sun-illumined Lantern held
In Midnight by the Master of the Show;

69

But helpless Pieces of the Game He plays   65
Upon this Checkerboard of Nights and Days;
   Hither and thither moves, and checks, and slays,
And one by one back in the Closet lays.

72

And that inverted Bowl they call the Sky,
Whereunder crawling cooped we live and die,   70
   Lift not your hands to *It* for help—for It
As impotently moves as you or I.

74

Yesterday *This* Day's Madness did prepare;
Tomorrow's Silence, Triumph, or Despair.
   Drink! for you know not whence you came, nor why;   75
Drink, for you know not why you go, nor where.

77

And this I know: whether the one True Light
Kindle to Love, or Wrath—consume me quite,
   One Flash of It within the Tavern caught
Better than in the Temple lost outright.   80

79

What! from his helpless Creature be repaid
Pure Gold for what he lent him dross-allayed—
   Sue for a Debt he never did contract,
And cannot answer—Oh, the sorry trade!

80

O Thou, who didst with pitfall and with gin   85
Beset the Road I was to wander in,
   Thou wilt not with Predestined Evil round
Enmesh, and then impute my Fall to Sin!

99

Ah, Love! could you and I with Him conspire
To grasp this sorry Scheme of Things entire,   90
   Would not we shatter it to bits—and then
Remold it nearer to the Heart's Desire!

EDWARD FITZGERALD

Life Is Struggle

To wear out heart, and nerves, and brain,
And give oneself a world of pain;
Be eager, angry, fierce, and hot,
Imperious, supple—God knows what,
For what's all one to have or not;   5
O false, unwise, absurd, and vain!
For 'tis not joy, it is not gain,
It is not in itself a bliss,
Only it is precisely this
   That keeps us all alive.   10

To say we truly feel the pain,
And quite are sinking with the strain;—
Entirely, simply, undeceived,

Believe, and say we ne'er believed
The object, e'en were it achieved,   15
A thing we e'er had cared to keep;
With heart and soul to hold it cheap,
And then to go and try it again;
O false, unwise, absurd, and vain!
Oh, 'tis not joy, and 'tis not bliss,   20
Only it is precisely this
   That keeps us still alive.

ARTHUR HUGH CLOUGH

Dover Beach

The sea is calm to-night,
The tide is full, the moon lies fair
Upon the straits;—on the French coast the light
Gleams and is gone; the cliffs of England stand,
Glimmering and vast, out in the tranquil bay.   5
Come to the window, sweet is the night air!
Only, from the long line of spray
Where the sea meets the moon-blanched land,
Listen! you hear the grating roar
Of pebbles which the waves draw back, and fling,   10
At their return, up the high strand,
Begin, and cease, and then again begin,
With tremulous cadence slow, and bring
The eternal note of sadness in.

Sophocles long ago   15
Heard it on the Ægean, and it brought
Into his mind the turbid ebb and flow
Of human misery; we
Find also in the sound a thought,
Hearing it by this distant northern sea.   20
The Sea of Faith
Was once, too, at the full, and round earth's shore
Lay like the folds of a bright girdle furled.
But now I only hear
Its melancholy, long, withdrawing roar,   25
Retreating, to the breath
Of the night wind, down the vast edges drear
And naked shingles of the world.

Ah, love, let us be true
To one another! for the world, which seems   30
To lie before us like a land of dreams,
So various, so beautiful, so new,
Hath really neither joy, nor love, nor light,
Nor certitude, nor peace, nor help for pain;
And we are here as on a darkling plain   35
Swept with confused alarms of struggle and flight
Where ignorant armies clash by night.

                              MATTHEW ARNOLD

I Never Saw a Moor

I never saw a moor,
I never saw the sea;
Yet know I how the heather looks,
And what a wave must be.

I never spoke with God,   5
Nor visited in Heaven;
Yet certain am I of the spot
As if the chart were given.

                              EMILY DICKINSON

Felix Randal

Felix Randal the farrier, O he is dead then? my duty all ended,
Who have watched his mold of man, big-boned and hardy-handsome
Pining, pining, till time when reason rambled in it and some
Fatal four disorders, fleshed there, all contended?

Sickness broke him. Impatient he cursed at first, but mended   5
Being anointed and all; though a heavenlier heart began some
Months earlier, since I had our sweet reprieve and ransom
Tendered to him. Ah well, God rest him all road ever he offended!
This seeing the sick endears them to us, us too it endears.
My tongue had taught thee comfort, touch had quenched thy tears, 10
Thy tears that touched my heart, child, Felix, poor Felix Randal;
How far from then forethought of, all thy more boisterous years,
When thou at the random grim forge, powerful amidst peers,
Didst fettle for the great grey drayhorse his bright and battering
  sandal!

                              GERARD MANLEY HOPKINS

Thou Art Indeed Just, Lord

Thou art indeed just, Lord, if I contend
With thee; but, sir, so what I plead is just.
Why do sinners' ways prosper? and why must
Disappointment all I endeavor end?
  Wert thou my enemy, O thou my friend,   5
How wouldst thou worse, I wonder, than thou dost
Defeat, thwart me? Oh, the sots and thralls of lust
Do in spare hours more thrive than I that spend,
Sir, life upon thy cause. See banks and brakes
Now, leavèd how thick; lacèd they are again   10
With fretty chervil, look, and fresh wind shakes
Them; birds build—but not I build; no, but strain,
Time's eunuch, and not breed one work that wakes.
Mine, O thou lord of life, send my roots rain.

GERARD MANLEY HOPKINS

The Chestnut Casts His Flambeaux

The chestnut casts his flambeaux, and the flowers
 Stream from the hawthorn on the wind away,
The doors clap to, the pane is blind with showers.
 Pass me the can, lad; there's an end of May.

There's one spoilt spring to scant our mortal lot,   5
 One season ruined of our little store.
May will be fine next year as like as not:
 Oh, ay, but then we shall be twenty-four.

We for a certainty are not the first
 Have sat in taverns while the tempest hurled   10
Their hopeful plans to emptiness, and cursed
 Whatever brute and blackguard made the world.

It is in truth iniquity on high
 To cheat our sentenced souls of aught they crave,
And mar the merriment as you and I   15
 Fare on our long fool's-errand to the grave.

Iniquity it is; but pass the can.
 My lad, no pair of kings our mothers bore;
Our only portion is the estate of man:
 We want the moon, but we shall get no more.   20

If here to-day the cloud of thunder lours
  To-morrow it will hie on far behests;
The flesh will grieve on other bones than ours
  Soon, and the soul will mourn in other breasts.

The troubles of our proud and angry dust   25
  Are from eternity, and shall not fail.
Bear them we can, and if we can we must.
  Shoulder the sky, my lad, and drink your ale.

A. E. HOUSMAN

The Laws of God, the Laws of Man

The laws of God, the laws of man,
He may keep that will and can;
Not I: let God and man decree
Laws for themselves and not for me;
And if my ways are not as theirs   5
Let them mind their own affairs.
Their deeds I judge and much condemn,
Yet when did I make laws for them?
Please yourselves, say I, and they
Need only look the other way.   10
But no, they will not; they must still
Wrest their neighbor to their will,
And make me dance as they desire
With jail and gallows and hell-fire.
And how am I to face the odds   15
Of man's bedevilment and God's?
I, a stranger and afraid
In a world I never made.
They will be master, right or wrong;
Though both are foolish, both are strong.   20
And since, my soul, we cannot fly
To Saturn nor to Mercury,
Keep we must, if keep we can,
These foreign laws of God and man.

A. E. HOUSMAN

Epilogue

"Terence, this is stupid stuff;
You eat your victuals fast enough;
There can't be much amiss, 'tis clear,
To see the rate you drink your beer.
But oh, good Lord, the verse you make,   5
It gives a chap the belly-ache.
The cow, the old cow, she is dead;
It sleeps well, the hornèd head:
We poor lads, 'tis our turn now
To hear such tunes as killed the cow.   10
Pretty friendship 'tis to rhyme
Your friends to death before their time
Moping melancholy mad:
Come, pipe a tune to dance to, lad."

Why, if 'tis dancing you would be,   15
There's brisker pipes than poetry.
Say, for what were hop-yards meant,
Or why was Burton built on Trent?
Oh many a peer of England brews
Livelier liquor than the Muse,   20
And malt does more than Milton can
To justify God's ways to man.
Ale, man, ale's the stuff to drink
For fellows whom it hurts to think:
Look into the pewter pot   25
To see the world as the world's not.
And faith, 'tis pleasant till 'tis past:
The mischief is that 'twill not last.
Oh, I have been to Ludlow fair
And left my necktie God knows where,   30
And carried half-way home, or near,
Pints and quarts of Ludlow beer:
Then the world seemed none so bad,
And I myself a sterling lad;
And down in lovely muck I've lain,   35
Happy till I woke again.
Then I saw the morning sky:
Heigho, the tale was all a lie;
The world, it was the old world yet,
I was I, my things were wet,   40

And nothing now remained to do
But begin the game anew.

Therefore, since the world has still
Much good, but much less good than ill,
And while the sun and moon endure   45
Luck's a chance, but trouble's sure,
I'd face it as a wise man would,
And train for ill and not for good.
'Tis true, the stuff I bring for sale
Is not so brisk a brew as ale: 50
Out of a stem that scored the hand
I wrung it in a weary land.
But take it: if the smack is sour,
The better for the embittered hour;
It should do good to heart and head   55
When your soul is in my soul's stead;
And I will friend you, if I may,
In the dark and cloudy day.

There was a king reigned in the East:
There, when kings will sit to feast,   60
They get their fill before they think
With poisoned meat and poisoned drink.
He gathered all that springs to birth
From the many-venomed earth;
First a little, thence to more,   65
He sampled all her killing store;
And easy, smiling, seasoned sound,
Sate the king when healths went round.
They put arsenic in his meat
And stared aghast to watch him eat;   70
They poured strychnine in his cup
And shook to see him drink it up:
They shook, they stared as white's their shirt:
Them it was their poison hurt.
—I tell the tale that I heard told.   75
Mithridates, he died old.

A. E. HOUSMAN

To a Friend Whose Work Has Come to Nothing

Now all the truth is out,
Be secret and take defeat
From any brazen throat,
For how can you compete,

Being honor bred, with one 5
Who, were it proved he lies,
Were neither shamed in his own
Nor in his neighbor's eyes?
Bred to a harder thing
Than Triumph, turn away 10
And like a laughing string
Whereon mad fingers play
Amid a place of stone,
Be secret and exult,
Because of all things known 15
That is most difficult.

WILLIAM BUTLER YEATS

Cliff Klingenhagen

Cliff Klingenhagen had me in to dine
With him one day; and after soup and meat,
And all the other things there were to eat,
Cliff took two glasses and filled one with wine
And one with wormwood. Then, without a sign 5
For me to choose at all, he took the draught
Of bitterness himself, and lightly quaffed
It off, and said the other one was mine.

And when I asked him what the deuce he meant
By doing that, he only looked at me 10
And grinned, and said it was a way of his.
And though I know the fellow, I have spent
Long time a-wondering when I shall be
As happy as Cliff Klingenhagen is.

EDWIN ARLINGTON ROBINSON

Credo

I cannot find my way: there is no star
In all the shrouded heavens anywhere;
And there is not a whisper in the air
Of any living voice but one so far
That I can hear it only as a bar 5
Of lost, imperial music, played when fair
And angel fingers wove, and unaware,
Dead leaves to garlands where no roses are.

No, there is not a glimmer, nor a call,
For one that welcomes, welcomes when he fears,   10
The black and awful chaos of the night;
But through it all,—above, beyond it all—
I know the far-sent message of the years,
I feel the coming glory of the Light!

EDWIN ARLINGTON ROBINSON

A Pact

I make a pact with you, Walt Whitman—
I have detested you long enough.
I come to you as a grown child
Who has had a pig-headed father;
I am old enough now to make friends.   5
It was you that broke the new wood,
Now is a time for carving.
We have one sap and one root—
Let there be commerce between us.

EZRA POUND

11
Providence and Destiny

The poems in this chapter reflect man's concern for his ultimate fate. It is a concern older than the great Greek tragedies and as new as today's folk ballad of protest. Philosophical man has usually insisted that there is a purposefulness and recognizable pattern to life. This pattern he may call fate or destiny. When he discerns a divine guidance in the pattern, it may be called providence.

Faith alone is sufficient for the devoutly religious man to accept the view that divinity has a hand in his ultimate fate. He seeks signs that reassure him of the divine, or at least the purposeful, hand. It is sufficient for some men that they find the signs in the formal doctrines and documents of the church, and faith in these often leads to a formal religious commitment. Some of the poets represented in Chapter 12 of this collection give evidence of the strength of this commitment. Other poets have been especially sensitive to nature as providing reassuring answers to basic philosophical and religious questions. Bryant, for example, accepts that the power that "guides through the boundless sky" the "certain flight" of the waterfowl will guide his steps. The slow accretions of the chambered nautilus comfort Holmes in much the same way.

The fate of the mouse and the mountain daisy does not bring Burns the same certainty, and a considerable number of the poems in this section indicate that other poets share his uncertainty. The discomforting thought occurs to some that there is no orderly plan. The fate of Blake's fly suggests to him that, if there is a guiding hand, it is indifferent or even capricious: "For I dance,/And drink, and sing,/ Till some blind hand/ Shall brush my wing." This lack of assurance of a divine providence has led some poets to accept a determinism as binding as a law of physics: "Around the ancient track marched, rank on rank,/ The army of unalterable law." As Hardy came to realize, this kind of impersonality does not leave man anything on which he can even vent his anger.

The theme of destiny or fate is at least implicit in a large body of literature. The problem and the mystery of why man ends as he does is the thematic backbone of Greek tragedy, and practically all tragedy since has had to grapple with it. The works listed below show that, as religious orthodoxy fades as a satisfying means of explaining man's fate, other explanations must be found, whether they go by the name of determinism, existentialism, or some other term.

READINGS IN OTHER GENRES

PLAYS

Aeschylus, *The Oresteia*
Maxwell Anderson, *Winterset*
Jean Anouilh, *Becket, The Lark*
Jean Cocteau, *The Infernal Machine*
Marc Connelly, *The Green Pastures*
T. S. Eliot, *Murder in the Cathedral, The Family Reunion*
Thomas Hardy, *The Dynasts*
Federico García Lorca, *The House of Bernarda Alba*
Christopher Marlowe, *The Tragical History of Doctor Faustus*
Eugene O'Neill, *Mourning Becomes Electra*
Jean-Paul Sartre, *The Flies*
William Shakespeare, *Hamlet, Macbeth*
George Bernard Shaw, *Saint Joan*
Sophocles, *Antigone, Oedipus Rex*
Thornton Wilder, *The Skin of Our Teeth*

NOVELS

Stephen Crane, *Maggie: A Girl of the Streets*
Theodore Dreiser, *An American Tragedy*
William Faulkner, *Light in August*
Graham Greene, *The Comedians, The Power and the Glory*
Thomas Hardy, *Jude the Obscure, Tess of the D'Urbervilles*
Ernest Hemingway, *To Have and Have Not*
Arthur Koestler, *Darkness at Noon*
Herman Melville, *Moby Dick, Pierre*
Frank Norris, *McTeague*
Jean-Paul Sartre, *Nausea*
John Steinbeck, *East of Eden*
Thornton Wilder, *The Bridge of San Luis Rey*
Emile Zola, *Germinal, L'Assommoir*

SHORT STORIES

Marcel Ayme, "Grace"
Charles Baudelaire, "The Rope"
Thomas Hardy, "The Three Strangers"
Nathaniel Hawthorne, "Ethan Brand," "The Birthmark," "Young Goodman Brown"
Ernest Hemingway, "A Clean, Well-Lighted Place"

Sir Patrick Spence

The king sits in Dumferling toune,
  Drinking the blude-reid wine:
"O whar will I get guid sailor,
  To sail this schip of mine?"

Up and spak an eldern knicht,   5
  Sat at the kings richt kne:
"Sir Patrick Spence is the best sailor
  That sails upon the se."

The king has written a braid letter,
  And signd it wi his hand,   10
And sent it to Sir Patrick Spence,
  Was walking on the sand.

The first line that Sir Patrick red,
  A loud lauch lauched he;
The next line that Sir Patrick red,   15
  The teir blinded his ee.

"O wha is this has don this deid,
  This ill deid don to me,
To send me out this time o' the yeir,
  To sail upon the se!   20

"Mak hast, mak haste, my mirry men all,
  Our guid schip sails the morne";
"O say na sae, my master deir,
  For I feir a deadlie storme.

"Late, late yestreen I saw the new moone,   25
  Wi the auld moone in hir arme,
And I feir, I feir, my deir master
  That we will cum to harme."

O our Scots nobles wer richt laith[1]
  To weet their cork-heild schoone;[2]   30
But lang owre[3] a' the play wer playd,
  Thair hats they swam aboone.

O lang, lang may their ladies sit,
  Wi thair fans into their hand,

_____
[1] Loath.   [2] Shoes.   [3] After.

Or eir[4] they se Sir Patrick Spence   35
   Cum sailing to the land.

O lang, lang may the ladies stand,
   Wi thair gold kems in their hair,
Waiting for thair ain deir lords,
   For they'll se thame na mair.   40

Haf-owre, haf-owre to Aberdour,
   It's fiftie fadom deip,
And thair lies guid Sir Patrick Spence,
   Wi the Scots lords at his feit.

                      ANONYMOUS

[4] Before.

Sic Vita[1]

Like to the falling of a star,
Or as the flights of eagles are,
Or like the fresh spring's gaudy hue,
Or silver drops of morning dew,

Or like a wind that chafes the flood,   5
Or bubbles which on water stood:
Even such is man, whose borrowed light
Is straight called in, and paid to night.

The wind blows out, the bubble dies,
The spring entombed in autumn lies,   10
The dew dries up, the star is shot,
The flight is past, and man forgot.

                      HENRY KING

[1] Such is life.

To a Mouse

Wee, sleekit, cow'rin', tim'rous beastie,
O what a panic's in thy breastie!
Thou need na start awa sae hasty,
        Wi' bickering brattle![1]

[1] Hurried scampering.

I wad be laith to rin an' chase thee   5
      Wi' murd'ring pattle!²

I'm truly sorry man's dominion
Has broken Nature's social union,
An' justifies that ill opinion
      Which makes thee startle   10
At me, thy poor earth-born companion,
      An' fellow-mortal!

I doubt na, whiles, but thou may thieve;
What then? poor beastie, thou maun live!
A daimen-icker in a thrave³   15
      'S a sma' request:
I'll get a blessin' wi' the lave,
      And never miss 't!

Thy wee bit housie, too, in ruin!
Its silly wa's the win's are strewin'!   20
An' naething, now, to big a new ane
      O' foggage green!
An' bleak December's winds ensuin',
      Baith snell⁴ an' keen!

Thou saw the fields laid bare and waste,   25
An' weary winter comin' fast,
An' cozie here, beneath the blast,
      Thou thought to dwell,
Till crash! the cruel coulter past
      Out-thro' thy cell.   30

That wee bit heap o' leaves an' stibble
Has cost thee mony a weary nibble!
Now thou's turned out, for a' thy trouble,
      But house or hald,⁵
To thole⁶ the winter's sleety dribble,   35
      An' cranreuch⁷ cauld!

But, Mousie, thou art no thy lane,
In proving foresight may be vain:
The best laid schemes o' mice an' men
      Gang aft a-gley,   40
An' lea'e us nought but grief an' pain
      For promised joy.

---

² Plow shaft.   ³ An occasional ear in twenty-four sheaves.

⁴ Bitter.   ⁵ Possessions.   ⁶ Endure.   ⁷ Frost.

Still thou art blest compared wi' me!
The present only toucheth thee:
But oh! I backward cast my e'e   45
       On prospects drear!
An' forward tho' I canna see,
        I guess an' fear!

ROBERT BURNS

To a Mountain Daisy

Wee modest crimson-tipped flow'r,
Thou's met me in an evil hour;
For I maun crush amang the stoure[1]
       Thy slender stem:
To spare thee now is past my pow'r,   5
       Thou bonnie gem.

Alas! it's no thy neibor sweet,
The bonnie lark, companion meet,
Bending thee 'mang the dewy weet
       Wi' spreckled breast,   10
When upward springing, blythe to greet
       The purpling east.

Cauld blew the bitter-biting north
Upon thy early humble birth;
Yet cheerfully thou glinted forth   15
       Amid the storm,
Scarce reared above the parent-earth
       Thy tender form.

The flaunting flow'rs our gardens yield
High shelt'ring woods and wa's maun shield,   20
But thou, beneath the random bield[2]
       O' clod or stane,
Adorns the histie[3] stibble-field,
       Unseen, alane.

There, in thy scanty mantle clad,   25
Thy snawy bosom sun-ward spread,
Thou lifts thy unassuming head
       In humble guise;

[1] Dust.   [2] Shelter.   [3] Bare.

But now the share uptears thy bed,
          And low thou lies!   30

Such is the fate of artless maid,
Sweet flow'ret of the rural shade,
By love's simplicity betrayed,
          And guileless trust,
Till she like thee, all soiled, is laid   35
          Low i' the dust.

Such is the fate of simple bard,
On life's rough ocean luckless starred:
Unskilful he to note the card
          Of prudent lore,   40
Till billows rage, and gales blow hard,
          And whelm him o'er!

Such fate to suffering worth is giv'n,
Who long with wants and woes has striv'n,
By human pride or cunning driv'n   45
          To mis'ry's brink,
Till wrenched of ev'ry stay but Heav'n,
          He ruined, sink!

Ev'n thou who mourn'st the Daisy's fate,
That fate is thine—no distant date;   50
Stern Ruin's ploughshare drives elate
          Full on thy bloom,
Till crushed beneath the furrow's weight
          Shall be thy doom!

ROBERT BURNS

The Tiger

Tiger! Tiger! burning bright
In the forests of the night,
What immortal hand or eye
Could frame thy fearful symmetry?

In what distant deeps or skies   5
Burnt the fire of thine eyes?
On what wings dare he aspire?
What the hand dare seize the fire?

And what shoulder, and what art,
Could twist the sinews of thy heart?   10
And when thy heart began to beat,
What dread hand? and what dread feet?

What the hammer? what the chain?
In what furnace was thy brain?
What the anvil? what dread grasp   15
Dare its deadly terrors clasp?

When the stars threw down their spears,
And watered heaven with their tears,
Did he smile his work to see?
Did he who made the Lamb make thee?   20

Tiger! Tiger! burning bright
In the forests of the night,
What immortal hand or eye,
Dare frame thy fearful symmetry?

WILLIAM BLAKE

The Fly

Little Fly,
Thy summer's play
My thoughtless hand
Has brushed away.

Am not I   5
A fly like thee?
Or art not thou
A man like me?

For I dance,
And drink, and sing,   10
Till some blind hand
Shall brush my wing.

WILLIAM BLAKE

To a Waterfowl

Whither, midst falling dew,
While glow the heavens with the last steps of day,
Far, through their rosy depths, dost thou pursue
    Thy solitary way?

    Vainly the fowler's eye   5
Might mark thy distant flight to do thee wrong,
As, darkly seen against the crimson sky,
    Thy figure floats along.

    Seek'st thou the plashy brink
Of weedy lake, or marge of river wide,   10
Or where the rocking billows rise and sink
    On the chafed ocean-side?

    There is a Power whose care
Teaches thy way along that pathless coast—
The desert and illimitable air—   15
    Lone wandering, but not lost.

    All day thy wings have fanned,
At that far height, the cold, thin atmosphere,
Yet stoop not, weary, to the welcome land,
    Though the dark night is near.   20

    And soon that toil shall end;
Soon shalt thou find a summer home, and rest,
And scream among thy fellows; reeds shall bend,
    Soon, o'er thy sheltered nest.

    Thou'rt gone, the abyss of heaven   25
Hath swallowed up thy form; yet, on my heart
Deeply hath sunk the lesson thou hast given,
    And shall not soon depart.

    He who, from zone to zone,
Guides through the boundless sky thy certain flight, 30
In the long way that I must tread alone
    Will lead my steps aright.

                WILLIAM CULLEN BRYANT

The Chambered Nautilus

This is the ship of pearl, which, poets feign,
  Sails the unshadowed main,—
    The venturous bark that flings
On the sweet summer wind its purpled wings
In gulfs enchanted, where the Siren sings,   5
  And coral reefs lie bare,
Where the cold sea-maids rise to sun their streaming hair.

Its webs of living gauze no more unfurl;
   Wrecked is the ship of pearl!
   And every chambered cell,   10
Where its dim dreaming life was wont to dwell,
As the frail tenant shaped his growing shell,
   Before thee lies revealed,—
Its irised ceiling rent, its sunless crypt unsealed!

Year after year beheld the silent toil   15
   That spread his lustrous coil;
   Still, as the spiral grew,
He left the past year's dwelling for the new,
Stole with soft step its shining archway through,
   Built up its idle door,   20
Stretched in his last-found home, and knew the old no more.

Thanks for the heavenly message brought by thee,
   Child of the wandering sea,
   Cast from her lap, forlorn!
From thy dead lips a clearer note is born   25
Than ever Triton blew from wreathèd horn!
   While on mine ear it rings,
Through the deep caves of thought I hear a voice that sings:—

Build thee more stately mansions, O my soul,
   As the swift seasons roll!   30
   Leave thy low-vaulted past!
Let each new temple, nobler than the last,
Shut thee from heaven with a dome more vast,
   Till thou at length art free,
Leaving thine outgrown shell by life's unresting sea!   35

OLIVER WENDELL HOLMES

Grief

I tell you, hopeless grief is passionless;
That only men incredulous of despair,
Half-taught in anguish, through the midnight air
Beat upward to God's throne in loud access
Of shrieking and reproach. Full desertness,   5
In souls as countries, lieth silent-bare
Under the blanching, vertical eye-glare
Of the absolute Heavens. Deep-hearted man, express
Grief for thy Dead in silence like to death—

Most like a monumental statue set 10
In everlasting watch and moveless woe
Till itself crumble to the dust beneath.
Touch it; the marble eyelids are not wet.
If it could weep, it could arise and go.

ELIZABETH BARRETT BROWNING

Revolutions

Before man parted for this earthly strand,
While yet upon the verge of heaven he stood,
God put a heap of letters in his hand,
And bade him make with them what word he could.

And man has turned them many times; made Greece, 5
Rome, England, France—yes, nor in vain essayed
Way after way, changes that never cease!
The letters have combined, something was made.

But ah! an inextinguishable sense
Haunts him that he has not made what he should; 10
That he has still, though old, to recommence,
Since he has not yet found the word God would.

And empire after empire, at their height
Of sway, have felt this boding sense come on;
Have felt their huge frames not constructed right, 15
And drooped, and slowly died upon their throne.

One day, thou say'st, there will at last appear
The word, the order, which God meant should be.
—Ah! we shall know *that* well when it comes near;
The band will quit man's heart, he will breathe free. 20

MATTHEW ARNOLD

A Noiseless Patient Spider
(*Manuscript Version*)

The Soul, reaching, throwing out for love,
As the spider, from some little promontory, throwing out filament after
filament, tirelessly out of itself, that one at least may catch and form a
link, a bridge, a connection

O I saw one passing alone, saying hardly a word—yet full of love I detected
    him, by certain signs
O eyes wishfully turning! O silent eyes!
For then I thought of you o'er the world   5
O latent oceans, fathomless oceans of love!
O waiting oceans of love! yearning and fervid! and of you sweet souls
    perhaps in the future, delicious and long:
But Dead, unknown on the earth—ungiven, dark here, unspoken, never
    born:
You fathomless latent souls of love—you pent and unknown oceans of love!

WALT WHITMAN

A Noiseless Patient Spider

A noiseless patient spider,
I marked where on a little promontory it stood isolated,
Marked how to explore the vacant vast surrounding,
It launched forth filament, filament, filament, out of itself,
Ever unreeling them, ever tirelessly speeding them.   5

And you O my soul where you stand,
Surrounded, detached, in measureless oceans of space,
Ceaselessly musing, venturing, throwing, seeking the spheres to connect
    them,
Till the bridge you will need be formed, till the ductile anchor hold,
Till the gossamer thread you fling catch somewhere, O my soul.   10

WALT WHITMAN

Spider and Poet: An Artist at Work

James T. F. Tanner

As a Romantic poet who insisted upon the primacy of the self over nature,
Walt Whitman wanted not so much to interpret nature as to interpret *himself*
through nature. Throughout *Leaves of Grass,* the dominant theme is the *self,*
its relation to other selves and to the cosmos. Indeed, Whitman's greatest poem
bears the title "Song of Myself." To adapt such a philosophical concept to poetry
(the problem confronting the poet in the poem under discussion), Whitman
needed an image of the poet's struggle to express himself and to communicate to
others the results of such self-expression. The question becomes something like
this: "What animate thing in the universe can best represent, metaphorically, the
struggle of a poet to express himself and to communicate with others?" Clearly

it is the spider, and nothing else but the spider, which satisfies both necessary conditions of self-expression and the urge to communicate, enabling the poet to compare himself to the spider.

When the spider spins its web, it does not procure the required materials from external nature; the spider takes a biological substance from *itself* to manufacture the web. And in a similar way, or so the poet wishes us to believe, the creative artist—when he seeks to express himself to others—must look deeply into his own soul, not to what is outside his own identity, and put down what he is able to take from *himself*. But expression is one thing, communication another. Both poet and spider, once they have produced from out of *themselves* a suitable substance, must find means of transmitting the substance to the world *outside themselves*. The spider must create a bridge, or a ductile anchor, and travel upon it to continue its work; likewise the poet, who is detached from everything outside his own personality, must span, somehow, the measureless oceans of space between *himself* and others. Success in such an undertaking requires patience and ceaseless musing, a continual "venturing, throwing, seeking the spheres to connect them." Finally the poet's web, like that of the spider, will catch hold somewhere, bridging the gap between himself and others; he will have achieved both expression and communication.

The form is simple and inevitable: five lines to the spider, five to the poet's soul. The poem is thus composed of only two sentences which *spin themselves out*. The first line in each stanza is the shortest line in that stanza, giving the poet room to lengthen the *web* of line as he goes. In both stanzas every line except the last ends with a comma; the period appears at the end of each sentence, symbolizing completion, success, contact. Observe the grammatical structure of the first stanza. First comes the spider, the direct object, then the subject *I* and the verb *marked;* then the poet *spins* two lines on two parallel adverbial phrases (*where* and *how,* two adverbs introducing the location of the spider and the means of improving its location); the fourth line is thereupon *spun* out of the third line, since the fact that the spider launched forth filament explains the *how* of line three. In line five the web continues to unreel both implicitly and explicitly; for the last line of the stanza is mere appositional repetition of the preceding line—a condition giving the desired effect of continued struggle. The student will observe a very similar grammatical structure for the second stanza. Thus the poet not only talks about spinning out of himself, he is careful—all the while—to see that his sentences obediently *spin themselves to conclusion* in much the same manner as a spider spins its web. The reader is rightly awed not only by *what* the poem means, but also by *how* the poem means.

It is clear that in this instance Walt Whitman wrote a perfect poem; perfect because all the parts fit precisely, because the image is simple and inevitable and true, and because the reader in contemplation of the poem finds nothing lacking, nothing unsaid, no part interchangeable with any other part. Not only does the poem tease the intellect, it touches the emotions. And what is more, the poem seems to be absolutely effortless.

But of course it was not effortless, as one may easily judge by comparing the unpublished manuscript of the poem with the published version. The manuscript is chaotic, wildly extravagant (it contains no less than six exclamation points), largely formless, and too highly personalized to pretend to universality. The pronoun *him* of the third line shocks the reader into an awareness of the poet's esoteric and idealized homosexuality, an awareness not in keeping with the mood of jubilancy, rhapsody, and cacophony which sweeps the reader into the sea of overly dramatized passion. Though he speaks of souls in the manuscript, it is bodies ("eyes wishfully turning," *et cetera*) that the poet is chiefly thinking of as the manuscript develops. The communication in which he is interested is undeniably sexual communication with other males, a love "unknown on the earth—ungiven, dark here, unspoken, never born."

The manuscript version is not devoid of poetic power. Intensity and honesty of emotion there are. Form and universality there are not. A way had to be found by the poet to utilize this intense and forbidden emotion for poetic purposes. The re-working of the manuscript's formless intensity has resulted in the admirably concise, well-formed poem that we see in the published version.

Whitman often found it necessary to sublimate his personal sexuality in order to objectify and universalize his poetic efforts. The Calamus emotion (Whitman's term for the love of comrades) *is* intense enough to undergo adaptation, expansion, and universalization. Might we not say that in some mystical way the intensity of the Calamus passion is somehow preserved even in a short poem like "A Noiseless Patient Spider"? One critic has said that the Calamus poems in *Leaves of Grass* constitute the "central nervous system" of the book; though the poem under discussion is not one of the Calamus poems superficially, surely it owes a debt to the overall concern of the poet to intensify expression by universalizing inward emotions. In any event, it is recognized by all that great poetry can be written only by one who thinks deeply and feels passionately and who can communicate passion and intelligence to others. In Whitman's work (and in that of most poets, incidentally) there is a great difference between passion and the expression of passion. That is why the comparison of published works with manuscripts is so interesting and important.

Lucifer in Starlight

On a starred night Prince Lucifer uprose.
Tired of his dark dominion swung the fiend
Above the rolling ball in cloud part screened,
Where sinners hugged their spectre of repose.
Poor prey to his hot fit of pride were those.   5

And now upon his western wing he leaned,
Now his huge bulk o'er Afric's sands careened,
Now the black planet shadowed Arctic snows.
Soaring through wider zones that pricked his scars
With memory of the old revolt from Awe,   10
He reached a middle height, and at the stars,
Which are the brain of heaven, he looked, and sank.
Around the ancient track marched, rank on rank,
The army of unalterable law.

GEORGE MEREDITH

Hap

If but some vengeful god would call to me
From up the sky, and laugh: "Thou suffering thing,
Know that thy sorrow is my ecstasy,
That thy love's loss is my hate's profiting!"

Then would I bear it, clench myself, and die,   5
Steeled by the sense of ire unmerited;
Half-eased in that a Powerfuller than I
Had willed and meted me the tears I shed.

But not so. How arrives it joy lies slain,
And why unblooms the best hope ever sown?   10
—Crass Casualty obstructs the sun and rain,
And dicing Time for gladness casts a moan. . . .
These purblind Doomsters had as readily strown
Blisses about my pilgrimage as pain.

THOMAS HARDY

The Convergence of the Twain

I

In a solitude of the sea
Deep from human vanity,
And the Pride of Life that planned her, stilly couches she.

II

Steel chambers, late the pyres
Of her salamandrine fires,   5
Cold currents thrid, and turn to rhythmic tidal lyres.

III

Over the mirrors meant
  To glass the opulent
The sea-worm crawls—grotesque, slimed, dumb, indifferent.

IV

Jewels in joy designed   10
  To ravish the sensuous mind
Lie lightless, all their sparkles bleared and black and blind.

V

Dim moon-eyed fishes near
  Gaze at the gilded gear
And query: "What does this vaingloriousness down here?"   15

VI

Well: while was fashioning
  This creature of cleaving wing,
The Immanent Will that stirs and urges everything

VII

Prepared a sinister mate
  For her—so gaily great—   20
A Shape of Ice, for the time far and dissociate.

VIII

And as the smart ship grew
  In stature, grace, and hue,
In shadowy silent distance grew the Iceberg too.

IX

Alien they seemed to be: 25
  No mortal eye could see
The intimate welding of their later history,

X

Or sign that they were bent
  By paths coincident
On being anon twin halves of one august event,   30

XI

Till the Spinner of the Years
   Said "Now!" And each one hears,
And consummation comes, and jars two hemispheres.

THOMAS HARDY

The Windhover:
To Christ Our Lord

I caught this morning morning's minion, king-
   dom of daylight's dauphin, dapple-dawn-drawn Falcon, in his riding
   Of the rolling level underneath him steady air, and striding
High there, how he rung upon the rein of a wimpling wing
In his ecstasy! then off, off forth on swing,   5
   As a skate's heel sweeps smooth on a bow-bend: the hurl and gliding
   Rebuffed the big wind. My heart in hiding
Stirred for a bird,—the achieve of, the mastery of the thing!

Brute beauty and valour and act, oh, air, pride, plume, here
   Buckle! AND the fire that breaks from thee then, a billion   10
Times told lovelier, more dangerous, O my chevalier!

   No wonder of it: shéer plód makes plough down sillion
Shine, and blue-bleak embers, ah my dear,
   Fall, gall themselves, and gash gold-vermilion.

GERARD MANLEY HOPKINS

Hopkins' "The Windhover"

Elisabeth Schneider

On "The Windhover" I am disposed to be dogmatic. The poem conveys one
direct meaning, and only one in which all the parts of the poem and all the
images find a place. Belt buckles and buckles in armor are not part of it; they
belong to some other poem, "in another country." Hopkins willingly employed
puns when double meaning might be "to one thing wrought" but not when two
meanings fractured a poem. The instinct of critics to hover around the word
buckle is nevertheless sound, for that word is the structural center, the pivot on
which the sonnet turns.

   Something buckles and something breaks through. Readers who buckle belts neglect the second half of this statement, though Hopkins capitalized the *AND* between the parts. It will not do to take *buckle* as an imperative either, as many writers do, for that leaves *AND* hanging loose and destroys the sentence. It is neither armor nor belt, nor Mr. Empson's bicycle wheel, that buckles or breaks; the pivotal image is of a higher order of magnitude. Deck or bulkheads of a ship buckle before fire breaks through; walls of a building buckle before they crash or burn. In "The Windhover" the whole material world buckles, "AND the fire" of the spiritual world—or Christ—"breaks" through. *Buckle* and *break* control the sestet as it subsides from the climax of spiritual illumination to the everyday imagery of the conclusion.

"The Windhover" is one of several variations on a theme that occupied Hopkins in 1877. Other sonnets, particularly "The Starlight Night" and "Spring," display the same pattern of thought: a progression from the concrete beauty of nature described in the octave, to its spiritual meaning or analogue in the sestet. As is so often true in Hopkins, the plan is simple and straightforward; only the execution is complex.

"The Windhover" is addressed "To Christ Our Lord," and though Christ is not mentioned till the tenth line, He is prepared for in the first by epithets given to the falcon—morning's favorite (minion), "kingdom of daylight's" crown prince— the Son, not the King or Father. *Dauphin* is more than an automatic bit of alliteration; it counts for the meaning and for unity. The falcon is an analogue, however, not a symbol of Christ. Though the power and beauty of its flight make it prince of the morning scene, it is not more than a bird, and it is described throughout the octave in the language of the material world. But the sight of it awakens the poet: "My heart [which had been] in hiding stirred." Beneath the word *hiding* I hear *hibernating,* but that may be an accidental personal association; at any rate, the poet's heart had been stagnant and perhaps reluctant to be moved (cf. *Letters* I, 66). Its awakening preludes the turn of the sonnet.

In the ninth line, the particularities of bird and morning are drained away, leaving abstractions and universals to represent the power and beauty in nature. This material world, so abstracted—"brute beauty and valour and act, oh, air, pride, plume"—"here [at this point, now] buckle[s]," and as it collapses before the poet's vision, the fire of Christ "breaks" through, "a billion times" more lovely and more dangerous. Only now does the poet address Christ directly: "the fire that breaks from thee then . . . O my chevalier." The image in Hopkins mind probably derives from the crackling of timbers or plates in a fire at sea, a kind of disaster with which his father was professionally concerned and which from time to time furnished Hopkins himself, landsman though he was, with a surprising quantity of imagery. Such an image gives double significance to the epithet *dangerous,* applied immediately afterwards to Christ. From this point on, tension relaxes and the pitch drops to a quiet conclusion with the imagery remaining under the shadow of *buckle* and *break.* "No wonder" this transformation occurs, Hopkins says, when the *breaking open* of the most drab things in life may reveal brightness within. Mere labor of plowing breaks open the earth and transforms dull clod into shining furrow ("the near hill glistening with very bright newly turned sods," he noted in his journal); and "blue-bleak" coals of an apparently dead fire fall and break apart to show bright living fire within.

In the outline of its thought, then, "The Windhover" is simple and strict. Its complexities lie, on the one hand, in the elaboration of the visual imagery interwoven with elaborately echoing patterns of sound, and, on the other, in the play between two counterpointed sets of opposites. The first is the opposition of the material and the spiritual which mark the two parts of the sonnet and are expressly brought together by the dauphin-Son parallel and more essentially by the primary theme of the poet's being stirred by one into more intense awareness of the other. The second pair of opposites appear in more shadowy form. The opposition of beauty and terror (or pain), present in so much of Hopkins' writing, runs through the poem without any reconciling of the two, though they are brought together in an uneasy harmony through the idea of power in the "mastery" of the bird and the "lovelier, more dangerous" fire of Christ. These opposites, however, are not evenly balanced in the poem: the terror or pain is no more than an undertone, reflected in one epithet of Christ, in the "gall" and "gash" of the close, possibly in the predatory character as well as the daring of the hawk and in the poet's "hiding" heart. The unresolved suggestions of terror and pain give an edge to the overriding spirit of breathless admiration.

These complexities are enough. Richness of symbolic meaning cannot be had merely by reading into the poem a mechanical, dictionary-flavored ambiguity in *buckle*. For the interpretation of "The Windhover" at least, an inveterate commitment to irony and paradox is apt to defeat itself by producing only disjointed structure and discordant associations that destroy, by neutralizing, the resonance of the poem. Quite a good deal of the resonance of "The Windhover" comes from simplicity of theme, clarity of structure, and directness of movement. This is true even though the final effect is of an extremely complex poem.

A Passer-By

Whither, O splendid ship, thy white sails
    crowding,
  Leaning across the bosom of the urgent
    West,
That fearest nor sea rising, nor sky cloud-
    ing,
  Whither away, fair rover, and what thy
    quest?
    Ah! soon, when Winter has all our vales
    opprest,   5
When skies are cold and misty, and hail
    is hurling,

Wilt thou glide on the blue Pacific, or
    rest
In a summer haven asleep, thy white sails
    furling.

I there before thee, in the country that
    well thou knowest,
    Already arrived am inhaling the odor-
    ous air: 10
I watch thee enter unerringly where thou
    goest,
    And anchor queen of the strange ship-
    ping there,
    Thy sails for awnings spread, thy masts
    bare;
Nor is aught from the foaming reef to
    the snow-capped, grandest
    Peak, that is over the feathery palms
    more fair   15
Than thou, so upright, so stately, and
    still thou standest.

And yet, O spendid ship, unhailed and
    nameless,
    I know not if, aiming a fancy, I rightly
    divine
That thou hast a purpose joyful, a courage
    blameless,
    Thy port assured in a happier land than
    mine.   20
    But for all I have given thee, beauty
    enough is thine,
As thou, aslant with trim tackle and
    shrouding,
    From the proud nostril curve of a
    prow's line
In the offing scatterest foam, thy white
    sails crowding.

ROBERT BRIDGES

Easter Hymn

If in that Syrian garden, ages slain,
You sleep, and know not you are dead in vain,

Nor even in dreams behold how dark and bright
Ascends in smoke and fire by day and night
The hate you died to quench and could but fan,   5
Sleep well and see no morning, son of man.

But if, the grave rent and the stone rolled by,
At the right hand of majesty on high
You sit, and sitting so remember yet
Your tears, your agony and bloody sweat,   10
Your cross and passion and the life you gave,
Bow hither out of heaven and see and save.

A. E. HOUSMAN

Leda and the Swan

A sudden blow: the great wings beating still
Above the staggering girl, her thighs caressed
By the dark webs, her nape caught in his bill,
He holds her helpless breast upon his breast.

How can those terrified vague fingers push   5
The feathered glory from her loosening thighs?
And how can body, laid in that white rush,
But feel the strange heart beating where it lies?

A shudder in the loins engenders there
The broken wall, the burning roof and tower   10
And Agamemnon dead.
                      Being so caught up,
So mastered by the brute blood of the air,
Did she put on his knowledge with his power
Before the indifferent beak could let her drop?

WILLIAM BUTLER YEATS

The Second Coming

Turning and turning in the widening gyre
The falcon cannot hear the falconer;
Things fall apart; the center cannot hold;
Mere anarchy is loosed upon the world,
The blood-dimmed tide is loosed, and everywhere   5
The ceremony of innocence is drowned;

The best lack all conviction, while the worst
Are full of passionate intensity.

Surely some revelation is at hand;
Surely the Second Coming is at hand.   10
The Second Coming! Hardly are those words out
When a vast image out of *Spiritus Mundi*[1]
Troubles my sight: somewhere in sands of the desert
A shape with lion body and the head of a man,
A gaze blank and pitiless as the sun,   15
Is moving its slow thighs, while all about it
Reel shadows of the indignant desert birds.

The darkness drops again; but now I know
That twenty centuries of stony sleep
Were vexed to nightmare by a rocking cradle,   20
And what rough beast, its hour come round at last,
Slouches towards Bethlehem to be born?

                                    WILLIAM BUTLER YEATS

[1] The soul of the world. Yeats uses the term to indicate the belief that all experience and all history are contained in the racial memory.

The Miracle

Who beckons the green ivy up
    Its solitary tower of stone?
What spirit lures the bindweed's cup
        Unfaltering on?
Calls even the starry lichen to climb   5
By agelong inches endless Time?

Who bids the hollyhock uplift
    Her rod of fast-sealed buds on high;
Fling wide her petals—silent, swift,
        Lovely to the sky?   10
Since as she kindled, so she will fade,
Flower above flower in squalor laid.

Ever the heavy billow rears
    All its sea-length in green, hushed wall;
But totters as the shore it nears,   15
        Foams to its fall;
Where was its mark? on what vain quest
Rose that great water from its rest?

So creeps ambition on; so climb
   Man's vaunting thoughts. He, set on high,   20
Forgets his birth, small space, brief time,
      That he shall die;
Dreams blindly in his stagnant air;
Consumes his strength; strips himself bare;

Rejects delight, ease, pleasure, hope,   25
   Seeking in vain, but seeking yet,
Past earthly promise, earthly scope,
      On one aim set:
As if, like Chaucer's child, he thought
All but "O Alma!" nought.   30

WALTER DE LA MARE

Fire and Ice

Some say the world will end in fire,
Some say in ice.
From what I've tasted of desire
I hold with those who favor fire.
But if it had to perish twice,   5
I think I know enough of hate
To say that for destruction ice
Is also great
And would suffice.

ROBERT FROST

Ballad for Gloom

For God, our God is a gallant foe
That playeth behind the veil.

I have loved my God as a child at heart
That seeketh deep bosoms for rest,
I have loved my God as a maid to man—   5
But lo, this thing is best:

To love your God as a gallant foe that plays behind the veil;
To meet your God as the night winds meet beyond Arcturus'[1] pale.

[1] The brightest star in the constellation Boötes.

I have played with God for a woman,
I have staked with my God for truth,   10
I have lost to my God as a man, clear-eyed—
    His dice be not of ruth.

For I am made as a naked blade,
    But hear ye this thing in sooth:

Who loseth to God as man to man   15
    Shall win at the turn of the game.
I have drawn my blade where the lightnings meet
    But the ending is the same:
Who loseth to God as the sword blades lose
    Shall win at the end of the game.   20

For God, our God is a gallant foe that playeth behind the veil.
Whom God deigns not to overthrow hath need of triple mail.

EZRA POUND

Heaven

Fish (fly-replete, in depth of June
Dawdling away their wat'ry noon)
Ponder deep wisdom, dark or clear,
Each secret fishy hope or fear.
Fish say, they have their Stream and Pond;   5
But is there anything Beyond?
This life cannot be All, they swear,
For how unpleasant, if it were!
One may not doubt that, somehow, good
Shall come of Water and of Mud;   10
And, sure, the reverent eye must see
A Purpose in Liquidity.
We darkly know, by Faith we cry,
The future is not Wholly Dry.
Mud unto Mud!—Death eddies near—   15
Not here the appointed End, not here!
But somewhere, beyond Space and Time,
Is wetter water, slimier slime!
And there (they trust) there swimmeth One
Who swam ere rivers were begun,   20
Immense, of fishy form and mind,
Squamous, omnipotent, and kind;
And under that Almighty Fin
The littlest fish may enter in.

Oh! never fly conceals a hook,   25
Fish say, in the Eternal Brook,
But more than mundane weeds are there,
And mud, celestially fair;
Fat caterpillars drift around,
And Paradisal grubs are found;   30
Unfading moths, immortal flies,
And the worm that never dies.
And in that Heaven of all their wish,
There shall be no more land, say fish.

RUPERT BROOKE

Lachrymae Christi

Whitely, while benzine
Rinsings from the moon
Dissolve all but the windows of the mills
(Inside the sure machinery
Is   still   5
And curdled only where a sill
Sluices its one unyielding smile),

Immaculate venom binds
The fox's teeth, and swart
Thorns freshen on the year's   10
First blood. From flanks unfended,
Twanged red perfidies of spring
Are trillion on the hill.

And the nights opening
Chant pyramids,—   15
Anoint with innocence,—recall
To music and retrieve what perjuries
Had galvanized the eyes.
                          While chime
Beneath and all around   20
Distilling clemencies,—worms'
Inaudible whistle, tunneling
Not penitence
But song, as these
Perpetual fountains, vines,—   25

Thy Nazarene and tinder eyes.

(Let sphinxes from the ripe
Borage of death have cleared my tongue
Once and again; vermin and rod
No longer bind. Some sentient cloud   30
Of tears flocks through the tendoned loam:
Betrayed stones slowly speak.)

Names peeling from Thine eyes
And their undimming lattices of flame,
Spell out in palm and pain   35
Compulsion of the year, O Nazarene.—

Lean long from sable, slender boughs,
Unstanched and luminous. And as the nights
Strike from Thee perfect spheres,
Lift up in lilac-emerald breath the grail   40
Of earth again—
                    Thy face
From charred and riven stakes, O
Dionysus, Thy
Unmangled target smile.   45

                    HART CRANE

Hart Crane's "Lachrymae Christi"

Martin Staples Shockley

I shall attempt to show that "Lachrymae Christi" is an intelligible poem, and
to suggest that as a poem it has some merit more than mere intelligibility.

The first sentence says:

Whitely, while benzine
Rinsings from the moon
Dissolve all but the windows of the mills,
(Inside the sure machinery
Is still
And curdled only where a sill
Sluices its one unyielding smile),

Immaculate venom binds
The fox's teeth, and swart
Thorns freshen on the year's
First blood.

That sentence makes two main statements: first, "Immaculate venom binds the
fox's teeth," and second, "Swart thorns freshen on the year's first blood." The
first part of the sentence consists of the adverb "whitely" and the adverbial clause

"while benzine rinsings from the moon dissolve all but the windows of t
mills." "Whitely" modifies both "dissolve" and "binds"; that is, the moonlig
whitely dissolves all but the windows of the mills, and the fox's teeth are white
bound. The description of the inside of the mill "(Inside the sure machine
is still and curdled only where a sill sluices its one unyielding smile)" is proper
a parenthetical insertion because it marks a shift in point of view. From a d
scription of the exterior of the mills in the moonlight, the poem shifts to a d
scription of the interior of a mill.

With syntax clear, let us look now at what the sentence says. The first lir
describe the moonlight, "benzine rinsings from the moon," shining on the mi
so that the buildings seem to dissolve, to merge into the landscape, except f
the windows from which the moonlight is reflected. Moonlight as "benzi
rinsings from the moon" is appropriate in that it fits the industrial setting
the mill town. A benzine solution was probably used to rinse cloth in the m
Benzine is a solvent, and the moonlight acts as a solvent, the mills dissolvi
in the moonlight.

The machinery is described as "sure"; that is, mechanically precise. T
machinery is sleek and shiny except where it is reflected in the water. T
water flows in a sluice or trough over a sill which breaks its smooth flow in
riffles which are reflected in the moonlight. This curve of riffles is the "one u
yielding smile." It is unyielding because it remains stationary, seemingly r
sisting the flow of the water. And the machinery is curdled in the riffles; that
the riffles distort the reflection of the machines so that they seem to be lum
or coagulated like curds in milk.

Now we come to the two statements: first, "Immaculate venom binds t
fox's teeth." The fox's teeth are the small, sharp needles which weave or kn
the cloth on the machines. The needles are white and sharp like fox's teeth, a
they shuttle in and out as they weave the cloth. "Immaculate venom" is t
threads or strands which are being woven. They stretch from one needle to a
other, seeming to bind the needles, or tie them together. They would be in
maculate, because the yarn or thread is white, immaculate in the moonligh
"Venom" is an appropriate word, because the yarn is strung between the needl
like a thread of saliva between the fox's teeth.

The second statement is: "Swart thorns freshen on the year's first blood." T
thorns prick blood from the newly shorn sheep. Here the word "thorns" su
gesting the crown of thorns is the first allusion to the subject of the poem, t
tears of Christ. The suggestion is picked up and elaborated later.

The next sentence is comparatively simple, and develops ideas which have
ready been suggested.

> From flanks unfended,
> Twanged red perfidies of spring
> Are trillion on the hill.

The unfended flanks refers, of course, to the shorn sheep. "Twanged" suggests the twanging of the thorn bush as the thorns catch and pull at the sheep, pricking them until they bleed. "Red perfidies of spring" are drops of blood from or on the flanks of the sheep. Here is another allusion to the subject of the poem. Christian tradition speaks of Christ as "the Lamb," and there is an easy association between the thorns pricking the sheep in spring and the crown of thorns pressed on the head of Christ, the paschal lamb.

Note the ironic tone of this passage in which the poet announces spring. The imagery is deliberately contradictory to the usual sentimental tone of "welcome sweet springtime." Instead of flowers, there are thorns; instead of gamboling in the meadow, the lambs are lacerated with thorns; instead of sweet songs, we have twanged red perfidies; and the word "trillion" is a conscious and ironic exaggeration.

The combination of the mill town and the pastoral scene is somewhat unusual, but logical. The relation between the sheep which produce the wool and the mills which knit the yarn serves to unify the pastoral and industrial imagery.

The next sentence is:

> And the nights opening
> Chant pyramids,
> Anoint with innocence,—recall
> To music and retrieve what perjuries
> Had galvanized the eyes.

The subject of the sentence is "nights." In saying that the nights, in opening or unfolding the beauty of the night, chant pyramids, Crane implies that the nights sing of the age-old mysteries of the world. The pyramids have always been regarded as one of the wonders of the world, associated with the Romantic and the exotic. Also, the nights "anoint with innocence." Many poets have written of the healing beauty of the night. The night anoints, or cleanses and purifies. In saying that the nights "recall to music," Crane is re-stating that the nights "chant pyramids." The night is beautiful like music; it chants, it sings, to us. And finally the nights "retrieve what perjuries had galvanized the eyes." The word "galvanized" is used in its literal sense of coated with metallic film. This film of perjuries, distortions, or illusions prevents us from seeing truth. The night retrieves these lies, enabling us to perceive the true beauty of the world.

The next sentence elaborates the idea of singing. Christ's eyes are singing while the night is chanting pyramids.

> While chime
> Beneath and all around
> Distilling clemencies,—worms'
> Inaudible whistle, tunneling
> Not penitence

> But song, as these
> Perpetual fountains, vines,—
>
> Thy Nazarene and tinder eyes.

The sentence is only apparently obscure. It says that while the night sings beauty, the tinder eyes of Christ the Nazarene chime distilling clemencies, even the inaudible whistle of tunneling worms is not penitence but song, as fountains and vines are song. Or, in other words, the eyes of Christ are like tinder because they kindle with beauty, a beauty which chimes beneath and all around as the eyes distill, or produce in its purest form, the gentleness and mercy which translates into music the inaudible whistle of tunneling worms, perpetual fountains, and vines.

The phrase "tinder eyes" is effective. More tritely, we say that eyes glow, or flash; but the metaphor of "tinder eyes" suggests both tenderness and flame. The word order, while it may seem illogical and twisted, is more effective in its striking combinations, and the passage achieves emphasis by its periodic structure, revealing its meaning in the last powerful line:

> Thy Nazarene and tinder eyes.

Possibly the "worms" refers to the workers in the mills, shut away from sunlight and fresh air, or it might suggest underground trains running between the mills. The words "whistle" and "tunneling" seem to suggest trains.

This is the last allusion to the mills. It relates stanza two to stanza one through the allusion in stanza two to the mills which are specifically mentioned in stanza one. The allusions are all tenuous, suggestive rather than direct, hence stimulating to the imagination. The words have double and triple meanings; they are cross-fertilized, so to speak, interlaced in subtle ways, and the poem is unified through these oblique relationships.

This oblique unity is illustrated in the next stanza:

> (Let sphinxes from the ripe
> Borage of death have cleared my tongue
> Once and again; vermin and rod
> No longer bind. Some sentient cloud
> Of tears flocks through the tendoned loam:
> Betrayed stones slowly speak.)

In stanza two, Crane used the pyramids: "And the nights opening chant pyramids." Now, the mention of the sphinxes recalls the pyramids. The phrase "vermin and rod" recalls the word "penitence" in stanza two. The statements are similar: "Not penitence but song"; "Vermin and rod no longer bind." Crane is saying that the old monastic practice of mortifying the flesh with vermin and rod is no longer binding. Christ wishes man to glorify God not through penitence, but with song.

The sentence contains words of different meanings and connotations. "Let" might mean either permitted or prevented. Sphinxes are symbols both of silence and of inscrutable wisdom and antiquity. Borage is a kind of plant and also a cordial made from the plant. The sentence says that sphinxes have been permitted to impart to the poet their wisdom, which has cleared his tongue, enabling him to speak out clearly time and again. The ripe borage of death probably means the sweet liquor of oblivion. This sweet intoxication with death the sphinxes have cleared from the poet's tongue, so that now he can speak the ancient wisdom imparted to him. This wisdom is, in part, the knowledge that Christ does not approve the old custom of penitence, the rule of vermin and rod. There is perhaps the suggestion that the tears of Christ are caused, in part, by man's misinterpretation of Christ's teaching, which has produced vermin and rod when Christ wishes song, the chimes of distilled clemencies.

In the next sentence—

> Some sentient cloud
> Of tears flocks through the tendoned loam:
> Betrayed stones slowly speak.)—

"sentient tears," of course, are tears produced by feeling. "Tendoned loam" is the human flesh. Man's body comes from dust, and the loam of the rich earth is held together by tendons; hence the human body is "tendoned loam." The phrase also suggests the tendoned earth, earth that is bound together by foliage, vines, roots; even the tunnels of the worms are tendons holding the soil together. The phrase has a double meaning; it suggests the identity of man with earth, an identity furthered by the line:

> Betrayed stones slowly speak.)

Here is a surging from the depths of nature. The tears of Christ speak for both man and nature. The very stones, betrayed nature as well as betrayed man, speak through the tears of Christ. The verb "flocks" is well chosen. The cloud of tears flocks through the body. The word conveys the feeling of gathering in a flock, of moving in one mass. It suggests the power of the emotion which produces the tears. Also, it recalls the earlier mention of the sheep flocking on the hillside.

In the next sentence—

> Names peeling from Thine eyes
> And their undimming lattice of flame,
> Spell out in palm and pain
> Compulsion of the year, O Nazarene.—

the phrase "lattices of flame" recalls the "tinder eyes" mentioned previously. "Palm and pain" refers, of course, to the triumph commemorated in Palm Sunday and the pain of the crucifixion. "Compulsion of the year" means that each is inevitable in its own time.

Logically developing the idea of crucifixion, the next lines:

> Lean long from sable, slender boughs,
> Unstanched and luminous.

image the crucified Christ, His long lean body suspended from the dark, slend
arms of the cross, His wounds unstanched, His eyes luminous. The lumino
eyes relates clearly enough to the "lattices of flame" and to the "tinder eyes."
The final sentence is:

> And as the nights
> Strike from Thee perfect spheres,
> Lift up in lilac-emerald breath the grail
> Of earth again—
> Thy face
> From charred and riven stakes, O
> Dionysus, Thy
> Unmangled target smile.

The "perfect spheres" are the tears of Christ. The beauty of the night strik
tears from His eyes. Notice here the allusion to the nights chanting pyrami
and to the sentient cloud of tears in preceding stanzas. The mention of lila
suggests spring (recall here the opening lines of the poem in which sheep a
on the hillsides in spring), but the meaning is a double one. Spring is of cour
the time of rebirth, of new life; but lilacs are a symbol of death and mournin
so there is a fusion of the symbolism of death and resurrection—the same fusi
which Crane's master, Whitman, had made before him.

The grail is, of course, the goal, the sacred object of a quest; and the grail
earth, the goal of life, is

> Thy face
> From charred and riven stakes, O
> Dionysus, Thy
> Unmangled target smile.

Dionysus is the Greek god of spring, hence of rebirth, of the eternal mirac
of renewed life which all peoples have associated with springtime and celebrate
in their festivals of spring. Christ and Dionysus, both images of resurrection, a
used interchangeably to indicate that life though constantly sacrificed is con
stantly renewed. Identification of Dionysus with Christ indicates that Cran
considers his theme not merely Christian, but universal. The sentence is im
perative. In simplest form, it says: "Lift up Thy face, O Dionysus."

The "unmangled smile" in this last sentence recalls the "unyielding smile" i
the first sentence where the water sluices over the sill. This "unmangled targe
smile" is the proof of resurrection and life. Although the smile is the targe
of death, of all evil and destructive forces, it survives, unmangled, the charre

and riven stakes. It is this smile, this image of suffering and sympathy, of compassion and love, of resurrection and life, which is the grail of earth, the goal of life.

In summary, we have in this poem a related sequence of vivid and powerful images, expressing in lyrical intensity a related body of ideas: the beauty of the world, the identity of man with nature, the universality of human suffering and human sympathy, the transcendent and eternal quality of love and life above suffering and beyond death—all symbolized in the tears of Christ.

Of course, the poem *is* more than that; it *communicates* more than that; but that, I think, is what the poem *says*.

Dirge

1-2-3 was the number he played but today the number came 3-2-1;
  bought his Carbide at 30 and it went to 29; had the favorite at Bowie
    but the track was slow—

O, executive type, would you like to drive a floating power, knee-action,
  silk-upholstered six? Wed a Hollywood star? Shoot the course in 58?
  Draw to the ace, king, jack?
O, fellow with a will who won't take no, watch out for three cigarettes
  on the same, single match; O, democratic voter born in August under
  Mars, beware of liquidated rails—

Denouement to denouement, he took a personal pride in the certain, certain
  way he lived his own, private life,   5
  but nevertheless, they shut off his gas; nevertheless, the bank foreclosed;
  nevertheless, the landlord called; nevertheless, the radio broke,
And twelve o'clock arrived just once too often,
  just the same he wore one grey tweed suit, bought one straw hat, drank
  one straight Scotch, walked one short step, took one long look, drew
  one deep breath,
  just one too many,
And wow he died as wow he lived,   10
  going whop to the office and blooie home to sleep and biff got married
  and bam had children and oof got fired,
  zowie did he live and zowie did he die,

With who the hell are you at the corner of his casket, and where the hell
  we going on the right hand silver knob, and who the hell cares walking
  second from the end with an American Beauty wreath from why the
  hell not,

Very much missed by the circulation staff of the New York Evening
　　Post; deeply, deeply mourned by the B.M.T.,[1]

Wham, Mr. Roosevelt; pow, Sears Roebuck; awk, big dipper; bop, summer
　　rain;
　bong, Mr., bong, Mr., bong, Mr., bong.

15

KENNETH FEARING

[1] Brooklyn-Manhattan Transit.

12
Duty, Responsibility, and Commitment

The poems included in this section discuss the questions of one's duty and responsibility, as well as the commitments that most men make to ideals. The poets urge the reader to commit himself to some honorable course in life, to be a responsible individual, to listen to the call of duty. Wordsworth calls duty "Stern Daughter of the Voice of God" and says that, if we are to answer God's call, we must do those tasks that we are convinced are right. Kipling admonishes his fellows to commit themselves to a cause, to "take up the white man's burden"; and though Kipling's cause is now disdained, the idea of commitment is a keystone of modern philosophy. The four poems in the section by Frost call upon the reader to discipline himself, to fortify himself against the ruins of time, to keep his promises before he sleeps.

The theme is represented in this section by both worthwhile ideals and those that are worthless. The tone in most of the section is serious, but there is even one humorous poem—Nash's satiric "Kind of an Ode to Duty." The whole complex of questions revolving around duty, responsibility, and commitment has been frequently and satisfactorily treated by poets, as our selections show. The list below indicates that the theme is widely treated in other genres also.

READINGS IN OTHER GENRES

PLAYS

Aeschylus, *Prometheus Bound, The Oresteia*
Maxwell Anderson, *Winterset*
Jean Anouilh, *Antigone, Becket, The Lark*
Robert Bolt, *A Man for All Seasons*
T. S. Eliot, *Murder in the Cathedral*
Gerhart Hauptmann, *The Sunken Bell*
Henrik Ibsen, *An Enemy of the People*
Sidney Kingsley, *Detective Story*
Jean-Paul Sartre, *The Flies*
William Shakespeare, *Coriolanus, Hamlet, Measure for Measure*

George Bernard Shaw, *Man and Superman*
Robert E. Sherwood, *Abe Lincoln in Illinois, There Shall Be No Night*
Sophocles, *Antigone*
James Thurber and Elliott Nugent, *The Male Animal*
Tennessee Williams, *The Night of the Iguana*

NOVELS

Pearl Buck, *The Good Earth*
Albert Camus, *The Plague*
Joseph Conrad, *Nostromo, Under Western Eyes, Victory*
William Faulkner, *Intruder in the Dust*
F. Scott Fitzgerald, *Tender Is the Night, The Great Gatsby*
Graham Greene, *The Power and the Glory*
Nathaniel Hawthorne, *The Scarlet Letter*
Ernest Hemingway, *For Whom the Bell Tolls*
Sinclair Lewis, *Arrowsmith*
Somerset Maugham, *The Moon and Sixpence*
Evelyn Waugh, *Brideshead Revisited*

SHORT STORIES

Albert Camus, "The Guest"
Joseph Conrad, "Heart of Darkness," "The Secret Sharer"
William Faulkner, "Barn Burning," "That Evening Sun"
Bret Harte, "The Luck of Roaring Camp," "The Outcasts of Poker Flat"
Ernest Hemingway, "The Killers"
Franz Kafka, "Metamorphosis"
Jean-Paul Sartre, "The Wall"

from *Milton*
Preface

And did those feet in ancient time
  Walk upon England's mountains green?
And was the holy Lamb of God
  On England's pleasant pastures seen?

And did the countenance divine   5
  Shine forth upon our clouded hills?
And was Jerusalem builded here
  Among these dark Satanic mills?

Bring me my bow of burning gold!
    Bring me my arrows of desire!   10
Bring me my spear! O clouds, unfold!
    Bring me my chariot of fire.

I will not cease from mental fight,
    Nor shall my sword sleep in my hand
Till we have built Jerusalem   15
    In England's green and pleasant land.

WILLIAM BLAKE

Ode to Duty

Stern Daughter of the Voice of God!
O Duty! if that name thou love
Who art a light to guide, a rod
To check the erring, and reprove;
Thou, who art victory and law
When empty terrors overawe;
From vain temptations dost set free;
And calm'st the weary strife of frail humanity!

There are who ask not if thine eye
Be on them; who, in love and truth,   1
Where no misgiving is, rely
Upon the genial sense of youth:
Glad hearts! without reproach or blot
Who do thy work, and know it not;
Oh! if through confidence misplaced   1
They fail, thy saving arms, dread Power! around them cast.

Serene will be our days and bright,
And happy will our nature be,
When love is an unerring light,
And joy its own security.   2
And they a blissful course may hold
Even now, who, not unwisely bold,
Live in the spirit of this creed;
Yet seek thy firm support, according to their need.

I, loving freedom, and untried,   2
No sport of every random gust,
Yet being to myself a guide,
Too blindly have reposed my trust,

And oft, when in my heart was heard
Thy timely mandate, I deferred   30
The task, in smoother walks to stray;
But thee I now would serve more strictly, if I may.

Through no disturbance of my soul,
Or strong compunction in me wrought,
I supplicate for thy control,   35
But in the quietness of thought;
Me this unchartered freedom tires;
I feel the weight of chance-desires;
My hopes no more must change their name,
I long for a repose that ever is the same.   40

Stern Lawgiver! yet thou dost wear
The Godhead's most benignant grace;
Nor know we anything so fair
As is the smile upon thy face;
Flowers laugh before thee on their beds   45
And fragrance in thy footing treads;
Thou dost preserve the stars from wrong;
And the most ancient heavens, through Thee, are fresh and strong.

To humbler functions, awful Power!
I call thee: I myself commend   50
Unto thy guidance from this hour;
Oh, let my weakness have an end!
Give unto me, made lowly wise,
The spirit of self-sacrifice;
The confidence of reason give;   55
And in the light of truth thy bondman let me live!

WILLIAM WORDSWORTH

Bright Star

Bright star, would I were steadfast as thou art—
    Not in lone splendor hung aloft the night
And watching, with eternal lids apart,
    Like nature's patient, sleepless Eremite,
The moving waters at their priest-like task   5
    Of pure ablution round earth's human shores,
Or gazing on the new soft-fallen mask
    Of snow upon the mountains and the moors—
No—yet still steadfast, still unchangeable,

Pillowed upon my fair love's ripening breast,   10
To feel for ever its soft fall and swell,
   Awake for ever in a sweet unrest,
Still, still to hear her tender-taken breath,
And so live ever—or else swoon to death.

JOHN KEATS

Excelsior

The shades of night were falling fast,
As through an Alpine village passed
A youth, who bore, 'mid snow and ice,
A banner with the strange device,
   Excelsior!   5

His brow was sad; his eye beneath,
Flashed like a falchion from its sheath,
And like a silver clarion rung
The accents of that unknown tongue,
   Excelsior!   10

In happy homes he saw the light
Of household fires gleam warm and bright;
Above, the spectral glaciers shone,
And from his lips escaped a groan,
   Excelsior!   15

"Try not the Pass!" the old man said;
"Dark lowers the tempest overhead,
The roaring torrent is deep and wide!"
And loud that clarion voice replied,
   Excelsior!   20

"O stay," the maiden said, "and rest
Thy weary head upon this breast!"
A tear stood in his bright blue eye,
But still he answered, with a sigh,
   Excelsior!   25

"Beware the pine tree's withered branch!
Beware the awful avalanche!"
This was the peasant's last good-night;
A voice replied, far up the height,
   Excelsior!   30

At break of day, as heavenward
The pious monks of Saint Bernard
Uttered the oft-repeated prayer,
A voice cried through the startled air,
   Excelsior!   35

A traveller, by the faithful hound,
Half-buried in the snow was found,
Still grasping in his hand of ice
That banner with the strange device,
   Excelsior!   40

There in the twilight cold and gray,
Lifeless, but beautiful, he lay,
And from the sky, serene and far,
A voice fell, like a falling star,
   Excelsior!   45

HENRY WADSWORTH LONGFELLOW

Ulysses

It little profits that an idle king,
By this still hearth, among these barren crags,
Matched with an aged wife, I mete and dole
Unequal laws unto a savage race,
That hoard, and sleep, and feed, and know not me.   5
I cannot rest from travel: I will drink
Life to the lees; all times I have enjoyed
Greatly, have suffered greatly, both with those
That loved me, and alone; on shore, and when
Through scudding drifts the rainy Hyades   10
Vexed the dim sea: I am become a name;
For always roaming with a hungry heart
Much have I seen and known; cities of men
And manners, climates, councils, governments,
Myself not least, but honoured of them all;   15
And drunk delight of battle with my peers,
Far on the ringing plains of windy Troy.
I am a part of all that I have met;
Yet all experience is an arch wherethrough
Gleams that untravelled world, whose margin fades   20
For ever and for ever when I move.
How dull it is to pause, to make an end,

To rust unburnished, not to shine in use!
As though to breathe were life! Life piled on life
Were all too little, and of one to me   25
Little remains; but every hour is saved
From that eternal silence, something more,
A bringer of new things; and vile it were
For some three suns to store and hoard myself,
And this grey spirit yearning in desire   30
To follow knowledge like a sinking star,
Beyond the utmost bound of human thought.
   This is my son, mine own Telemachus,
To whom I leave the sceptre and the isle—
Well-loved of me, discerning to fulfil   35
This labour, by slow prudence to make mild
A rugged people, and through soft degrees
Subdue them to the useful and the good.
Most blameless is he, centered in the sphere
Of common duties, decent not to fail   40
In offices of tenderness, and pay
Meet adoration to my household gods,
When I am gone. He works his work, I mine.
   There lies the port; the vessel puffs her sail:
There gloom the dark broad seas. My mariners,   45
Souls that have toiled and wrought, and thought with me—
That ever with a frolic welcome took
The thunder and the sunshine, and opposed
Free hearts, free foreheads—you and I are old;
Old age hath yet his honour and his toil;   50
Death closes all; but something ere the end,
Some work of noble note, may yet be done,
Not unbecoming men that strove with Gods.
The lights begin to twinkle from the rocks:
The long day wanes: the slow moon climbs: the deep   55
Moans round with many voices. Come, my friends,
'Tis not too late to seek a newer world.
Push off, and sitting well in order smite
The sounding furrows; for my purpose holds
To sail beyond the sunset, and the baths   60
Of all the western stars, until I die.
It may be that the gulfs will wash us down:
It may be we shall touch the Happy Isles,
And see the great Achilles, whom we knew.
Though much is taken, much abides; and though   65
We are not now that strength which in old days
Moved earth and heaven; that which we are, we are;
One equal temper of heroic hearts,

Made weak by time and fate, but strong in will
To strive, to seek, to find, and not to yield.   70

ALFRED, LORD TENNYSON

The Lost Leader

Just for a handful of silver he left us,
    Just for a riband to stick in his coat—
Found the one gift of which fortune bereft us,
    Lost all the others she lets us devote;
They, with the gold to give, doled him out silver,   5
    So much was theirs who so little allowed;
How all our copper had gone for his service!
    Rags—were they purple, his heart had been proud!
We that had loved him so, followed him, honored him,
    Lived in his mild and magnificent eye,   10
Learned his great language, caught his clear accents,
    Made him our pattern to live and to die!
Shakespeare was of us, Milton was for us,
    Burns, Shelley, were with us—they watch from
        their graves!
He alone breaks from the van and the freemen—   15
    He alone sinks to the rear and the slaves!

We shall march prospering—not through his presence;
    Songs may inspirit us—not from his lyre;
Deeds will be done—while he boasts his quiescence,
    Still bidding crouch whom the rest bade aspire;   20
Blot out his name, then, record one lost soul more,
    One task more declined, one more footpath untrod,
One more devils'-triumph and sorrow for angels,
    One wrong more to man, one more insult to God!
Life's night begins; let him never come back to us!   25
    There would be doubt, hesitation, and pain,
Forced praise on our part—the glimmer of twilight,
    Never glad confident morning again!
Best fight on well, for we taught him—strike gallantly,
    Menace our heart ere we master his own;   30
Then let him receive the new knowledge and wait us,
    Pardoned in heaven, the first by the throne!

ROBERT BROWNING

Say Not the Struggle Nought Availeth

Say not the struggle nought availeth,
   The labour and the wounds are vain,
The enemy faints not, nor faileth,
   And as things have been they remain.

If hopes were dupes, fears may be liars;   5
   It may be, in yon smoke concealed,
Your comrades chase e'en now the fliers,
   And, but for you, possess the field.

For while the tired waves, vainly breaking,
   Seem here no painful inch to gain,   10
Far back, through creeks and inlets making,
   Comes silent, flooding in, the main.

And not by eastern windows only,
   When daylight comes, comes in the light,
In front, the sun climbs slow, how slowly,   15
   But westward, look, the land is bright.

ARTHUR HUGH CLOUGH

Pis-Aller[1]

"Man is blind because of sin;
Revelation makes him sure.
Without that, who looks within,
Looks in vain, for all's obscure."

Nay, look closer into man!   5
Tell me, can you find indeed
Nothing sure, no moral plan
Clear prescribed, without your creed?

"No, I nothing can perceive!
Without that, all's dark for men.   10
That, or nothing, I believe."—
For God's sake, believe it then!

MATTHEW ARNOLD

[1] A last resource.

The Better Part

Long fed on boundless hopes, O race of man,
How angrily thou spurn'st all simpler fare!
"Christ," someone says, "was human as we are;
No judge eyes us from heaven, our sin to scan;
We live no more, when we have done our span."—   5
"Well, then, for Christ," thou answerest, "who can care?
From sin, which heaven records not, why forbear?
Live we like brutes our life without a plan!"
So answerest thou; but why not rather say:
"Hath man no second life?—*Pitch this one high!*   10
Sits there no judge in heaven, our sin to see?
More strictly, then, the inward judge obey!
Was Christ a man like us? *Ah! let us try*
If we then, too, can be such men as he!"

MATTHEW ARNOLD

East London

'Twas August, and the fierce sun overhead
Smote on the squalid streets of Bethnal Green,
And the pale weaver, through his windows seen
In Spitalfields, looked thrice dispirited.
I met a preacher there I knew, and said: 5
"Ill and o'erworked, how fare you in this scene?"—
"Bravely!" said he; "for I of late have been
Much cheered with thoughts of Christ, *the living bread.*"
O human soul! as long as thou canst so
Set up a mark of everlasting light,   10
Above the howling senses' ebb and flow,
To cheer thee, and to right thee if thou roam—
Not with lost toil thou laborest through the night!
Thou mak'st the heaven thou hop'st indeed thy home.

MATTHEW ARNOLD

The Last Word

Creep into thy narrow bed,
Creep, and let no more be said!

Vain thy onset! all stands fast.
Thou thyself must break at last.

Let the long contention cease!   5
Geese are swans, and swans are geese.
Let them have it how they will!
Thou art tired; best be still!

They out-talked thee, hissed thee, tore thee.
Better men fared thus before thee;   10
Fired their ringing shot and passed,
Hotly charged—and broke at last.

Charge once more, then, and be dumb!
Let the victors, when they come,
When the forts of folly fall,   15
Find thy body by the wall!

MATTHEW ARNOLD

Song of the Chattahoochee

Out of the hills of Habersham,
  Down the valleys of Hall,
I hurry amain to reach the plain,
Run the rapid and leap the fall,
Split at the rock and together again,   5
Accept my bed, or narrow or wide,
And flee from folly on every side
With a lover's pain to attain the plain
  Far from the hills of Habersham,
  Far from the valleys of Hall.   10

All down the hills of Habersham,
  All through the valleys of Hall,
The rushes cried *Abide, abide,*
The willful waterweeds held me thrall,
The laving laurel turned my tide,   15
The ferns and the fondling grass said *Stay,*
The dewberry dipped for to work delay,
And the little reeds sighed *Abide, abide,*
  Here in the hills of Habersham,
  Here in the valleys of Hall.   20

High o'er the hills of Habersham,
  Veiling the valleys of Hall,

The hickory told me manifold
Fair tales of shade, the poplar tall
Wrought me her shadowy self to hold,   25
The chestnut, the oak, the walnut, the pine,
Overleaning, with flickering meaning and sign,
Said, *Pass not, so cold, these manifold*
  Deep shades of the hills of Habersham,
  These glades in the valleys of Hall.   30

  And oft in the hills of Habersham,
  And oft in the valleys of Hall,
The white quartz shone, and the smooth brook-stone
Did bar me of passage with friendly brawl,
And many a luminous jewel lone   35
—Crystals clear or a-cloud with mist,
Ruby, garnet and amethyst—
Made lures with the lights of streaming stone
  In the clefts of the hills of Habersham,
  In the beds of the valleys of Hall.   40

  But oh, not the hills of Habersham,
  And oh, not the valleys of Hall
Avail: I am fain for to water the plain.
Downward the voices of Duty call—
Downward, to toil and be mixed with the main,   45
The dry fields burn, and the mills are to turn,
And a myriad flowers mortally yearn,
And the lordly main from beyond the plain
  Calls o'er the hills of Habersham,
  Calls through the valleys of Hall.   50

                           SIDNEY LANIER

Invictus

  Out of the night that covers me,
    Black as the Pit from pole to pole,
  I thank whatever gods may be
    For my unconquerable soul.

  In the fell clutch of circumstance   5
    I have not winced nor cried aloud.
  Under the bludgeonings of chance
    My head is bloody, but unbowed.

Beyond this place of wrath and tears
   Looms but the horror of the shade,   10
And yet the menace of the years
   Finds, and shall find, me unafraid.

It matters not how strait the gate,
   How charged with punishments the scroll,
I am the master of my fate: 15
   I am the captain of my soul.

WILLIAM ERNEST HENLEY

The White Man's Burden

Take up the White Man's burden—
   Send forth the best ye breed—
Go bind your sons to exile
   To serve your captives' need;
To wait in heavy harness,   5
   On fluttered folk and wild—
Your new-caught, sullen peoples,
   Half-devil and half-child.

Take up the White Man's burden—
   In patience to abide,   10
To veil the threat of terror
   And check the show of pride;
By open speech and simple,
   An hundred times made plain,
To seek another's profit,   15
   And work another's gain.

Take up the White Man's burden—
   The savage wars of peace—
Fill full the mouth of Famine
   And bid the sickness cease;   20
And when your goal is nearest
   The end for others sought,
Watch Sloth and heathen Folly
   Bring all your hope to nought.

Take up the White Man's burden—   25
   No tawdry rule of kings,
But toil of serf and sweeper—
   The tale of common things.

The ports ye shall not enter,
    The roads ye shall not tread,   30
Go make them with your living,
    And mark them with your dead.

Take up the White Man's burden—
    And reap his old reward:
The blame of those ye better,   35
    The hate of those ye guard—
The cry of hosts ye humour
    (Ah, slowly!) toward the light:—
"Why brought ye us from bondage,
    "Our loved Egyptian night?"   40

Take up the White Man's burden—
    Ye dare not stoop to less—
Nor call too loud on Freedom
    To cloak your weariness;
By all ye cry or whisper,   45
    By all ye leave or do,
The silent, sullen peoples
    Shall weigh your Gods and you.

Take up the White Man's burden—
    Have done with childish days—   50
The lightly proffered laurel,
    The easy, ungrudged praise.
Comes now, to search your manhood
    Through all the thankless years,
Cold-edged with dear-bought wisdom,   55
    The judgment of your peers!

RUDYARD KIPLING

I Saw a Man

I saw a man pursuing the horizon;
Round and round they sped.
I was disturbed at this;
I accosted the man.
"It is futile," I said,   5
"You can never—"
"You lie," he cried,
And ran on.

STEPHEN CRANE

The Road Not Taken

Two roads diverged in a yellow wood,
And sorry I could not travel both
And be one traveler, long I stood
And looked down one as far as I could
To where it bent in the undergrowth;   5

Then took the other, as just as fair,
And having perhaps the better claim,
Because it was grassy and wanted wear;
Though as for that the passing there
Had worn them really about the same,   10

And both that morning equally lay
In leaves no step had trodden black.
Oh, I kept the first for another day!
Yet knowing how way leads on to way,
I doubted if I should ever come back.   15

I shall be telling this with a sigh
Somewhere ages and ages hence:
Two roads diverged in a wood, and I—
I took the one less traveled by,
And that has made all the difference.   20

ROBERT FROST

Stopping by Woods on a Snowy Evening

Whose woods these are I think I know.
His house is in the village though;
He will not see me stopping here
To watch his woods fill up with snow.

My little horse must think it queer   5
To stop without a farmhouse near
Between the woods and frozen lake
The darkest evening of the year.

He gives his harness bells a shake
To ask if there is some mistake.   10
The only other sound's the sweep
Of easy wind and downy flake.

The woods are lovely, dark and deep,
But I have promises to keep,
And miles to go before I sleep,   15
And miles to go before I sleep.

ROBERT FROST

Choose Something like a Star

O Star (the fairest one in sight),
We grant your loftiness the right
To some obscurity of cloud—
It will not do to say of night,
Since dark is what brings out your light.   5
Some mystery becomes the proud,
But to be wholly taciturn
In your reserve is not allowed.
Say something to us we can learn
By heart and when alone repeat.   10
Say something! And it says "I burn."
But say with what degree of heat.
Talk Fahrenheit, talk Centigrade.
Use language we can comprehend.
Tell us what elements you blend.   15
It gives us strangely little aid,
But does tell something in the end.
And steadfast as Keats' Eremite,
Not even stooping from its sphere,
It asks a little of us here.   20
It asks of us a certain height,
So when at times the mob is swayed
To carry praise or blame too far,
We may choose something like a star
To stay our minds on and be staid.   25

ROBERT FROST

Provide, Provide

The witch that came (the withered hag)
To wash the steps with pail and rag,
Was once the beauty Abishag,

The picture pride of Hollywood.
Too many fall from great and good   5
For you to doubt the likelihood.

Die early and avoid the fate.
Or if predestined to die late,
Make up your mind to die in state.

Make the whole stock exchange your own!   10
If need be occupy a throne,
Where nobody can call *you* crone.

Some have relied on what they knew;
Others on being simply true.
What worked for them might work for you.   15

No memory of having starred
Atones for later disregard,
Or keeps the end from being hard.

Better to go down dignified
With boughten friendship at your side   20
Than none at all. Provide, provide!

ROBERT FROST

The Listeners

"Is there anybody there?" said the Traveller,
    Knocking on the moonlit door;
And his horse in the silence champed the grasses
    Of the forest's ferny floor:
And a bird flew up out of the turret,   5
    Above the Traveller's head:
And he smote upon the door again a second time;
    "Is there anybody there?" he said.
But no one descended to the Traveller;
    No head from the leaf-fringed sill   10
Leaned over and looked into his grey eyes,
    Where he stood perplexed and still.
But only a host of phantom listeners
    That dwelt in the lone house then
Stood listening in the quiet of the moonlight   15
    To that voice from the world of men:
Stood thronging the faint moonbeams on the dark stair
    That goes down to the empty hall,

Hearkening in an air stirred and shaken
   By the lonely Traveller's call.   20
And he felt in his heart their strangeness,
   Their stillness answering his cry,
While his horse moved, cropping the dark turf,
   'Neath the starred and leafy sky;
For he suddenly smote on the door, even   25
   Louder, and lifted his head:—
"Tell them I came, and no one answered,
   That I kept my word!" he said.
Never the least stir made the listeners,
   Though every word he spake   30
Fell echoing through the shadowiness of the still house
   From the one man left awake.
Ay, they heard his foot upon the stirrup,
   And the sound of iron on stone,
And how the silence surged softly backward,   35
   When the plunging hoofs were gone.

WALTER DE LA MARE

In Waste Places

As a naked man I go
Through the desert, sore afraid;
Holding high my head, although
I'm as frightened as a maid.

The lion crouches there! I saw   5
In barren rocks his amber eye!
He parts the cactus with his paw!
He stares at me as I go by!

He would pad upon my trace
If he thought I was afraid!   10
If he knew my hardy face
Veils the terrors of a maid.

He rises in the night-time, and
He stretches forth! He snuffs the air!
He roars! He leaps along the sand!   15
He creeps! He watches everywhere!

His burning eyes, his eyes of bale
Through the darkness I can see!

He lashes fiercely with his tail!
He makes again to spring at me! 20

I am the lion, and his lair!
I am the fear that frightens me!
I am the desert of despair!
And the night of agony!

Night or day, whate'er befall, 25
I must walk that desert land,
Until I dare my fear and call
The lion out to lick my hand.

JAMES STEPHENS

Nevertheless

you've seen a strawberry
    that's had a struggle; yet
        was, where the fragments met,

a hedgehog or a star-
    fish for the multitude 5
        of seeds. What better food

than apple-seeds—the fruit
    within the fruit—locked in
        like counter-curved twin

hazel-nuts? Frost that kills 10
    the little rubber-plant-
        leaves of *kok-saghyz*-stalks, can't

harm the roots; they still grow
    in frozen ground. Once where
        there was a prickly-pear- 15

leaf clinging to barbed wire,
    a root shot down to grow
        in earth two feet below;

as carrots form mandrakes
    or a ram's-horn root some- 20
        times. Victory won't come

to me unless I go
     to it; a grape-tendril
     ties a knot in knots till

knotted thirty times,—so   25
     the bound twig that's under-
     gone and over-gone, can't stir.

The weak overcomes its
     menace, the strong over-
     comes itself. What is there   30

like fortitude! What sap
     went through that little thread
     to make the cherry red!

                           MARIANNE MOORE

Kind of an Ode to Duty

O Duty,
Why hast thou not the visage of a sweetie or a cutie?
Why glitter thy spectacles so ominously?
Why art thou clad so abominously?
Why art thou so different from Venus   5
And why do thou and I have so few interests mutually in common
    between us?
Why art thou fifty per cent martyr
And fifty-one per cent Tartar?

Why is it thy unfortunate wont
To try to attract people by calling on them either to leave undone
    the deeds they like or to do the deeds they don't?   10
Why art thou so like an April post-mortem
On something that died in the ortumn?
Above all, why dost thou continue to hound me?
Why art thou always albatrossly hanging around me?

Thou so ubiquitous,   15
And I so iniquitous.
I seem to be the one person in the world thou art perpetually
    preaching at who or to who;
Whatever looks like fun, there art thou standing between me and it,
    calling yoo-hoo.
O Duty, Duty!

How noble a man should I be hadst thou the visage of a sweetie
    or a cutie!   20
But as it is thou art so much forbiddinger than a Wodehouse hero's
    forbiddingest aunt
That in the words of the poet, When Duty whispers low, Thou
    must, this erstwhile youth replies, I just can't.

OGDEN NASH

13
Death

Of all the subjects of poetry, none has occupied the poet more than death. As might be assumed from a mystery so overwhelming as death, there is a wide range of tones and attitudes toward it. The selections in this group represent some of the finest and most moving statements about death to be found in our language.

Some poets see death as a release from the hard bitterness of life, while others see it as the greatest of evils and find its prospect horrifying. Donne, in "Death Be Not Proud," addresses his comments to death and says that in the end, when one comes to God, death itself will die. There are poems in this section that are written to ease the pain of death, to teach one that he should go to the final end joyously, or at least with resignation. But Dylan Thomas's "Do Not Go Gentle into That Good Night" admonishes the dying to fight the evil of darkness to the last—"rage, rage against the dying of the light." And finally there is Cummings's poem, in which the speaker sees death as very desirable sometimes. She likes "to think of dead" and believes it has "a smile like the nicest man you've never met."

READINGS IN OTHER GENRES

PLAYS

Leonid Andreyev, *The Life of Man*
Albert Camus, *Caligula*
Euripides, *Alcestis*
Everyman
Archibald MacLeish, *J. B.*
Arthur Miller, *Death of a Salesman*
Ferenc Molnar, *Liliom*
Eugene O'Neill, *Lazarus Laughed*
Jean-Paul Sartre, *No Exit, The Victors*
Sutton Vane, *Outward Bound*

NOVELS

James Agee, *A Death in the Family*
William Faulkner, *As I Lay Dying*
Ernest Hemingway, *Death in the Afternoon*
William Saroyan, *The Human Comedy*
Leo Tolstoy, *The Death of Ivan Ilyich*
Evelyn Waugh, *The Loved One*

SHORT STORIES

Conrad Aiken, "Secret Snow, Silent Snow"
Sherwood Anderson, "Brother Death"
Leonid Andreyev, "The Seven Who Were Hanged"
Isaac Babel, "The Death of Dolgushov"
Ivan Bunin, "The Gentleman from San Francisco"
William Faulkner, "A Rose for Emily"
Ernest Hemingway, "The Snows of Kilimanjaro"
D. H. Lawrence, "The Rocking-Horse Winner"
Thomas Mann, "Death in Venice"
Edgar Allan Poe, "Ligeia"
Katherine Anne Porter, "The Jilting of Granny Weatherall"
J. D. Salinger, "A Perfect Day for Banana Fish"
Jean-Paul Sartre, "The Wall"
Jean Stafford, "The Interior Castle"
Eudora Welty, "Death of a Traveling Salesman"

On the Life of Man

What is our life? a play of passion,
Our mirth the music of division,
Our mothers' wombs the tiring houses be,
Where we are dressed for this short comedy,
Heaven the judicious sharp spectator is,   5
That sits and marks still who doth act amiss,
Our graves that hide us from the searching sun,
Are like drawn curtains when the play is done,
Thus march we playing to our latest rest,
Only we die in earnest, that's no jest.   10

                    SIR WALTER RALEIGH

To Be, or Not to Be

To be, or not to be—that is the question.
Whether 'tis nobler in the mind to suffer
The slings and arrows of outrageous fortune,
Or to take arms against a sea of troubles
And by opposing end them. To die, to sleep—   5
No more, and by a sleep to say we end
The heartache and the thousand natural shocks
That flesh is heir to. 'Tis a consummation
Devoutly to be wished. To die, to sleep,
To sleep—perchance to dream. Aye, there's the rub,   10
For in that sleep of death what dreams may come
When we have shuffled off this mortal coil
Must give us pause. There's the respect
That makes calamity of so long life.
For who would bear the whips and scorns of time,   15
The oppressor's wrong, the proud man's contumely
The pangs of despised love, the law's delay,
The insolence of office, and the spurns
That patient merit of the unworthy takes,
When he himself might his quietus make   20
With a bare bodkin? Who would fardels bear,
To grunt and sweat under a weary life,
But that the dread of something after death,
The undiscovered country from whose bourn
No traveler returns, puzzles the will,   25
And makes us rather bear those ills we have
Than fly to others that we know not of?
Thus conscience does make cowards of us all,
And thus the native hue of resolution
Is sicklied o'er with the pale cast of thought,   30
And enterprises of great pith and moment
With this regard their currents turn awry
And lose the name of action.

WILLIAM SHAKESPEARE
(from Hamlet)

Upon the Image of Death

Before my face the picture hangs
   That daily should put me in mind
Of these cold names and bitter pangs
   That shortly I am like to find;

But yet, alas, full little I   5
Do think hereon that I must die.

I often look upon a face
    Most ugly, grisly, bare, and thin;
I often view the hollow place
    Where eyes and nose had sometimes been;   10
I see the bones across that lie,
Yet little think that I must die.

I read the label underneath,
    That telleth me whereto I must;
I see the sentence eke that saith   15
    Remember, man, that thou art dust!
But yet, alas, but seldom I
Do think indeed that I must die.

Continually at my bed's head
    A hearse doth hang, which doth me tell   20
That I ere morning may be dead,
    Though now I feel myself full well;
But yet, alas, for all this, I
Have little mind that I must die.

The gown which I do use to wear,   25
    The knife wherewith I cut my meat,
And eke that old and ancient chair
    Which is my only usual seat,—
All those do tell me I must die,
And yet my life amend not I.   30

My ancestors are turned to clay,
    And many of my mates are gone;
My youngers daily drop away,
    And can I think to 'scape alone?
No, no, I know that I must die,   35
And yet my life amend not I.

Not Solomon for all his wit,
    Nor Samson, though he were so strong,
No king nor person ever yet
    Could 'scape but death laid him along;   40
Wherefore I know that I must die,
And yet my life amend not I.

Though all the East did quake to hear
    Of Alexander's dreadful name,

And all the West did likewise fear   45
  To hear of Julius Caesar's fame,
Yet both by death in dust now lie;
Who then can 'scape but he must die?

If none can 'scape death's dreadful dart,
  If rich and poor his beck obey,   50
If strong, if wise, if all do smart,
  Then I to 'scape shall have no way.
Oh, grant me grace, Oh God, that I
My life may mend, sith I must die.

ROBERT SOUTHWELL

Death, Be Not Proud

Death, be not proud, though some have callèd thee
Mighty and dreadful, for thou art not so;
For those whom thou think'st thou dost overthrow
Die not, poor Death; nor yet canst thou kill me.
From rest and sleep, which but thy pictures be,   5
Much pleasure; then from thee much more must flow;
And soonest our best men with thee do go—
Rest of their bones and souls' delivery!
Thou'rt slave to fate, chance, kings, and desperate men,
And dost with poison, war, and sickness dwell;   10
And poppy or charms can make us sleep as well
And better than thy stroke. Why swell'st thou then?
One short sleep past, we wake eternally,
And Death shall be no more: Death, thou shalt die.

JOHN DONNE

Mortification

How soon doth man decay!
When clothes are taken from a chest of sweets
  To swaddle infants, whose young breath
    Scarce knows the way,
  Those clouts are little winding-sheets   5
Which do consign and send them unto death.

  When boys go first to bed,
They step into their voluntary graves;

> Sleep binds them fast; only their breath
>   Makes them not dead.   10
> Successive nights, like rolling waves,
> Convey them quickly who are bound for death.
>
> When youth is frank and free,
> And calls for music, while his veins do swell,
>   All day exchanging mirth and breath   15
>   In company,
>   That music summons to the knell
> Which shall befriend him at the house of death.
>
> When man grows staid and wise,
> Getting a house and home, where he may move   20
>   Within the circle of his breath,
>   Schooling his eyes,
>   That dumb inclosure maketh love
> Unto the coffin that attends his death.
>
> When age grows low and weak,   25
> Marking his grave, and thawing ev'ry year,
>   Till all do melt and drown his breath
>   When he would speak,
>   A chair or litter shows the bier
> Which shall convey him to the house of death.   30
>
> Man, ere he is aware,
> Hath put together a solemnity,
>   And dressed his hearse, while he has breath
>   As yet to spare;
>   Yet, Lord, instruct us so to die,   35
> That all these dyings may be life in death.

GEORGE HERBERT

On My First Son

> Farewell, thou child of my right hand, and joy;
>   My sin was too much hope of thee, loved boy:
> Seven years thou wert lent to me, and I thee pay,
>   Exacted by thy fate, on the just day.
> Oh, could I lose all father now! for why   5
> Will man lament the state he should envy—
> To have so soon 'scaped world's and flesh's rage,
>   And, if no other misery, yet age?

Rest in soft peace, and asked, say, "Here doth lie
   Ben Jonson his best piece of poetry;   10
For whose sake henceforth all his vows be such
   As what he loves may never like too much."

BEN JONSON

Elegy
Written in a Country Churchyard

The curfew tolls the knell of parting day,
   The lowing herd wind slowly o'er the lea,
The plowman homeward plods his weary way,
   And leaves the world to darkness and to me.

Now fades the glimmering landscape on the sight,   5
   And all the air a solemn stillness holds,
Save where the beetle wheels his droning flight,
   And drowsy tinklings lull the distant folds;

Save that from yonder ivy-mantled tower
   The moping owl does to the moon complain   10
Of such, as wandering near her secret bower,
   Molest her ancient solitary reign.

Beneath those rugged elms, that yew-tree's shade,
   Where heaves the turf in many a mouldering heap,
Each in his narrow cell for ever laid,   15
   The rude forefathers of the hamlet sleep.

The breezy call of incense-breathing morn,
   The swallow twittering from the straw-built shed,
The cock's shrill clarion, or the echoing horn,
   No more shall rouse them from their lowly bed.   20

For them no more the blazing hearth shall burn,
   Or busy housewife ply her evening care;
No children run to lisp their sire's return,
   Or climb his knees the envied kiss to share.

Oft did the harvest to their sickle yield,   25
   Their furrow oft the stubborn glebe has broke;
How jocund did they drive their team afield!
   How bowed the woods beneath their sturdy stroke!

Let not Ambition mock their useful toil,
    Their homely joys, and destiny obscure;   30
Nor Grandeur hear with a disdainful smile
    The short and simple annals of the poor.

The boast of heraldry, the pomp of power,
    And all that beauty, all that wealth e'er gave,
Awaits alike the inevitable hour.   35
    The paths of glory lead but to the grave.

Nor you, ye proud, impute to these the fault,
    If Memory o'er their tomb no trophies raise,
Where through the long-drawn aisle and fretted vault
    The pealing anthem swells the note of praise.   40

Can storied urn or animated bust
    Back to its mansion call the fleeting breath?
Can Honor's voice provoke the silent dust,
    Or Flattery sooth the dull cold ear of Death?

Perhaps in this neglected spot is laid   45
    Some heart once pregnant with celestial fire;
Hands, that the rod of empire might have swayed,
    Or waked to ecstasy the living lyre.

But Knowledge to their eyes her ample page
    Rich with the spoils of time did ne'er unroll;   50
Chill Penury repressed their noble rage,
    And froze the genial current of the soul.

Full many a gem of purest ray serene,
    The dark unfathomed caves of ocean bear:
Full many a flower is born to blush unseen,   55
    And waste its sweetness on the desert air.

Some village-Hampden, that with dauntless breast
    The little Tyrant of his fields withstood;
Some mute inglorious Milton here may rest,
    Some Cromwell guiltless of his country's blood.   60

The applause of listening senates to command,
    The threats of pain and ruin to despise,
To scatter plenty o'er a smiling land,
    And read their history in a nation's eyes,

Their lot forbade: nor circumscribed alone   65
    Their growing virtues, but their crimes confined;

Forbade to wade through slaughter to a throne,
   And shut the gates of mercy on mankind,

The struggling pangs of conscious truth to hide,
   To quench the blushes of ingenuous shame,
Or heap the shrine of Luxury and Pride
   With incense kindled at the Muse's flame.

Far from the madding crowd's ignoble strife,
   Their sober wishes never learned to stray;
Along the cool sequestered vale of life
   They kept the noiseless tenor of their way.

Yet even these bones from insult to protect,
   Some frail memorial still erected nigh,
With uncouth rhymes and shapeless sculpture decked,
   Implores the passing tribute of a sigh.

Their name, their years, spelt by the unlettered muse,
   The place of fame and elegy supply:
And many a holy text around she strews,
   That teach the rustic moralist to die.

For who to dumb Forgetfulness a prey,
   This pleasing anxious being e'er resigned,
Left the warm precincts of the cheerful day, .
   Nor cast one longing lingering look behind?

On some fond breast the parting soul relies,
   Some pious drops the closing eye requires;
Ev'n from the tomb the voice of Nature cries,
   Ev'n in our ashes live their wonted fires.

For thee, who mindful of the unhonored dead
   Dost in these lines their artless tale relate,
If chance, by lonely contemplation led,
   Some kindred spirit shall inquire thy fate,

Haply some hoary-headed swain may say,
   "Oft have we seen him at the peep of dawn
Brushing with hasty steps the dews away
   To meet the sun upon the upland lawn.

"There at the foot of yonder nodding beech
   That wreathes its old fantastic roots so high,
His listless length at noontide would he stretch,
   And pore upon the brook that babbles by.

"Hard by yon wood, now smiling as in scorn,   105
   Muttering his wayward fancies he would rove;
Now drooping, woeful-wan, like one forlorn,
   Or crazed with care, or crossed in hopeless love.

"One morn I missed him on the customed hill,
   Along the heath, and near his favorite tree;   110
Another came; nor yet beside the rill,
   Nor up the lawn, nor at the wood was he;

"The next with dirges due in sad array
   Slow through the church-way path we saw him borne,—
Approach and read (for thou can'st read) the lay,   115
   Graved on the stone beneath yon agèd thorn."

The Epitaph

Here rests his head upon the lap of earth
   A youth to fortune and to fame unknown;
Fair Science frowned not on his humble birth,
   And Melancholy marked him for her own.   120

Large was his bounty, and his soul sincere;
   Heaven did a recompense as largely send:
He gave to Misery (all he had) a tear,
   He gained from Heaven ('twas all he wished) a friend.

No farther seek his merits to disclose,   125
   Or draw his frailties from their dread abode
(There they alike in trembling hope repose),
   The bosom of his Father and his God.

THOMAS GRAY

Tithonus

The woods decay, the woods decay and fall,
The vapours weep their burthen to the ground,
Man comes and tills the field and lies beneath,
And after many a summer dies the swan.
Me only cruel immortality   5
Consumes: I wither slowly in thine arms,
Here at the quiet limit of the world,
A white-haired shadow roaming like a dream
The ever-silent spaces of the East,
Far-folded mists, and gleaming halls of morn.   10

Alas! for this gray shadow, once a man—
So glorious in his beauty and thy choice,
Who madest him thy chosen, that he seemed
To his great heart none other than a God!
I asked thee, "Give me immortality."   15
Then didst thou grant mine asking with a smile,
Like wealthy men who care not how they give.
But thy strong Hours indignant worked their wills,
And beat me down and marred and wasted me,
And though they could not end me, left me maimed   20
To dwell in presence of immortal youth,
Immortal age beside immortal youth,
And all I was, in ashes. Can thy love,
Thy beauty, make amends, though even now
Close over us, the silver star, thy guide,   25
Shines in those tremulous eyes that fill with tears
To hear me? Let me go; take back thy gift;
Why should a man desire in any way
To vary from the kindly race of men,
Or pass beyond the goal of ordinance   30
Where all should pause, as is most meet for all?

A soft air fans the cloud apart; there comes
A glimpse of that dark world where I was born.
Once more the old mysterious glimmer steals
From thy pure brows, and from thy shoulders pure,   35
And bosom beating with a heart renewed.
Thy cheek begins to redden through the gloom,
Thy sweet eyes brighten slowly close to mine,
Ere yet they blind the stars, and the wild team
Which love thee, yearning for thy yoke, arise,   40
And shake the darkness from their loosened manes,
And beat the twilight into flakes of fire.

Lo! ever thus thou growest beautiful
In silence, then before thine answer given
Departest, and thy tears are on my cheek.   45
Why wilt thou ever scare me with thy tears,
And make me tremble lest a saying learnt,
In days far-off, on that dark earth, be true?
"The Gods themselves cannot recall their gifts."

Ay me! ay me! with what another heart   50
In days far-off, and with what other eyes
I used to watch—if I be he that watched—
The lucid outline forming round thee; saw
The dim curls kindle into sunny rings;

Changed with thy mystic change, and felt my blood   55
Glow with the glow that slowly crimsoned all
Thy presence and thy portals, while I lay,
Mouth, forehead, eyelids, growing dewy-warm
With kisses balmier than half-opening buds
Of April, and could hear the lips that kissed   60
Whispering I knew not what of wild and sweet,
Like that strange song I heard Apollo sing,
While Ilion like a mist rose into towers.

    Yet hold me not for ever in thine East:
How can my nature longer mix with thine?   65
Coldly thy rosy shadows bathe me, cold
Are all thy lights, and cold my wrinkled feet
Upon thy glimmering thresholds, when the steam
Floats up from those dim fields about the homes
Of happy men that have the power to die,   70
And grassy barrows of the happier dead.
Release me, and restore me to the ground;
Thou seëst all things, thou wilt see my grave:
Thou wilt renew thy beauty morn by morn;
I earth in earth forget these empty courts,   75
And thee returning on thy silver wheels.

ALFRED, LORD TENNYSON

Crossing the Bar

Sunset and evening star,
   And one clear call for me!
And may there be no moaning of the bar,
   When I put out to sea,

But such a tide as moving seems asleep,   5
   Too full for sound and foam,
When that which drew from out the boundless deep
   Turns again home.

Twilight and evening bell,
   And after that the dark!   10
And may there be no sadness of farewell,
   When I embark;

For though from out our bourne of Time and Place
   The flood may bear me far,

I hope to see my Pilot face to face   15
  When I have crossed the bar.

ALFRED, LORD TENNYSON

Requiescat

Strew on her roses, roses,
  And never a spray of yew!
In quiet she reposes;
  Ah, would that I did too!

Her mirth the world required;   5
  She bathed it in smiles of glee,
But her heart was tired, tired,
  And now they let her be.

Her life was turning, turning,
  In mazes of heat and sound.   10
But for peace her soul was yearning,
  And now peace laps her round.

Her cabined, ample spirit,
  It fluttered and failed for breath.
To-night it doth inherit   15
  The vasty hall of death.

MATTHEW ARNOLD

Song

When I am dead, my dearest,
  Sing no sad songs for me;
Plant thou no roses at my head,
  Nor shady cypress tree:
Be the green grass above me   5
  With showers and dewdrops wet,
And if thou wilt, remember,
  And if thou wilt, forget.

I shall not see the shadows,
  I shall not feel the rain;   10
I shall not hear the nightingale
  Sing on as if in pain;

And dreaming through the twilight
   That doth not rise nor set,
Haply I may remember,   15
   And haply may forget.

CHRISTINA ROSSETTI

Because I Could Not Stop for Death

Because I could not stop for Death,
He kindly stopped for me;
The carriage held but just ourselves
And Immortality.

We slowly drove, he knew no haste,   5
And I had put away
My labor, and my leisure too,
For his civility.

We passed the school where children played
At wrestling in a ring;   10
We passed the fields of gazing grain,
We passed the setting sun.

We paused before a house that seemed
A swelling of the ground;
The roof was scarcely visible,   15
The cornice but a mound.

Since then 'tis centuries; but each
Feels shorter than the day
I first surmised the horses' heads
Were toward eternity.   20

EMILY DICKINSON

I Heard a Fly Buzz When I Died

I heard a fly buzz when I died;
The stillness in the room
Was like the stillness in the air
Between the heaves of storm.

The eyes around had wrung them dry,   5
And breaths were gathering firm
For that last onset when the king
Be witnessed in the room.

I willed my keepsakes, signed away
What portion of me be   10
Assignable—and then it was
There interposed a fly,

With blue, uncertain, stumbling buzz
Between the light and me;
And then the windows failed, and then   15
I could not see to see.

EMILY DICKINSON

Dickinson's "I Heard a Fly Buzz When I Died"
Gerhard Friedrich

This poem seems to present two major problems to the interpreter. First, w
is the significance of the buzzing fly in relation to the dying person, and seco
what is the meaning of the double use of "see" in the last line? An analysis
the context helps to clear up these apparent obscurities, and a close para
found in another Dickinson poem reinforces such interpretation.

In an atmosphere of outward quiet and inner calm, the dying person c
lectedly proceeds to bequeath his or her worldly possessions, and while engag
in this activity of "willing," finds his attention withdrawn by a fly's buzzi
The fly is introduced in intimate connection with "my keepsakes" and "w
portion of me be assignable"; it follows—and is the culmination of—the dyi
person's preoccupation with cherished material things no longer of use to
departing owner. In the face of death, and even more of a possible spiritual
beyond death, one's concern with a few earthly belongings is but a triviality, a
indeed a distraction from a momentous issue. The obtrusiveness of the inferi
physical aspects of existence, and the busybody activity associated with them,
poignantly illustrated by the intervening insect (cf. the line "Buzz the dull fl
on the chamber window," in the poem beginning "How many times these l
feet staggered"). Even so small a demonstrative, demonstrable creature
sufficient to separate the dying person from "the light," i.e. to blur the vision,
short-circuit mental concentration, so that spiritual awareness is lost. The last li
of the poem may then be paraphrased to read: "Waylaid by irrelevant, tangib
finite objects of little importance, I was no longer capable of that deeper perce

tion which would clearly reveal to me the infinite spiritual reality." As Emily Dickinson herself expressed it, in another, Second Series poem beginning "Their height in heaven comforts not":

> I'm finite, I can't see.
>
> .   .   .   .
>
> This timid life of evidence
> Keeps pleading, "I don't know."

The dying person does in fact not merely suffer an unwelcome external interruption of an otherwise resolute expectancy, but falls from a higher consciousness, from liberating insight, from faith, into an intensely skeptical mood. The fly's buzz is characterized as "blue, uncertain, stumbling," and emphasis on the finite physical reality goes hand in hand with a frustrating lack of absolute assurance. The only portion of a man not properly "assignable" may be that which dies and decomposes! To the dying person, the buzzing fly would thus become a timely, untimely reminder of man's final, cadaverous condition and putrefaction.

The sudden fall of the dying person into the captivity of an earth-heavy skepticism demonstrates of course the inadequacy of the earlier pseudo-stoicism. What seemed then like composure, was after all only a pause "between the heaves of storm"; the "firmness" of the second stanza proved to be less than veritable peace of mind and soul; and so we have a profoundly tragic human situation, namely the perennial conflict between two concepts of reality, most carefully delineated.

The poem should be compared with its illuminating counterpart of the Second Series, "Their height in heaven comforts not," and may be contrasted with "Death is a dialogue between," "I heard as if I had no ear," and the well-known "I never saw a moor."

Afterwards

When the Present has latched its postern behind my tremulous stay,
    And the May month flaps its glad green leaves like wings,
Delicate-filmed as new-spun silk, will the neighbors say,
    "He was a man who used to notice such things"?

If it be in the dusk when, like an eyelid's soundless blink,   5
    The dewfall-hawk comes crossing the shades to alight
Upon the wind-warped upland thorn, a gazer may think,
    "To him this must have been a familiar sight."

If I pass during some nocturnal blackness, mothy and warm,
   When the hedgehog travels furtively over the lawn,   10
One may say, "He strove that such innocent creatures should come to no
      harm,
   But he could do little for them; and now he is gone."

If, when hearing that I have been stilled at last, they stand at the door,
   Watching the full-starred heavens that winter sees,
Will this thought rise on those who will meet my face no more,   15
   "He was one who had an eye for such mysteries"?

And will any say when my bell of quittance is heard in the gloom,
   And a crossing breeze cuts a pause in its outrollings,
Till they rise again, as they were a new bell's boom,
   "He hears it not now, but used to notice such things"?   20

THOMAS HARDY

To an Athlete Dying Young

The time you won your town the race
We chaired you through the market-place;
Man and boy stood cheering by,
And home we brought you shoulder-high.

Today, the road all runners come,   5
Shoulder-high we bring you home,
And set you at your threshold down,
Townsman of a stiller town.

Smart lad, to slip betimes away
From fields where glory does not stay,   10
And early though the laurel grows
It withers quicker than the rose.

Eyes the shady night has shut
Cannot see the record cut,
And silence sounds no worse than cheers   15
After earth has stopped the ears:

Now you will not swell the rout
Of lads that wore their honors out,
Runners whom renown outran
And the name died before the man.   20

So set, before its echoes fade,
The fleet foot on the sill of shade,
And hold to the low lintel up
The still-defended challenge-cup.

And round that early-laureled head   25
Will flock to gaze the strengthless dead,
And find unwithered on its curls
The garland briefer than a girl's.

A. E. HOUSMAN

Danny Deever

"What are the bugles blowin' for?" said Files-on-Parade.
"To turn you out, to turn you out," the Color-Sergeant said.
"What makes you look so white, so white?" said Files-on-Parade.
"I'm dreadin' what I've got to watch," the Color-Sergeant said.
For they're hangin' Danny Deever, you can 'ear the Dead March play,   5
The Regiment's in 'ollow square—they're hangin' him today;
They've taken of his buttons off an' cut his stripes away,
An' they're hangin' Danny Deever in the mornin'.

"What makes the rear-rank breathe so 'ard?" said Files-on-Parade.
"It's bitter cold, it's bitter cold," the Color-Sergeant said.   10
"What makes that front-rank man fall down?" said Files-on-Parade.
"A touch o' sun, a touch o' sun," the Color-Sergeant said.
They are hangin' Danny Deever, they are marchin' of 'im round,
They 'ave 'alted Danny Deever by 'is coffin on the ground;
An' 'e'll swing in 'arf a minute for a sneakin' shootin' hound—   15
O they're hangin' Danny Deever in the mornin'!

" 'Is cot was right-'and cot to mine," said Files-on-Parade.
" 'E's sleepin' out an' far to-night," the Color-Sergeant said.
"I've drunk 'is beer a score o' times," said Files-on-Parade.
" 'E's drinkin' bitter beer alone," the Color-Sergeant said.   20
They are hangin' Danny Deever, you must mark 'im to 'is place,
For 'e shot a comrade sleepin'—you must look 'im in the face;
Nine 'undred of 'is county an' the Regiment's disgrace,
While they're hangin' Danny Deever in the mornin'.

"What's that so black agin the sun?" said Files-on-Parade.   25
"It's Danny fightin' 'ard for life," the Color-Sergeant said.
"What's that that whimpers over'ead?" said Files-on-Parade.
"It's Danny's soul that's passin' now," the Color-Sergeant said.

For they're done with Danny Deever, you can 'ear the quickstep play,
The Regiment's in column, an' they're marchin' us away;   30
Ho! the young recruits are shakin', an' they'll want their beer to-day,
After hangin' Danny Deever in the mornin'!

RUDYARD KIPLING

How Annandale Went Out

"They called it Annandale—and I was there
To flourish, to find words, and to attend:
Liar, physician, hypocrite, and friend,
I watched him; and the sight was not so fair
As one or two that I have seen elsewhere: 5
An apparatus not for me to mend—
A wreck, with hell between him and the end,
Remained of Annandale; and I was there.

"I knew the ruin as I knew the man;
So put the two together, if you can,   10
Remembering the worst you know of me.
Now view yourself as I was, on the spot—
With a slight kind of engine. Do you see?
Like this—You wouldn't hang me? I thought not."

EDWIN ARLINGTON ROBINSON

Bells for John Whiteside's Daughter

There was such speed in her little body,
And such lightness in her footfall,
It is no wonder her brown study
Astonishes us all.

Her wars were bruited in our high window.   5
We looked among orchard trees and beyond,
Where she took arms against her shadow,
Or harried unto the pond

The lazy geese, like a snow cloud
Dripping their snow on the green grass,   10
Tricking and stopping, sleepy and proud,
Who cried in goose, Alas,

For the tireless heart within the little
Lady with rod that made them rise
From their noon apple-dreams and scuttle   15
Goose-fashion under the skies!

But now go the bells, and we are ready,
In one house we are sternly stopped
To say we are vexed at her brown study,
Lying so primly propped.   20

                    JOHN CROWE RANSOM

gee i like to think of dead

gee i like to think of dead it means nearer because deeper
firmer since darker than little round water at one end of
the well   it's too cool to be crooked and it's too firm
to be hard but it's sharp and thick and it loves,   every
old thing falls in rosebugs and jackknives and kittens and   5
pennies they all sit there looking at each other having the
fastest time because they've never met before

dead's more even than how many ways of sitting on
your head your unnatural hair has in the morning

dead's clever too like POF goes the alarm off and the   10
little striker having the best time tickling away everybody's brain so everybody just puts out their finger
and they stuff the poor thing all full of fingers

dead has a smile like the nicest man you've never met
who maybe winks at you in a streetcar and you pretend   15
you don't but really you do see and you are My how
glad he winked and hope he'll do it again

or if it talks about you somewhere behind your back it
makes your neck feel pleasant and stoopid   and if
dead says may i have this one and was never intro-   20
duced you say Yes because you know you want it to
dance with you and it wants to and it can dance and
Whocares

dead's fine like hands do you see that water flowerpots
in windows but they live higher in their house than   25
you so that's all you see but you don't want to

dead's happy like the way underclothes All so differ-
ently solemn and inti and sitting on one string

dead never says my dear,Time for your musiclesson
and you like music and to have somebody play who   30
can but you know you never can and why have to?

dead's nice like a dance where you danced simple hours
and you take all your prickley-clothes off and squeeze-
into-largeness without one word   and you lie still as
anything   in largeness and this largeness begins to   35
give you,the dance all over again and you,feel all again
all over the way men you liked made you feel when they
touched you(but that's not all)because largeness tells
you so you can feel what you made,men feel when,you
touched,them   40

dead's sorry like a thistlefluff-thing which goes landing away all by himself on somebody's roof or something where who-ever-heard-of-growing and nobody
expects you to anyway

dead says come with me he says(andwhyevernot)into   45
the round well and see the kitten and the penny and
the jackknife and the rosebug
                    and you say Sure you
say (like that) sure i'll come with you you say for i
like kittens i do and jackknives i do and pennies i do   50
and rosebugs i do

                    E. E. CUMMINGS

Buffalo Bill's

Buffalo Bill's
defunct

        who used to
        ride a watersmooth-silver
                            stallion   5
and break onetwothreefourfive pigeonsjustlikethat
                                        Jesus

he was a handsome man
                    and what i want to know is
how do you like your blueeyed boy   10
Mister Death

                    E. E. CUMMINGS

The Irony of E. E. Cummings

David Ray

. . . To understand the poem's ["Buffalo Bill's"] irony it is necessary to make the chronological perspective within the poem very clear. The persona is that of a mature man who, as a child, was awed by Bill (in quite the all-out way described in the Sandburg poem) and who, hearing of Bill's death, first grieves for him, and then (and these functions are simultaneous) adds additional fuel to his hatred of "Mister Death," the destroyer of everything, by reflecting that he was defrauded and deprived by Bill as well as by "Mister Death." In this sense the poet both laments and curses the fraudulence of his childhood hero-worship. These shifts are clearly signalled by the change of tense from present to past (to the boy's view) and back again to the angry persona of the present tense. There is, of course, a very obvious shift of tone that goes along with the shift of tense; the mellifluous "watersmooth-silver stallion" image, almost caressed, is a sharp contrast to such a nasty word as *defunct* or to such a sneering phrase as "how do you like your blueeyed boy."

It is important to note, in making a case for the redirection of the poet's fury to Bill, that Bill, in the poem, functions as a destroyer, an agent of death. What has been destroyed, of course, is rather all-embracing. Bill has been destroyed; the poet's childhood, and the kind of innocent faith and wonder that went along with it has been destroyed by his subsequent disillusionment with Bill;[1] the clay pigeons have been destroyed. The poet is in many ways blaming Bill for disappointing both his expectations of childhood and of America, for delivering him rather treacherously to a tawdry world of cheapened values, for America is Bill's "sponsor" as well as that of freedom and breakfast foods. In other words, the poet allows his reminiscence of his child's attitude toward Bill (what the psychiatric observers would call an "introject") to respond elegiacally to Bill's death; he then turns on this entire reaction with his adult's awareness that Bill

---

[1] [Since this is an excerpt from a longer article, the footnotes have been re-numbered. Eds.] Innocent wonder (a major *love* of Cummings, who as a primitivist and a symbolist recurrently voices his *hates* and his *loves* rather rawly) is frequently, in his poems, delivered over to a shady adult knowledge, the treachery of lurking sin and death. The children at play in *Chansons Innocentes* are threatened by the lurking, seductive "goat-footed balloon Man," a Pan image. His "far and wee" whistle signals the adult world waiting, anticipates their betrayal, the giving over of the world of childhood innocence to that of tainted knowledge and death. This quite innocent awe of the boy telling of his Uncle Sol's death (and, ironically, of his final success in a business venture when he starts a worm farm), in *nobody loses all the time*—a wonder at the sheer gadgetry of the button that sends the coffin into the earth—is betrayed again by the sudden awareness of death. Once again, wonder is delivered up to death. The theme of the delivery of all precious things to worms is a most common one in his work. In *Three*, Cummings writes: "Requiescat./carry/carefully the blessed large silent him/into nibbling final worms."

was, historically, a fraud. The result is an angry assault on all that disappoints, deprives, defrauds; both "Mister Death" and his "blueeyed boy" (companion, agent; "fair-haired" boy) are arraigned. There are many other poems in which death is similarly personified (and sometimes confused with love or sex); in *Chimneys* a prostitute's "slippery body is Death's littlest pal, skilled in quick softness"; death is also variously personified as "Farmer Death" and "O crazy daddy of death." In *Post Impressions* "young death sits in a café" with considerable purchasing power; the first line of "if i should sleep with a lady called death" tells its own story.

It would not be at all inappropriate to wonder what further connotations the figure of Bill on horseback might evoke. The skeletal figure of death riding through plague-tainted streets is a traditional association; death has more than once been pictured on horseback with a scythe, if not with a rifle. Katherine Anne Porter employed this image developmentally in her *Pale Horse, Pale Rider*. One recalls even William Butler Yeats's epitaph. Death and man on horseback are associations as old as our literary heritage.[2] If the "Portrait" of Buffalo Bill is a mere elegy, without irony for the victim it laments, it is only because, doubly gulled, the poet has been seduced into pity for death's henchman.

Cummings's poem is, then, an assault on everything held dear by a sentimentalist or a hero-worshipper. Following his usual practice, his first offense is directed at the grammarians; he then turns to attack the tradition of a respectful stance toward the subject of death ("Mister Death" is a mocking appellation, a dimension of irony long ago pointed out by Brooks and Warren), the heroism of Buffalo Bill, and—most importantly—the entire convention of the elegy. Cummings assaults everything, in short, in this finest of his "hate" poems[3] except what he manages to assert by this anger—a sense of fundamental decency outraged with everything that corrupts life or makes it fraudulent. He curses a culture that makes a hero of Bill while he expresses fury toward a death that

[2] I am indebted to Professor Baxter Hathaway for this point.

[3] Since Cummings's basic recurrent images usually have the same or similar values attached to them (the recurrence of words like *rain, green, moon, hands, snow*), there is a systematic frame of values easily discoverable in his work. A concordance would provide a key to his principal themes, and to a wider awareness that as a primitivist his basic work as a poet is usually the raw expression of his loves and hates. Major hates like war and death would top a list of more topical hates, like those of mothers, anthologists, tourists, Fourth of July orators and psychoanalysts. His major loves are for nature, integrity, childhood innocence, and the body. His weapons of irony are most frequently employed in his hate poems, sometimes against materialists, phrasemongers, parvenus, salesmen and the rich who have not the wisdom to love or enjoy life. He is, of course, always attacking "fifteenth rate ideas," "hypercivic zeal," and "marriageable nymphs" with his more obvious irony. Since Cummings is so systematic (despite himself, for this is surely not intentional), a concordance would quickly lead many readers to an understanding of his basic metaphors (whether for love-making, for spring, or for death), and it is particularly regrettable that his *Collected Poems* is not provided with an alphabetical index of first lines. This is doubly troublesome for a teacher since he frequently reuses titles or uses none.

kills even those for whom he has learned contempt. By building up the
hackneyed elegiac theme of a great man brought to ruin, Cummings merely
prepares for its demolishment. The question "how do you like your blueeyed
boy" throws the supposedly admiring description into doubt, makes us realize
that the inspired "Jesus he was a handsome man" has been spoken by the childhood introject rather than by the persona of the adult poet; at this point the
"admiring" description of Bill is reversed and the reader responds to the func-
tioning of the poet's rapid passing over of the facile tricks; we realize the two-
dimensionality of Bill's "blueeyed" image is deliberate; it reflects Bill's shallow-
ness. The poet who seems to have been taken in by Bill suddenly asks a question
with such obvious sarcasm that it constitutes a sneering indictment of Bill's
reputation and makes the reader completely reassess the earlier images. The
reader grieves for and then sees through Bill, just as the poet has in the lengthier
scope of his experiencing of Bill's heroism. Yet these are simultaneous responses
for many readers; poetic language is often at its greatest when it is performing
many functions at once; a kind of anti-language is at work which can express
doubt while praise is rhetorically developed. Bill is at once worshipped and ex-
posed, and blamed for the mode of experiencing he represents and our culture encourages; the great man for whom we have grieved is reduced to the
level of fraud, a flash in the pan, a hero of whom one remembers only the blue
eyes. Cummings has discovered another wooden nickel in the Parthenon.

At last Bill belongs literally to "Mister Death's" team. The poet triumphs
over death by having come to an insight into Bill's fraudulence before "Mister
Death," who is only now presumably finding out that he has been tricked into
treating a sham performer as a great man, cut down with all the panoply of
tragedy. The poet has beaten Mister Death to the draw, literally, and leaves the
great destroyer to find out that he has the commonest of food for his worms.
Perhaps, then, as *The Greek Anthology* occasionally leads us to feel, the best
elegies are for the least heroic of victims, not for those figures who are true
heroes in our lives, but for those who have functioned in our lives at their most
tawdry, misguided, or commonplace moments. The lingering evocations of Cummings's "portrait" are not those of Bill's "watersmooth-silver stallion" nor of
his "blue eyes" but of the stale smell of the carnival tent and sawdust.

And Death Shall Have No Dominion

And death shall have no dominion.
Dead men naked they shall be one
With the man in the wind and the west moon;
When their bones are picked clean and the clean bones gone,
They shall have stars at elbow and foot;   5

Though they go mad they shall be sane,
Though they sink through the sea they shall rise again;
Though lovers be lost love shall not;
And death shall have no dominion.

And death shall have no dominion.   10
Under the windings of the sea
They lying long shall not die windily;
Twisting on racks when sinews give way,
Strapped to a wheel, yet they shall not break;
Faith in their hands shall snap in two,   15
And the unicorn evils run them through;
Split all ends up they shan't crack;
And death shall have no dominion.

And death shall have no dominion.
No more may gulls cry at their ears   20
Or waves break loud on the seashores;
Where blew a flower may a flower no more
Lift its head to the blows of the rain;
Though they be mad and dead as nails,
Heads of the characters hammer through daisies;   25
Break in the sun till the sun breaks down,
And death shall have no dominion.

DYLAN THOMAS

Do Not Go Gentle into That Good Night

Do not go gentle into that good night,
Old age should burn and rave at close of day;
Rage, rage against the dying of the light.

Though wise men at their end know dark is right,
Because their words had forked no lightning they   5
Do not go gentle into that good night.

Good men, the last wave by, crying how bright
Their frail deeds might have danced in a green bay,
Rage, rage against the dying of the light.

Wild men who caught and sang the sun in flight,   10
And learn, too late, they grieved it on its way,
Do not go gentle into that good night.

Grave men, near death, who see with blinding sight
Blind eyes could blaze like meteors and be gay,
Rage, rage against the dying of the light.   15

And you, my father, there on the sad height,
Curse, bless, me now with your fierce tears, I pray.
Do not go gentle into that good night.
Rage, rage against the dying of the light.

DYLAN THOMAS

Glossary of Terms

Accent (or **stress**). The emphasis given a vocalized syllable. In scansion, accented syllables are usually marked /, unaccented ᴜ, as in the following line:

ᴜ / ᴜ / ᴜ / ᴜ /
The stag at eve had drunk his fill.   (Scott)

Alexandrine. A line of verse with six *iambic feet* (*see* Meter).

A needless Alexandrine ends the song,
That, like a wounded snake, drags its slow length along.   (Pope)

Alliteration. The repetition of consonant sounds at the beginning of words. Old English and some Middle English verse is based on alliteration rather than rhyme:

In a *s*omer *s*esun whon *s*ofte was the *s*onne,
I *sch*op me into a *sch*roud a *sch*eep as I were;   (from *Piers Plowman*)

In modern verse, alliteration is not usually used as a substitute for rhyme but is often used in connection with rhyme:

When first my way to fair I took
   Few pence in purse had I,
And long I used to stand and look
   At things I could not buy.   (Housman)

Amphibrach. *See* Meter.

Anacrusis. One or more unaccented syllables at the beginning of a line of verse which regularly starts with an accented syllable.

Alas! for the rarity
Of Christian charity   (Hood)

Analogy. Similarity between two different things; usually the poet uses the more familiar of the two objects to explain something unfamiliar. In Donne's "A Valediction Forbidding Mourning," the compass is analogous to the two lovers.

Anapestic meter. *See* Meter.

Apostrophe. A figure of speech in which a person or an abstract quality not present is addressed.

> Milton, thou shouldst be living at this hour.   (Wordsworth)

Assonance. The repetition of like vowel sounds, usually in accented syllables:

> Of beechen green, and shadows numberless,   (Keats)

Ballad. A short narrative poem or song with a simple, repeated stanza form, usually *abcb:*

> The King sits tonight in Dumferline toun
> Drinking his blude-red wine
> "O where will I get a gude sailor
> To sail this ship of mine?"   (from "Sir Patrick Spence")

> Literary ballads are written in imitation of popular (or folk) ballads.
> *See* Keats's "La Belle Dame sans Merci."

Ballad stanza. *See* Stanza.

Blank verse. Unrhymed *iambic pentameter* (*see* Meter).

> $\overset{\cup}{\text{Was}}$ $\overset{/}{\text{this}}$ $\overset{\cup}{\text{the}}$ $\overset{/}{\text{face}}$ $\overset{\cup}{\text{that}}$ $\overset{/}{\text{launched}}$ $\overset{\cup}{\text{a}}$ $\overset{/}{\text{thou}}$ $\overset{\cup}{\text{sand}}$ $\overset{/}{\text{ships}}$
> And burnt the topless towers of Ilium?   (Marlowe)

Caesura. A pause within a line of verse, usually near the middle of the line.

> Know then thyself, / / presume not God to scan.   (Pope)

Catalexis. Omission of one or more syllables at the end of a line of poetry. (Such a line is often called a *truncated line.*)

> Tiger! Tiger! burning bright.   (Blake)

Conceit. A type of metaphor or simile which employs an involved and usually extended *analogy.* The term is most often associated with the metaphysical poets; the compass image in Donne's "A Valediction Forbidding Mourning" is an example of an elaborate and ingenious conceit.

Connotation. Ideas suggested by a word aside from its explicit meaning (deno-tion). For instance, the word "exotic" means "foreign," but it connote lotus blossoms, sloe-eyed maidens, and strange, melliflu names.

Consonance. Repetition of final consonant sounds where the vowels are differe Its use in rhyme is called near rhyme or slant rhyme: *seem / su read / hid*.

Couplet. Two rhyming lines of verse, usually in the same meter.

> And malt does more than Milton can
> To justify God's ways to man.   (Housman)

Dactylic meter. *See* Meter.

Denotation. The strictly defined meaning of a word apart from all connotatio

Diction. The words used in prose or verse. In criticizing writing, one m always take into account the aptness of the words the author choos *Poetic diction* is the term used to refer to words and phrases thou to be especially appropriate to poetry. The fashion in poetic dicti changes; for example, words such as "o'er," "ere," and "whilst" not used by modern poets, but Dylan Thomas's "a springful of lar is perfectly acceptable.

Dimeter. *See* Meter.

Dissonance. The use of harsh, unpleasant sounds. The term also is sometin used as a synonym for consonance—rhymes that are not qu perfect because of differences in vowels in the rhyming wor *found / fond*.

Double rhyme. *See* Rhyme.

Dramatic monologue. A poem in which the speaker is addressing some ot character present "on stage" with him, not just the reader. The ot character often apparently speaks back, but the reader must infer comments from what the speaker says. Browning's "My Last Duche is an excellent example of a dramatic monologue.

Elegy. A formal, serious poem, usually on the theme of death. Milton's "L idas," Shelley's "Adonais," and Yeats's "In Memory of Major Rob

Gregory" are examples of elegies devoted to an individual. Gray's "Elegy Written in a Country Churchyard" is an example of an elegy on death in general.

Elision. The omission of a syllable or more to gain some rhythmic effect: *o'er* for *over*.

Ellipsis. The omission of a word or words for a rhetorical effect. The reader must be aware, if he is to understand the sentence, what words have been left out:

> Nor mouth had, no nor mind, expressed
> What heart heard of, ghost guessed.   (Hopkins)

End-stopped line. A line that has a grammatical pause at the end.

> The laws of God, the laws of man,
> He may keep that will and can.   (Housman)

Enjambment. The use of run-on lines; that is, the sense and the grammatical structure run over from one line into the next.

> That's my last duchess, painted on the wall
> Looking as if she were alive. I call
> That piece a wonder now.   (Browning)

Epigram. A compressed, pity, and pointed saying; usually witty, often ironic. Pope's "Intended for Sir Isaac Newton" is epigrammatic, as is the phrase:

> Divorces are made in heaven.   (Wilde)

Epithet. The use of a word or apt phrase to characterize a person or thing: Jack *the Ripper*.

Feminine ending. The use of an extra, unstressed syllable at the end of a line.

> He is gone on the mountain
>   He is lost to the forest
> Like a summer-dried fountain
>   When our need is the sorest   (Scott)

Feminine rhyme. *See* Rhyme.

Figure of speech. Any linguistic device which allows the writer to enrich his language beyond the means of ordinary speech; among the most com-

mon are *analogy, irony, simile, metaphor, hyperbole, apostro,*
metonymy, and *synecdoche* (*see* separate listings). The following
employs several figures of speech:

While memory holds a seat in this distracted globe.   (Shakespeare)

Foot.   *See* Meter.

Free verse.   Verse which has no regular metrical or rhyming pattern, but re
instead upon the cadences of normal speech for its metrical effect. '
selections from Whitman are examples of free verse.

Heroic couplet.   Two rhymed *iambic pentameter* (*see* Meter) lines, usually v
a pause after the first line. First used by Chaucer, the heroic cou
reached its height of popularity with Dryden and Pope.

Know then thyself, presume not God to scan,
The proper study of mankind is man.   (Pope)

Hexameter.   A line of six feet. This line is infrequent in English, though
classical verse it was the standard line for the epic. *See* Meter.

Hyperbole.   Exaggeration used as a figure of speech.

And I will luve thee still, my dear,
'Till a' the seas gang dry.   (Burns)

Iamb.   *See* Meter.

Image.   Literally a likeness, one in which the words evoke a sensory represe
tion or mental impression.

Imagery.   In contemporary critical usage, a somewhat ambiguous term, gener;
synonymous with figures of speech; often used to designate a group
collection of images within a given work or in the work of a spec
writer.

Internal rhyme.   *See* Rhyme.

Irony.   (1) A figure of speech in which the words convey a meaning other th
or different from what is literally stated.

And malt does more than Milton can
To justify God's ways to man.   (Housman)

(2) A situation in which there is a disparity between the real situation and the way it is viewed or interpreted by others, as in Browning's "My Last Duchess."

Lyric. A major kind of poetry, usually a short subjective poem expressing personal emotion or feeling; originally lyric poems were written to be sung.

Masculine ending. A metrical line in which the final syllable is stressed.

> Full many a flower is born to blush unseen   (Gray)

Metaphor. A figure of speech involving the direct comparison of two objects; the compared objects are equated, and the connective "like" or "as" is omitted. (*See also* Simile.)

> Your mind and you are our Sargasso Sea.   (Pound)

Meter. The pattern of stressed and unstressed syllables in a line of poetry. The basic metrical unit is called a *foot*. Most feet contain one accented syllable and one or two unaccented syllables. The number of units, or feet, in a line is indicated by one of the following terms: monometer (one foot), dimeter (two feet), trimeter (three feet), tetrameter (four feet), pentameter (five feet), hexameter (six feet), heptameter (seven feet), octameter (eight feet). The rhythmic pattern of stressed and unstressed syllables within the unit or foot is indicated by one of the following terms: *iambic* (u/), *anapestic* (uu/), *trochaic* (/u), *dactylic* (/uu), *amphibrachic* (u/u). *Spondaic* (//) and *pyrrhic* (uu) feet also occur occasionally. The following patterns are among the most common:

Iambic tetrameter

<pre>
 u / | u / | u / | u /
The Sun came up upon the left   (Coleridge)
</pre>

Iambic pentameter

<pre>
  u   / | u   / | u / | u / | u /
Who says my tears have overflowed his ground   (Donne)
</pre>

Anapestic tetrameter

<pre>
   u   u   / | u u / | u   u / | u u /
Like the leaves of the forest when Summer is green,   (Byron)
</pre>

Trochaic tetrameter

<pre>
 /   u | /   u | / u | / u
Happy field or mossy cavern   (Keats)
</pre>

Metonymy. A figure of speech in which a word is used in place of anot█ with which it is associated. Used by some as synonymous with sy█ doche. In the following passage, the word *rhyme* is used in plac█ *poem* or *sonnet:*

> Not marble, nor the gilded monuments
> Of princes, shall outlive this powerful *rhyme.* (Shakespeare)

Monometer. *See* Meter.

Ode. A major kind of lyric poem, varied in length, usually treating a digni█ or exalted theme. Originally the ode was choral, meant to be sung █ public occasion. The term as used today has lost specific reference the Greek ode. In English prosody three main types are recogniz█ the Greek, or Pindaric; the Roman, or Horatian; and the Irregu█ *See* Wordsworth's "Ode to Duty," Keats's "Ode on Melancholy."

Onomatopoeia. A figure of speech in which a word or words imitate or res█ ble the sound of the object or occurrence they refer to: "buz█ "murmur," and "ring."

> Cold currents thrid, and turn to rhythmic tidal lyres. (Hardy)

Ottava rima. *See* Stanza.

Overstatement. *See* Hyperbole.

Paradox. A statement or situation in which a contradiction or seeming con█ diction is incorporated:

> The Child is father of the Man. (Wordsworth)

Paraphrase. A rewriting or restatement of a given piece of writing, usually explain and clarify it.

Pentameter. *See* Meter.

Personification. A figure of speech in which an abstract idea or inanimate obj█ is treated in human terms or endowed with human characteristics.

> Death, be not proud, though some have called thee
> Mighty and dreadful, for thou art not so, (Donne)

Poetic diction. *See* Diction.

Pyrrhic. *See* Meter.

Quatrain. A grouping of four lines of verse—sometimes a stanza, sometimes a part of a longer stanza. Gray's "Elegy Written in a Country Churchyard" is a good example of stanza form in quatrains.

Refrain. A phrase, line, or group of lines repeated at intervals throughout a poem, usually at the end of a stanza.

> An' they're hangin' Danny Deever in the Mornin'.   (Kipling)

Rhyme. The repetition or duplication of approximate or exact sounds, usually in a pattern, and usually involving terminal sounds of words at the ends of lines of verse. Rhymes may be classified according to position: beginning rhyme, internal rhyme, and end rhyme. Rhymes also may be classified on the basis of numbers of syllables with corresponding sounds: *masculine rhyme,* where the final syllables are stressed and are identical in sound (*hood / good*); *feminine rhyme,* sometimes called *double rhyme,* where stressed rhyming syllables are followed by identical unstressed syllables (*testing / resting*). When feminine rhyme has three consecutive rhyming syllables (*gracefully / tastefully*), it is called *triple* or *polysyllabic rhyme.* Rhymes which are not true but only approximate are often called *slant rhyme.*

Rime royal. *See* Stanza.

Run-on lines. *See* Enjambment.

Scansion. A detailed analysis to determine the meter and rhythm of a poetic line by marking off the feet and marking the stressed (/) and unstressed (u) syllables within each foot.

> u / | u / | u / | u   /
> The wrinkled sea beneath him crawls;
> u / | u / | u / | u   /
> He watches from his mountain walls,   (Tennyson)

Sestet. A grouping of six lines of verse, either as a separate stanza or the last six lines of an Italian sonnet.

Simile. A figure of speech in which two essentially unlike things are compared; in contrast to metaphor, the simile makes use of the word "like" or "as."

> The Assyrian came down like a wolf on the fold.   (Byron)

Sonnet. A fourteen-line lyric poem that usually follows one of two main patterns: (1) The Italian, or Petrarchan, sonnet has two parts, an octave that rhymes *abba abba* and a sestet that usually rhymes *cde cde* or *cd cd cd;* (2) the English, or Shakespearean, sonnet is comprised of three quatrains and a concluding couplet, rhyming *abab cdcd efef gg.* A variant of the English sonnet is the Spenserian form, with linked quatrains rhyming *abab bcbc cdcd ee.* Sonnets may be separate poems, or they may be grouped in a sonnet sequence with a common theme or other linking factors.

Spenserian stanza. *See* Stanza.

Spondee. *See* Meter.

Sprung rhythm. A term invented by Gerard Manley Hopkins to designate the rhythmical pattern based on a foot with one stressed syllable and any number of unstressed syllables:

/ /   /
Margaret, are you grieving

Stanza. Formal groups of lines into which a poem may be divided. Usually, both the number of lines and the rhyme scheme follow a recurring pattern. There is often unity of thought or theme within a stanza. The number of lines in a given stanza varies widely. Some of the commonest stanza forms in English are the *couplet* (two lines rhyming *aa*); the *triplet,* or *tercet* (three lines rhyming *aaa,* or linked *aba, bcb,* etc., as in terza rima); *ballad stanza* (four lines of alternating iambic tetrameter and trimeter rhyming *abcb*); *rime royal* (seven lines of iambic pentameter rhyming *ababbcc*); *ottava rima* (eight lines of iambic pentameter rhyming *abababcc*); and the Spenserian stanza (eight lines of iambic pentameter and an alexandrine in the ninth line, rhyming *ababbcbcc*).

Stress. *See* Accent.

Symbol. Quite simply, a thing that stands for or represents something else, such as a flag or a wedding ring. Literary symbols function in much the same way as other symbols. They evoke meanings beyond the literal object and may embody an idea or quality. They may be broad, nearly universal, symbols, such as winter for aging or white for purity. They may be more private, such as the gyre in the poetry of Yeats.

Synecdoche.   A figure of speech in which a part stands for the whole. *See* Metonymy.

Tail rhymes.   Short rhyming lines in a stanza of otherwise longer lines. *See* "Go, and Catch a Falling Star" by John Donne.

Tercet.   Three rhyming lines in a single rhyme or in linked triplets. *See* Tennyson's "The Eagle."

Terza rima.   Linked triplets in continuing sequence (*aba bcb cdc,* etc.). *See* Shelley's "Ode to the West Wind."

Tetrameter.   *See* Meter.

Theme.   As a literary term, the basic idea incorporated in or developed by a piece of literature. In a short poem, a single theme may be developed, such as the mutability, or *carpe diem,* theme in Marvell's "To His Coy Mistress." A longer work may develop several themes, although there may be only one dominant theme.

Tone.   Tone is determined for the most part by the author's attitude toward his subject and his audience. It should be distinguished from atmosphere, which is determined by locale or setting.

Trimeter.   *See* Meter.

Trochaic meter.   *See* Meter.

Truncated line.   *See* Catalexis.

Understatement.   A kind of irony in which something is spoken of as less important than it is; the opposite of hyperbole.

Index of Authors and Titles

Index of First Lines